THE FOOD AND COOKING OF
RUSSIA & POLAND

THE FOOD AND COOKING OF
RUSSIA & POLAND

EXPLORE THE RICH AND VARIED CUISINE OF EASTERN EUROPE IN MORE THAN 150
CLASSIC STEP-BY-STEP RECIPES ILLUSTRATED WITH OVER 740 PHOTOGRAPHS

Elena Makhonko and Ewa Michalik

LORENZ BOOKS

This edition is published by Lorenz Books, an imprint of Anness Publishing Ltd, Blaby Road, Wigston, Leicestershire LE18 4SE
Email: info@anness.com

Web: www.lorenzbooks.com;
www.annesspublishing.com

If you like the images in this book and would like to investigate using them for publishing, promotions or advertising, please visit our website www.practicalpictures.com for more information.

Publisher: Joanna Lorenz
Editorial Director: Helen Sudell
Executive Editor: Joanne Rippin
Designer: Adelle Morris
Food styling: Jenny White, Claire Ptak and Joy Skipper
Food photography: Jon Whitaker
Prop styling: Penny Markham
Production controller: Wendy Lawson

ETHICAL TRADING POLICY

Because of our ongoing ecological investment programme, you, as our customer, can have the pleasure and reassurance of knowing that a tree is being cultivated on your behalf to naturally replace the materials used to make the book you are holding. For further information about this scheme, please visit www.annesspublishing.com/trees

A CIP catalogue record for this book is available from the British Library.

Previously published in two separate volumes, *Russian Food & Cooking* and *Poland: Food & Cooking*

NOTES

Bracketed terms are intended for American readers.
For all recipes, quantities are given in both metric and imperial measures and, where appropriate, in standard cups and spoons. Follow one set of measures, but not a mixture, because they are not interchangeable.
Standard spoon and cup measures are level. 1 tsp = 5ml, 1 tbsp = 15ml, 1 cup = 250ml/8fl oz.
Australian standard tablespoons are 20ml. Australian readers should use 3 tsp in place of 1 tbsp for measuring small quantities.
American pints are 16fl oz/2 cups. American readers should use 20fl oz/2.5 cups in place of 1 pint when measuring liquids.

Electric oven temperatures in this book are calculated for conventional ovens. When using a fan oven, the temperature will probably need to be reduced by about 10–20°C/20–40°F. Since ovens vary, you should check with your manufacturer's instruction book for guidance.
The nutritional analysis given for each recipe is calculated per portion (i.e. serving or item), unless otherwise stated. If the recipe gives a range, such as Serves 4–6, then the nutritional analysis will be for the smaller portion size, i.e. 6 servings. The analysis does not include optional ingredients, such as salt added to taste, etc.
Medium (US large) eggs are used unless otherwise stated.

Main front cover image shows Pashka – for recipe, see pages 220–1.

PUBLISHER'S NOTE

Contents

Introduction

Mention Russian food, and most people will conjure up an image of a tureen of ruby-red borscht served with sour cream, imperial salmon pie, tiny little dumplings, or chilled champagne and caviar. Polish cuisine uses many of the same elements, and both of these countries share not only similar dishes but also a great pride in their traditional cuisine, handed down from one generation to the next, using ingredients that follow the seasonal rhythms of the year.

Climates

Poland is more or less on the same latitude as southern and western Russia, where most of the Russian population, its industry and its agriculture are to be found. This means that both Poland and southern Russia enjoy warm summers and suffer long, cold, bleak winters, with the briefest of spring or autumn seasons to divide them. The crops that are grown, therefore, are those that can withstand the onslaught of the cold winter weather, such as root vegetables, or that flourish during the short summer growing season and come to fruition well before the snows fall, such as cereal crops.

Preserving food

There are years in both countries when the crops fail, or prolonged snow or ice prevents the farmer from ploughing his land. But both Russians and Poles have developed skilful ways of preserving the food for such eventualities, and these traditional recipes for pickled vegetables, smoked fish, cured meat and sausages are the lifeblood of both cuisines.

Wild food

The other natural resource that links the two countries is the vast larder of wild food to be found in the forests. Russians and Poles love to hunt, whether it's

mushrooms or rabbits, and this tradition is maintained today, by local people and by tourists who come to these ancient woodlands to experience the thrill of the chase. There are plenty of recipes in both cuisines for delicious game pies, stews and soups made with wild boar, venison, hare and game birds, or using the

Above: A typical farming village in the north of Russia, one of the most fertile areas of the country.

freshwater fish from the rivers and lakes. These tend to be flavoured with the tasty field mushrooms, herbs, spices and berries just waiting to be picked.

Another well-loved tradition is for whole families, from the youngest to the oldest, to spend a day in the brief autumn season wandering in the deciduous woodlands, berry-picking or foraging for mushrooms in the undergrowth, with a delightful picnic of cold pies and sweet pastries to sustain the hard workers.

Left: The many varieties of delicious dried and cured meats and sausages are still very popular in Poland, even though it is no longer necessary as a method of preserving meat. Many of them are also exported to Russia.

Foreign influences

Southern and western Russia's strongest trading routes have always been with Europe, and through these they have had access to goods from far-flung countries all around the world. Poland, too, sits in a prime position for trading, alongside the Baltic Sea, with the thrusting economy of Germany to the west, the developing Baltic states to the east, and the stability of Denmark, Sweden and Finland to the north. This means that links with other countries are well established, and trading of food and culinary ideas from and through Poland has been conducted for hundreds of years.

However, northern and eastern Russia suffer extreme Arctic temperatures. These parts of the country are much more remote from world commerce, and have to rely on their own foodstuffs and traditional cuisines, owing to the difficulty of transporting goods. Despite this, there are still delicious recipes from Siberia to enjoy, such as the much-loved dumplings, pelmeni, known in Poland as pierogi.

Below: Classic recipes, such as borscht, rely on the best seasonal ingredients.

Above: The forested areas of Poland are huge, and people still fish, hunt game and gather fruit and mushrooms there.

About this book

Most Russian and Polish food is based on good-quality, fresh ingredients, enhanced by preserved vegetables such as sauerkraut or dried mushrooms, or cured meat such as sausage and ham. Here you will find recipes that reflect this tradition.

All the recipes are carefully explained with simple step-by-step instructions and colour pictures. The final appearance of the dish is an important element for every cook – Russians and Poles have a good eye for presentation – and the vivid colours of beetroot (beets), black rye bread, white sour cream, green herbs and rich dark meat stand out on the plate.

Russian and Polish cooking is all about enjoying the taste, texture and aroma of these hearty traditional foods. The reward for the cook comes from making an impressive dish that sustains good health while pleasing the senses.

Below: Both Russia and Poland have many recipes for little pies and dumplings.

Religious traditions

Russians have their own religious faith, based on the Eastern Orthodox Christian tradition. Even though this was suppressed during the 20th century under Communism, the rituals of the church year were preserved by many families. The main festivals, with their major family feasts, were celebrated quietly in people's homes, with the traditional dishes associated with each one, such as Pashka (above), made for the Easter holiday, or roasted carp, eaten on Good Friday. In Poland, too, the Communist years meant that Catholic rituals had to be celebrated quietly at home, but the Christmas and Easter festival meals were carefully prepared in the same way as they had been for centuries, with delicious treats such as Christmas almond soup or angels' wings biscuits.

Below: Salmon pie, or koulibiac, was devised for the Russian imperial court.

Russian Land and History

The huge land mass that is Russia spreads out across a great proportion of the Northern Hemisphere. It touches Europe at one end and Japan at the other. Its history is similarly complex, holding together extremes of class, income, religion and ethnic diversity, as well as the cultural characteristics of East and West. The resulting culinary inheritance of this nation is one of its unifying factors, with Russians sharing a love of their recipes and the joy of hospitality.

Left: The distinctive towers of The Kremlin, Moscow. Now the seat of Russia's democratic government, it was once the stronghold of the Communist regime, and before that the palace of the tsars.

foods in the cold winter months became a matter of life and death, and from this necessity arose many delicious recipes for pickled or preserved foods that are still made and enjoyed in Russian households today.

The rise of the tsars
The first time the whole of Russia was pulled together into one country was in the 16th century, when Ivan the Terrible began his reign. His brutal regime enforced obedience over a vast land mass containing many different tribes and religions, with their own customs. Later, the more settled reigns of Peter the Great and Catherine the Great allowed for more interaction with other countries, and at this point a European influence arrived in Russian cuisine. It is difficult to believe that wheat was unknown in Russia before the 16th century; it is now one of Russia's major exports and makes up half the country's grain crop. At the same time,

Russia's beginnings
The first settlements in Russia grew up on the western side of the country, where the warmer weather and abundant wild food make it easier to have permanent arrangements for living, working and feeding the family. Moscow grew out of one of these early settlements, developing as the centre of power and government in the 16th century. The wonderfully fertile 'black earth' of the surrounding countryside enabled the first farmers to grow plenty of rye, oats, barley and buckwheat to make dark, tasty bread, pancakes, dumplings and grain spirits such as vodka, the staples of the Russian diet. The freshwater fish in many rivers and lakes, plus the wild game from the forests, formed the protein element of people's diet. Learning to preserve these

Below: Many city dwellers also own a smallholding in the country that supplies the family with fresh fruit and vegetables.

Below: Buckwheat in blossom, one of the earliest cereal crops grown in Russia and still a staple ingredient today.

Below: The once familiar symbol of the Communist Party was the national flag of the Soviet Union.

Above: The vast forested taiga region in the north is an area still abundant with wild food, including fish and game.

Above: The fertile land on the banks of the Volga River in western Russia provides rich pasture for sheep and cattle.

green vegetables and salads first appeared on the tables of the nobility, as well as chocolate, sweet pastries and other luxurious delicacies that have since become great favourites.

Turmoil and revolution

The upheavals of the 20th century, the Russian Revolution, Communism and the subsequent collapse of the Soviet Union by the end of the century, caused many hardships all the way from west to east. The Russian people generally had enough to eat, although the diet of most people was rather monotonous, being based on bread, potatoes, cabbage and vodka. It was supplemented, as it had been through the centuries, by wild produce such as mushrooms, honey, berries and game to be found in the forests, according to the annual rhythm of the seasons.

The 21st century

Life since the end of the Cold War and the fall of Communism has been extremely hard for many Russians. While a few people made huge fortunes in the rush to embrace capitalism, others were left without savings, pensions or any income. The beginning of the 21st century has seen an upturn in Russia's fortunes and a more equable regime has begun to emerge. Luckily, many Russians have access to a small plot of land that

they can cultivate for food. A quite astonishing 80 per cent of the country's vegetables are grown on these individual smallholdings, and are then used fresh, preserved in people's own kitchens, or sold to their neighbours.

The traditions of the Russian way of life have been maintained through all these upheavals. Religious festivals are still extremely important markers throughout the year, and are celebrated with

Below: Grayling are hung to dry during the brief Siberian summer, to be stored for the long, harsh winter months.

reverence for the old ways, using recipes handed down through the generations. With the recent expansion of links with the outside world, Russian food culture has exploded into life, and today the people of this huge country once more take great pride in their national cuisine.

A giant among countries

The sheer size of Russia is astonishing. Even after the break-up of the Soviet Union and its satellite states, Russia still stretches over 8,000 kilometres (4,971 miles), covering 11 time zones from the Baltic States and the Black Sea in the west to the Sea of Japan in the east. There are 40 National Parks and more than 100 nature reserves in this wild, sometimes bleak landscape. The most important

element, which dominates life in Russia, is the climate, which is influenced by the mountain ranges that encircle the country.

The mountains of Russia

The Urals run roughly north to south, dividing the western, European part of Russia from the eastern, Siberian plains. By far the majority of Russia's population lives in the shelter of the more temperate western side of the mountains. Here it is possible to grow a very good variety of crops to feed millions of people, and therefore this is where most people have chosen to settle.

Much higher than the Urals, the Caucasus mountains form the south-western border between Russia, Georgia and Azerbaijan. This region has a warmer climate and provides the people of Russia with wheat, vegetables, herbs, honey and dairy produce. Vineyards, orchards and olive groves have been established here in the sheltered foothills for centuries.

Below: Russia's size and geographical complexity is unique, and this, combined with the climate, and the influences of its many neighbours, has given the country a rich and varied cuisine.

Russia's two capitals

Moscow (seen above at night) and St Petersburg are the two main power centres of the Russian Federation. Moscow is by far the older settlement, with records going back to the 12th century, whereas St Petersburg was constructed on the barren, waterlogged landscape of the far northern Baltic coast. It was founded in the early 18th century, on the orders of Peter the Great, one of Russia's most innovative and dynamic tsars. Both cities have at one time or another been the nation's capital. Moscow, with its vast size and longer history, finally won out in 1918 and is the bustling, thriving centre of government and commerce today. St Petersburg's position on the Baltic Sea means that it has become a major hub for importing and exporting goods, but its main attraction is as the artistic centre of Russia. Its citizens are proud of their wonderful art, music and theatres, and the well-developed and cosmopolitan cuisine in its many restaurants.

Above: This riverside village is typical of the Russian settlements found in the fertile valleys of the Ural mountains.

To the south of Russia, running roughly along its border with China and Mongolia, lies a vast mountainous region, which has had an even stronger influence on the way Russia has developed over the centuries. These unmapped and often un-named mountain ranges prevent the warmer tropical air currents from the Pacific Ocean and the Chinese mainland from reaching Russia from the south, while there is no corresponding mountain range to protect the country from the Arctic winds blowing from the north. This is the main reason why so much of northern Russia is unproductive tundra, a land of permafrost where the low temperatures, as well as the many swamps and lagoons dotting the landscape, make it impossible to grow any kind of crops or to keep animals for food.

Agriculture in Russia
Below the northern tundra belt, stretching across most of Russia, is a more temperate zone known as the taiga. Here, forests of pine trees lie undisturbed for thousands of kilometres (miles). The taiga protects the more productive agricultural land to the south from the harsh climate of northern Russia. Hunters love the taiga for its sources of game and freshwater fish, which thrive in its cold temperatures, and there are many wonderful Russian recipes for warming stews and soups using game and fish as the main ingredients. The taiga also contains an abundance of wild berries, many of which find their way into both savoury and sweet dishes. Local people have always known the best way of using the sparse produce of the taiga, from adding juniper berries and wild mushrooms to flavour hunter's stew, to savouring wild strawberries, sweetened with local honey, in a tangy dessert.

Further south still, the landscape softens into a more productive zone known as the 'steppe'. Western Russia, in particular, has a fantastic natural resource in the 'black earth' zone to be found around Moscow, fed by the long Volga River. This black earth, or *chernozem*, allows the farmers to grow nourishing food crops such as grains of all kinds, vegetables, sunflower seeds and pasture for cattle, sheep and pigs. The collapse of the Communist system of collective farms left much of this fertile land uncultivated for a few years, but now both local and European entrepreneurs are beginning to see its potential and are working on bringing the land back to life.

Northern Russia, including the whole of Siberia, is very sparsely populated, even in the 21st century, when transport links have traversed the wildest places on Earth. Here time seems to stand still, and life is very harsh. Meat is a rarity and is enjoyed only on special occasions. People in Siberia eat the same type of food that people in this region have always consumed: a relatively restricted, but healthy, diet of dark rye bread, root vegetables, game, fish and dairy products.

The fishing industry
Fishing is a very important food industry in Russia. The country adjoins three major oceans: the Arctic, the Atlantic and the Pacific. Russia also has borders with the smaller Caspian Sea and the Black Sea, and contains hundreds of lakes and rivers teeming with freshwater fish.

Russian fishing fleets go out to sea every day of the year, and come back loaded with cod, herring, crab and haddock from the cold northern waters. Russian caviar, renowned all over the world, comes from sturgeon that grow to a great size in the warm Caspian Sea. All of these different kinds of fish and shellfish are used in traditional recipes, particularly on those days when meat is banned by the church for religious reasons, such as the period of Lent.

Below: In contrast to Russia's fertile areas is the harsh and extensive Baikal steppe of the Chinese-Russian borderlands.

Russian Cuisine

The cooking of Russia has its roots in how to make the most of a sometimes limited number of local ingredients and how to sustain the body against the bitter cold of a Russian winter. There is still time and energy, however, to express the Russian love of food and hospitality.

The cuisine of the past

Many years ago, this huge country had a largely rural population. The peasants would work on land owned by the nobility, and traditional methods of food production lasted for centuries. All kinds of grain, particularly wheat, corn and buckwheat, were grown on the wide, flat fields, and this encouraged the development of recipes for different kinds of bread, pastry and cakes. Bread is an absolute staple of the Russian diet – no meal would be complete without it.

21st-century changes

The hoarding instinct became more pronounced, if anything, during the food shortages of the 20th century, when Communism changed the way the land was farmed, not always for the better as far as feeding the people was concerned. When Communism fell in the late 20th century, a small but influential new upper class appeared, the 'new Russians', along

Below: The samovar may have been replaced by the electric kettle, but it is still held in great affection by Russians.

with a growing lower class, whose access to wealth was strictly limited. The new Russians are affluent, sometimes super-wealthy, and this spending power has introduced a new spectrum of luxury items in the food stores as well as Western-style restaurants and cafés.

Eating out

When Russians cook at home they do not think or care about which region the dish originates from. That is not the case when eating out, as restaurants are strictly of a type: a Georgian restaurant would never dream of serving a course from Ukraine, for example.

As well as these specialist regional restaurants, in recent times Russian fast-food places have become popular. Here a buffet of hot and cold traditional Russian courses is offered for a low price. The most perfect Russian fast food is actually a traditional dish, pelmeni, which can be made with around 20 different fillings. Another Russian classic to be found on the streets of most towns is the beer stand, the beer being served warm when the weather is cold, and always accompanied by a salty snack such as salted fish or boiled crayfish.

Above: There are many different versions of the famous Russian borscht.

Shopping and cooking

Russians love to eat and drink, especially in the company of family and friends. Hence they are also very generous and hospitable hosts, and eating at home with family and friends is an important part of life. Many Russians today shop at supermarkets, where they can buy typical Russian fare as well as imported delicacies. But special food-market stalls entirely devoted to either pickled vegetables or many kinds of dried fruit still thrive, while fresh bread is usually bought every morning from the baker.

The typical Russian way of cooking is to make large batches of food at one time. Casseroles and soups are made in large 7-litre (12-pint) pans and nobody thinks twice about eating the same food for four consecutive days.

Food of the day

Breakfast is usually a cup of tea with sugar and a slice of lemon, and maybe a piece of bread or cake to go with it. The classic Russian lunch is often taken in a *stolovaja*. These are simple cafeterias where students and employees eat an inexpensive lunch of genuine Russian food. Usually there are three dishes to choose from, inevitably including a soup. As always in Russia, bread and tea is served with the meal.

Dinner is the main meal of the day. In past times, when many people were working hard on the land, it would be a substantial affair to keep up the energy levels. The nobility stretched this meal into several courses, while peasants might be on basic rations of bread and soup, maybe with a little meat or fish.

These days, if it is a special occasion there will be some appetizers (zakuski), a thick, rich soup, then a main course of meat, fish or poultry. Desserts are usually light and based on fruit after the rich and substantial savoury courses.

Pelmeni

These tiny pasta rolls, filled with meat and eaten all over Russia, are something between dim sum and ravioli and originally came from China.

Pelmeni are at their best when home-made, but these days they can be bought frozen. Making these snacks is a fantastic way of spending quality time with friends and family, as pelmeni are usually made in big batches, often around 100 at a time. There is always a bottle of vodka and a plate of simple zakuski around to help yourself from while the baking goes on. One person takes care of the dough, another mixes the meat, and a third fills the little rolls with the filling. Once ready, pelmeni are placed in perfect straight rows on cutting boards, carefully counted and placed in the freezer. They taste best 'frost-bitten', according to the Russians.

When it is time to eat, the pelmeni are boiled from frozen in water and stock, and served with refreshing sour smetana, a couple of drops of vinegar, salt and ground black pepper – simple, yet elegant. Around 20 pelmeni per person is a normal portion, and vodka is the only possible drink to go with them.

Blinis

For Russians, blinis have symbolized life and fertility since pagan times. Perfectly round, golden and warm, the blini also symbolizes the sun. During Maslenitsa, a happy festival where the return of the spring is celebrated, blinis are the main food for a whole week. They are also

Above: Russian vodka must be served ice cold and in large quantities.

eaten to excess before the start of Lent. In the old days they were served to women in childbirth to help them gather their strength and sustain them through labour. 'Life begins and ends with blini', according to the Russians.

Champagne, vodka and tea

Russian champagne is often served throughout a good dinner; it is sweet and served at room temperature, but the new generation has learned to appreciate French champagne served chilled.

Vodka is made from wheat grain and often has a touch of sweetness from sugar, berries or fruits. Roots and herbs are also used to season vodka. Chilli pepper vodka is bottled with a whole red chilli. Vodka is usually enjoyed straight, and Russians always have a piece of dark

Below: Frost-bitten pelmeni ready to be dropped in boiling stock.

bread or a salted cucumber to go with it. To have a toast with vodka is a way of showing respect for the host. The tradition is to empty the glass in a single gulp. There is a Russian saying, 'To leave vodka in the glass is to leave tear drops for the host'.

Tea, served from the samovar, once had almost ritual status. Today kettles and tea bags are commonplace, but the samovar, also now likely to be electric, is still used at parties. Russians take their tea with sugar and lemon rather than milk.

Zakuski

The tradition of zakuski first appeared in Russian manor houses when a table of food and drink was always ready in the hallway, to greet guests any time of day or night. On the table a carafe containing vodka was given the place of honour, and during the winter the samovar was constantly sizzling with hot tea, together with dishes of salted cucumbers, smetana (sour cream), pickles, black bread and a simple fish or meat dish. Gradually the number of dishes on the table increased, and eventually people were sometimes too full to eat dinner once it was time to sit down for the main meal of the day.

Nowadays zakuski often consists of black sourdough bread, boiled potatoes mixed with dill, salted herring and smoked fish. There should also be some sort of caviar on the table. Often the famous salat olivje is included, and there will be some kind of 'poor man's caviar' made of vegetables.

Pickles are always a part of the zakuski table. Sauerkraut should be there, of course, but also marinated tomatoes and pickled mushrooms.

Russian Festivals and Celebrations

Hospitality is very important in most Russian households, and food and drink must be offered to visitors as they arrive to celebrate any holiday. As in most countries, special recipes are connected to the various festivals and religious ceremonies, and even at christenings no one would expect to leave without a glass or two of vodka and a plate or two of food.

New Year

According to the Russian calendar, New Year is before Christmas. During the years when Christmas was banned, some of the activities that belonged to Christmas were transferred to the New Year celebration, so now the decorated fir tree and Father Frost (Ded Moroz), are part of the New Year celebrations. On New Year's Eve, 31 December, Russians like to celebrate with a party of vodka and zakuski. At midnight there is champagne and festive fireworks.

The highlight of New Year for children is the arrival of Father Frost. According to Russian tradition he is offered a glass of vodka at every place he visits and cannot refuse without being rude. Father Frost carries a staff and wears a long blue coat. His helper, the Snow Maiden, represents frozen rivers and lakes and is dressed in a sparkling blue gown.

Christmas

Orthodox Christians follow the Julian calendar, so Christmas Day falls on 7 January, and is a quiet family celebration in comparison to the more extravagant New Year celebrations.

Below: A girl lights a candle in St Petersburg's Cathedral. In the Orthodox church Christmas Day falls on 7 January.

During the Soviet era it was actually forbidden to celebrate Christmas for several years. However, many people continued to celebrate in secret. Today, Christmas once again is regarded as a religious festival and a national holiday. Many people follow the tradition of fasting before Christmas, when they will

Below: An impressive display of New Year fireworks begins over St Basil's Cathedral in Moscow's Red Square.

Above: Father Frost, the Russian equivalent of Father Christmas, and his assistant, the beautiful Snow Maiden, arrive in central Moscow for the traditional New Year parade on 31 December.

avoid dishes that contain fat and meat. Many traditional Russian dishes have been specifically created to be eaten during the fasting period, including the 'caviars' made from vegetables, especially beetroot (beets) and mushrooms. A meal of 13 of these dishes is eaten on Christmas Eve, one of which is kutja, a porridge made with honey and raisins that is also served at funerals. The meal begins with zakuski, after which there will be a borscht, or another rich soup. Pasties with mushrooms, fish or cabbage are served with the soup.

On Christmas Day the fast is finally over and a huge meal is served featuring the foods that were forbidden during the past few weeks. The main course is often roasted goose, suckling pig or turkey. Finally the dessert table is laid with gingerbread, fruit compotes and kiselj, a soup made of cranberry juice thickened with cornflour (cornstarch).

Right: A lavishly spread Easter zakuski table, decorated with Fabergé eggs.

Maslenitsa

Originally an ancient pagan festival to welcome spring, today Maslenitsa is a big public party for both children and adults, with theatrical performances, dances and lots of games.

During the week of Maslenitsa, also known as 'Butter Week', the children ride sledges, build snow forts and have snowball fights, while the adults take sleigh rides and drink cognac served from samovars. Outside the cities, large bonfires are built and people burn *tjutjelo*, dolls made with straw symbolizing winter.

Blinis are the absolute favourite food during Maslenitsa. In Russia it is said that when you eat a blini you get a share of the warmth and the strength from the sun, and during the week of Maslenitsa everyone eats them to excess.

Lent

During Lent the rule for Orthodox Christians is to abstain from meat and eggs. Instead they are allowed to eat food such as fresh and pickled vegetable and mushrooms fried in vegetable oil. Over the centuries, much creativity has gone into inventing filling dishes avoiding the proscribed meat and fish: stews, pelmeni, soups, vegetable caviar, pastries with vegetables, mushrooms and fruits.

Easter

Called Pascha in Russian, Easter is the most important festival in the Christian calendar. In Russia it occurs at the same time of year as an old pagan feast marking the end of winter. One Easter tradition is to select perfect, white eggs to cook and paint. The eggs can also be dyed red by boiling them with onion skins. These brightly painted eggs are used to brighten up the table and are also given as presents to friends and family. Tsar Nikolai II gave bejewelled eggs made by Fabergé in St Petersburg to his wife and his mother. Today these extravagant eggs represent a piece of Russian imperial history and the tradition of giving bejewelled eggs has been revived.

The grand pashka, the Easter dessert, dominates the festive table. It is made in a wooden pyramid mould decorated with religious symbols and the letters 'XB', meaning 'Christ is Risen'. Another favourite Easter cake is kulich, a tall, round confection glazed with sugar and filled with raisins and nuts.

A modern Easter party in the 21st century starts with vodka and zakuski (often including chicken liver mousse, marinated mushrooms, and fish salad) and ends with pashka and kulich. In between come many different meat, poultry or fish dishes which have been off the menu for the last seven weeks, such as rabbit in smetana, roast chicken stuffed with sauerkraut and dried fruits, or oven-baked fish. Family and friends are invited to share the Easter feast.

Below: Russian monks enjoy traditional Easter foods; cake, red caviar and wine.

Below: Street parades in traditional costume often mark national holidays.

Polish Land and History

Surrounded on most of its borders by powerful neighbouring countries, Poland was for centuries subjected to repression and occupation by other nations. This is not surprising, for it was a prize worth capturing: the fertile countryside abounds with all manner of good things to eat – from vast fields of grain and lakes and rivers teeming with freshwater fish, to large forests inhabited by animals and birds suitable for the table.

The first Polish kingdom

Prior to 966, the year of the earliest recorded historical event and first written reference to a Polish state, the region that is now known as Poland was inhabited by various tribes, including the Polanie, Wislanie, Pomorzanie and Mazovians. With the baptism of Mieszko I, duke of the Slavic tribe of Polans, in 966, the tribes, known collectively as the West Slavs, were united, and within 25 years had become one of the most powerful states in eastern Europe.

For the next 800 years Poland was a flourishing sovereign state, which made trade and cultural links with other countries through a combination of adventurous exploration and royal marriages. In addition, from 1569 to 1791 Poland joined with Lithuania to form a commonwealth that was beneficial to both countries and made them a strong force in eastern Europe.

With hunting parties providing venison, hare, pheasant and duck from the woods; mushrooms and herbs growing abundantly in the deep forests; and fish filling the lakes, ready to be fried, simmered, or made into soup, medieval Poland already had a strong and diverse culinary culture.

With the formation of strong links with the rest of Europe, however, cooking techniques and ingredients from western and southern Europe, especially Italy and France, started to have a huge influence on Polish food. In addition, spices from the East started to be incorporated, being used, in particular, to disguise the flavour of any meat or game that was perhaps past its best.

With the arrival in 1518 of an Italian princess, Queen Bona Sforza, to marry King Sigismund I, Polish cooking began to evolve into the rich cuisine of today. Homesick for Italy, the new queen encouraged French and Italian cooks to travel to Poland, bringing with them more delicate recipes for soups and stews, as well as new ingredients, including cabbage, leeks, lettuce and celeriac, which were adopted with enthusiasm.

Division of the spoils

From the end of the 18th century until the end of the 20th century, the history of Poland has been one of occupation and turmoil. For many years the land was controlled by different powers, including Russia, Prussia and Austria. This was followed by a brief period of independence in 1918–39, which ended abruptly when Nazi Germany invaded in 1939. After the war the country fell under Communist rule and the domination of the USSR until 1989.

Over 20 per cent of the population of Poland died during World War II, most of them Jews and members of other ethnic minorities who were transported to concentration camps. Survivors had their natural food stocks to fall back on when imports became scarce, but even these were often taken from them in the later 20th century to feed other mouths, or wasted under the centralized Communist system. Despite an attempt to establish collective farms under this system after 1945, however, the traditional Polish system of small-scale agriculture somehow survived, along with many closely guarded age-old local recipes and ingredients.

The 21st century

Poland has changed radically since the uprising against the Communist leaders in the 1980s, which was led by Lech Walesa and the Solidarity trade union, based in the Gdansk shipyards. It now has its own democratic government, although several Communist party members have been returned to power now that the people are free to choose their own representatives. It has also joined NATO and the EU, and a free flow of goods and people passes once again into and out of the country.

Left: Deer have been hunted in the forests of Poland since medieval times, and venison is still very popular.

As with many changing countries in Eastern Europe, a large number of Polish workers go abroad to further their careers in more prosperous parts of the world. And wherever Polish workers go, they take cultural traditions with them. As a result, although Polish restaurants and food stores have long been a feature of the larger cities in Europe, especially since World War II, these outlets are now spreading further afield as they find new opportunities for work abroad.

The geography of the country

Poland's shape – a square with the south-western corner chewed away – is dominated by the natural boundaries of

Below: Carp, a favourite on the Polish table at Christmas, are found in the many lakes.

Above: The stunning Baltic coastline is home to many different types of fish.

the Baltic Sea to the north and the Sudeten, Tatra and Carpathian mountain ranges to the south. On its western and eastern borders, however, there are no such physical delineations. On the western border the only sign that you are passing from Germany to Poland is the Oder river, which winds its way from south to north towards the sea. On the eastern side,

nothing separates Poland from its neighbours, Kaliningrad, Lithuania, Belarus and Ukraine.

This lack of natural boundaries has proved inviting to Poland's neighbours, who have, in the past, been tempted to take advantage of Poland's abundant natural resources for their own use.

Below: Because it is bordered by seven other countries, Poland has enjoyed the influence of many different cultures.

However, Poland's position as a kind of pivot nestling between Western and Eastern Europe, as well as between the warm south and the chilly north, also has its advantages. One of these is the country's exposure to different cultures and their corresponding trade links. As a result, Poles have been able to adapt their cuisine to mix local ingredients with imported crops, such as potatoes and salad vegetables, which now flourish in the fertile soil.

Southern mountains

To the south, Poland's natural border is formed by the spectacular mountain ranges that divide the country from the Czech Republic and Slovakia. With most of Poland's hills rarely rising to more than 300m/1,000ft above sea level, the

Above: The beautiful Tatra mountain range forms a natural border with Slovakia.

contrast between the plains and the southern fringe is extreme. The highest mountain, Mount Rysy, in the Tatra range on the border with Slovakia, is 2,499m/8,200ft above sea level, while the lowest point, located west of the village of Raczki Elblaskie, plunges to 1.8m/5.9ft below sea level.

The foothills to these mountains support a range of animals, including sheep, pigs and cattle. Hay fields rising gently up the slopes are a common sight and are cultivated in order to feed the animals. Despite the abundance of sheep, lamb is not a favourite meat in Poland – and flocks of sheep are more often kept for their wool, to be made into clothing

City life

The capital city, Warsaw, like many of the other major cities of Poland, is situated in the central region of the country. Now that the restrictions of earlier years have been lifted, there is a flourishing restaurant trade in these cities, and people love to go out on special occasions to eat their favourite foods – dumplings (pierogi) filled with savoury or sweet mixtures, filling soups, hunter's stew (bigos) and the delectable cakes and pastries made by the many bakers to be found in Polish cities.

ready for the cold winters, and their milk, to be made into a much-loved sharp-tasting sheep's cheese.

Despite the winter cold, the southern mountain region is well-populated, with family farms predominating. Some entrepreneurial inhabitants now take advantage of their position in the fresh mountain air to encourage tourists to stay for walking holidays, fortified by hearty stews and maybe the fierce local plum brandy (Sliwowica Lacka). Other local industries include food-processing plants, which now package and despatch the abundant meat, dairy and food crops of the region.

Left: The sweeping grasslands of Poland provide hay to feed the cattle, sheep and pigs throughout the winter.

A good farming climate

Temperatures and growing conditions in Poland vary only slightly from one side of the country to the other, with warmer, wetter weather in the south-west and colder, drier areas in the north-east. The whole country can be very cold in the winter as the biting north-westerly winds sweep across mainland Europe and Scandinavia, picking up rain and snow clouds from the Baltic.

Summer temperatures are rather more variable, depending on the prevailing air currents, although the reliable gentle summer rains bring stable growing conditions for the crops of central Poland and ensure that there is always enough summer pasture for the cattle and food for the pigs.

To make the most of such fertile conditions the people of Poland developed many ways of working with the climate to maximize crop yields from the land. They also knew how to make sure there was enough food to see them through the lean times of year, and this led to many excellent, tasty recipes based on meat, game, root vegetables, grains and freshwater fish, combined with preserved foods such as sauerkraut, curd cheese, sour cream and, of course, the famously potent local vodka.

Northern lakes

The region in northern Poland that borders the Baltic Sea is a flat wetland dominated by waterways and home to many of the country's 10,000 lakes. These lakes are teeming with a great variety of freshwater fish, a fantastic source of protein that has been part of Polish cuisine since the earliest days. Pike, carp and trout in particular grow to a good size, and are served to the whole family on feast days such as Christmas, where carp is set in jelly or simmered in a wine stock. In the past a successfully caught carp was kept alive until the last moment before it was cooked to ensure its freshness – often even swimming in the family's bathtub!

The Baltic coastline is smooth, with the strong currents of the Baltic driving shoals of fish past Poland and on to the Baltic states and Scandinavia. Poland's relatively short sea border ends with a swirl at Gdansk, where the Vistula river meets the sea and a long spit of silt from the river has formed a natural lagoon.

Above: The fertile grasslands in central Poland are ideally suited for farming.

Poland's fishing fleets based on the coast still catch sardines, haddock, lobster and other seafood, but over-fishing and pollution in the Baltic means that many have to travel much longer distances to find enough fish.

In this spongy northern terrain, some of which is below sea level, there is little room between the lakes and forests for large-scale agriculture. Farms tend to be very small family affairs, with just a few pigs and cattle and the growing of root crops, particularly potatoes – a staple of many Polish dishes, including pancakes and dumplings.

Central plains

Like the northern lake region, the central part of Poland is also very flat, but less liberally sprinkled with lakes. This gives the farmers more room to grow cereals and to keep cattle, although family farms tend to be rather small and many still produce only enough food for their owners and for local markets, rather than trading on a national scale.

Shaped by the glaciers of the Ice Age, this flat landscape is rich in natural resources, particularly coal, and this led to considerable industrialization during the 19th and 20th centuries. In later years, these heavy industries have moved elsewhere, leaving a legacy of pollution, run-down housing and a lack of jobs for the local people.

Church festivals

The Catholic church – a hugely important part of life in Poland throughout its recorded history – retains its influence today. Nearly all Poles regard themselves as Catholics, with 75 per cent of them being regular churchgoers. A symbol of hope, the church helped to preserve traditional feast days and foods, and provided something to look forward to in the long dark years of food shortages and repression.

Polish Cuisine

In a country where the people have had to battle for independence, it is a matter of national pride that the traditions of Polish cuisine have been so well preserved. Faced with bitterly cold winters, the Poles know how to make expert use of their natural resources to produce hearty and sustaining meals. Polish food is not for slimmers!

Family life – the daily routine

From the shipyard communities of Gdansk in the north to the villages in the Tatra mountains in the south, Polish people take their daily meals seriously. Many dishes require long, slow cooking, and as most meals are eaten at home (restaurants are mainly for special occasions), time must be taken to plan, shop and cook for the family.

Breakfast

Although breakfast can be quite a quick meal – the working day often starts at 8am – it is still quite substantial. Poles like to base their morning meal on dark rye bread, cooked meats, hard-boiled eggs, cheese or jam. In the old days, people ate soup for breakfast, often thickened with grains (kasza) or based on sweetened milk with rice – a sustaining bowl of goodness to start the day. These days the liquid is more likely to be a cup of tea or coffee.

Lunch

Traditionally the main meal of the day in Poland, lunch is often eaten at home, although people who travel long distances to work might take lunch with them. If at all possible, everyone in the family will

Right: Steaming, hearty soups are often served in bread as a nourishing winter meal.

return home sometime between 1pm and 3pm to eat a two- or three-course meal that is designed to set them up with enough energy for the rest of the day.

The first course of this meal is nearly always soup. Poles love hearty vegetable and meat soups, and also make a range of chilled ones for summer. The famous soup borscht (barszcz), based on the beautiful ruby-red colour of beetroot (beets), is a universal dish, which pleases the eye as well as the stomach. Other favourite appetizers might be fish in aspic or a selection of cold cooked meats and vegetable side dishes. Next comes a sustaining main dish, such as hunter's stew (bigos) or pork cutlets served with sauerkraut and other vegetables. This course is generally based on meat, apart from on fasting days ordained by Catholic ritual, where fish takes its place.

Finally, the Poles love their desserts and will often find room for a cake such as poppy seed cake (makowiec), a substantial pastry such as plum dumplings (knedle ze sliwkami), or a dish of ice cream in hot weather.

Supper

At the end of the long working day, families will gather together again to eat supper, normally between 6pm and 8pm This is usually a lighter meal than lunch, with similar dishes – soup, fish, sweet desserts – being served, but this time omitting the heavier main course. Both lunch and supper may be accompanied by wine, vodka or fruit juice.

Snacks

Apart from the three main meals of the day, Poles enjoy eating snacks. Many Polish people have a sweet tooth, and there are a multitude of bakeries in every town and village. These bakeries sell a range of breads, of course, but their speciality is more often the delectable cakes and pastries that are so popular with their clientele.

Many of these delicacies are based on yeast dough, for example doughnuts (paczki z roza) or jam puffs, plum cake and seasonal favourites such as babka, an Easter cake made with citrus fruit, raisins and spices. Other sweet snacks are pastry-based, such as mazurek, a delicious tart

Far left: There is an abundance of fresh produce available at Polish markets.

Left: Bakeries selling bread and a range of cakes are visited on a daily basis.

Polish vodka

Picasso once said that 'the three most astonishing things in the past half-century have been the blues, cubism and Polish vodka'. This endorsement is well founded, as the amazingly strong spirit, made from potatoes and selected grains, flavoured with herbs, berries and spices, is now popular around the world and has a reputation for quality. In Poland, vodka is often drunk with meals as well as at other times.

made of pastry enriched with egg yolks and topped with all kinds of sweet things – soft cheese, honey, fruits, jam or nuts.

Preserving food

In any country that has extremely cold winters and where very little fresh food is available for weeks on end, techniques for preserving food needed to be developed to make sure everyone had enough to eat through the bleak months. This tradition is still practised in Poland today, and there are a range of pickled foods that feature on the winter menu.

Sauerkraut is perhaps the most famous of these. It originated as a way of preserving cabbage for use when fresh vegetables could not be dug from the snow-covered fields, but has now become a staple ingredient that is used in all types of weather. In past times, country households would keep a barrel of the pickle in the kitchen, while townspeople could buy a ladleful at a time from a similar barrel in the grocer's shop. Today,

Right: The oven is the key feature of this beautiful traditional Polish kitchen.

sauerkraut is widely available in jars and cans. Other vegetables, such as cucumbers, gherkins, beetroot (beets) and kohlrabi, can also be pickled, while others, such as the many varieties of mushrooms found in the forests, can be dried and added to marinades and stews.

In past years, before fresh fish could be easily and quickly transported around the country, only people who lived near the coast could eat seafood all year round, until a recipe for soused herring made with spices and vinegar was developed. Like sauerkraut, this is a staple dish that is found in most European countries with a Baltic Sea or North Sea coastline, ranging from Belgium to Norway.

Regional and ethnic dishes

The shape and terrain of Poland means that it has always been well served by trade links within and outside of the country. Linked by the mountain ranges to the south to its Czech and Slovak neighbours, and with no geographical barriers further north, Poland trades freely with Germany and France on one side and Russia on the other. With such open borders, any localized recipes soon spread over the whole country.

Despite this, some regions are known for certain foods. The northern lakes produce freshwater fish in abundance, and these became a major part of many

Above: Hot doughnuts filled with rosehip jam are a favourite snack in Poland.

Christmas feasts. Further south, fields of grain provide the basic ingredients for all sorts of bread, particularly the dense, robust rye bread found throughout Poland and its neighbouring countries. In the high southern mountains, sure-footed sheep provide milk to be made into a fresh, sharp cheese (oszczypek).

The influence of the many Jewish people who lived in Poland before World War II can be seen in several dishes, especially the traditional Jewish fish dish, pike or carp in aspic, which has been incorporated into Polish Catholic tradition and has become a regular part of Christmas feasts.

Polish Festivals and Celebrations

Many of the festivals celebrated in Poland are linked to the rituals of the Catholic calendar, with its emphasis on Christmas and Easter. These two major Christian celebrations are marked with a quite magnificent seriousness in Poland, and the religious basis is never forgotten. Other, more secular celebrations are also noted during the year, including hunting feasts in rural areas and name-day parties everywhere, as well as weddings and other family get togethers.

Christmas

Celebrations start early in Poland, with St Nicholas arriving on his sleigh on 6 December to hand out presents of honey and almond cookies and apples to the children, along with religious pictures of the Nativity. Traditionally, good children were rewarded for reciting their prayers to St Nicholas; naughty ones who had not bothered to learn them by heart could expect a severe rebuke, and no presents!

After a few weeks' wait the biggest celebration of the year on Christmas Eve (Wigilia) takes place. Wigilia means 'waiting', and it is the anticipation of Christ's birth that is all-important.

Wigilia is a huge affair of long meals and family rituals involving dressing the tree and opening gifts. The presence of as many family members as possible is a vital element, and guests and strangers are welcomed in as part of the family, sometimes with an ulterior motive – to make up the numbers – odd numbers at the table are thought to bring bad luck.

Below: Carp in aspic is just one of the many dishes served for the Wigilia feast.

In past times, people in rural areas would bring a sheaf of corn into the house or spread hay under the white tablecloth to remind them of the manger in the stable where Jesus was laid. Most of all it is a day for telling the story of the Christmas angel, Aniolek, who brings the presents (and sometimes the sparkling tree, too) into the house while no one is looking; for dressing up in your best clothes; for waiting for the appearance of the first star in the sky, which signals the beginning of the feast; and, most of all, for eating the traditional food of this special day.

The Wigilia feast

This Christmas Eve meal is a major event in the Polish calendar. No meat is eaten, according to religious tradition, and people even try to avoid using animal fats

Below: A decorated Christmas tree in Bytom market square in Silesia, Poland.

Above: Honey and almond cookies are given to children during Advent.

in the cooking. In past years, the feast was a huge affair of 12 courses (to represent the 12 apostles), but nowadays three or four courses are considered plenty. First, the family and guests will break and share a plate of oplatek, the thin wafers associated with the

communion service in church. Then follows a warming beetroot (beet) or sweet almond soup and some dishes of vegetables from the surrounding fields, such as sauerkraut, stuffed kohlrabi, mushrooms and potatoes.

The main dish is usually a magnificent whole carp or pike, and the meal ends with a dried fruit compote, and then the special Christmas pudding, kutia, made from wheat grains, honey, poppy seeds, cherry jam, dried fruit and nuts. Those who are still hungry might nibble the traditional honey cookies or a yeasty poppy seed roll, and the grown-ups can open their presents with a glass or two of fiery vodka to hand.

After the feast
Midnight Mass follows the Christmas Eve celebration, and the family service is a chance to focus on the real reason for the feast. It also marks the end of Wigilia as the birth of Christ is celebrated by the

A Wigilia feast
This joyful family feast will include some of the following:
- Christmas borscht
- Christmas Eve almond soup
- Herring in sour cream
- Carp in aspic, or wine sauce, or fried in breadcrumbs
- Pike with hard-boiled eggs and parsley
- Dumplings (pierogi)
- Sauerkraut with mushrooms
- Noodles with poppy seeds
- Dried fruit compote
- Poppy seed rolls
- Christmas pudding (kutia)
- Wine with the savoury dishes and vodka with the pudding

Above: At Easter time Polish women and girls traditionally spend Good Friday hand-decorating eggs. These are then used as table decorations or gifts.

congregation. After all this splendour, Christmas Day lunch is often a smaller and quieter affair. Some families eat a roast turkey, but more often the meal consists of leftovers from the previous day served cold with plenty of salad and vegetables. It is a time to enjoy visiting friends or family, where you will be offered a piece of honey cake or cookies.

New Year's Eve
This is a time to shake off the excesses of Christmas and start afresh with a party, either at home or out at a restaurant if you are lucky enough to be able to book a place. There may well be a full dinner during the evening, followed by champagne and a buffet after midnight.

Twelfth Night
Christmas finally winds down on 6 January, with a quiet celebration marking the arrival of the wise men at Christ's nativity. On this day, known as Twelfth Night, many families still mark the initials of the three kings above their front door with chalk, and burn incense in order to protect the home and family against hardship during the coming year.

Good Friday
On Good Friday, the main focus is religious. Many families visit several churches, to pray, but also to inspect and compare the decorated tombs found in each church, with an effigy of the Christ figure surrounded by flowers. A simple meal will follow that evening – maybe soused herring and potatoes – and the women spend the day decorating eggs.

Easter
It's hard to know how to top the festivities of Wigilia, but Polish people certainly try to go one better at Easter (Wielkanoc), when this most important Christian festival is celebrated with lavish feasting and partying alongside the traditional religious ritual.

There is a longer build-up to Easter than at Christmas, starting with the quiet and serious weeks of Lent. During this period everyone tries to give up some favourite food, and meat is eaten far less often than at other times of the year.

Easter also coincides with the annual spring cleaning season, a ritual that symbolizes death and re-birth. In Holy Week, just before Easter, the cooking and cleaning in every household rises to such a pitch that many men take themselves quietly out of the way to the local tavern or restaurant for a restorative meal or just some shots of excellent vodka.

Easter weekend

Saturday is a day of anticipation. In past times, the local priest would visit as many houses as possible to bless the family and the Easter feast laid out on the table, ready for the following day's celebrations. Finally, at midday on Easter Sunday, after another church service in the morning, the family gather for a long feast lasting through to the evening.

In the centre of the Easter Sunday table there is often a white lamb made of sugar or butter, usually standing on a little hill of greenery made of cress grown specially for the occasion, and surrounded by sweetly scented hyacinths. Once the

Above: The Easter table is laid on Easter Saturday and is often blessed by a priest.

Left: Lambs made from sugar or butter are sold during Easter.

family has gathered, a plate of quartered hard-boiled eggs is passed around and the feast can begin. This consists of cold meats including sausage, roast pork, turkey and ham; cold vegetables and salads; mazurki, the sweet, decorated pastries; and the Easter cake known as babka, baked in a special tall tin with fluted edges.

Harvest festival

A traditional rural feast day, the harvest festival is celebrated in most parts of the world. In Poland, the most popular and hardworking girl in a village (or maybe just the prettiest?) is chosen to represent the farm workers, and will carry a harvest wreath on her head from church to present to the local landowner. He will then reward the company with an array of dishes containing all the good things gathered during the harvest – grains, fruit, nuts and plenty of vodka.

Weddings and christenings

The traditional family celebrations of weddings and christenings are, of course, another good excuse for a great

Left: The annual harvest is a time of celebration and feasting.

meal with family members and friends, as they are everywhere in the world. In Poland, wedding traditions dictate that the bride and groom must pass a bottle of vodka to their neighbours before they can be allowed to walk through the spectators into the church.

After the ceremony there is a lavish wedding banquet for all the family and friends. Before it starts, however, another little ritual is always carried out, whereby the respective parents of the bride and groom offer them bread (ensuring that they always have plenty to eat); salt (to remind them of the hardships they may have to overcome); and a bottle of champagne (to celebrate the good things in life). The couple then drink the champagne and throw the glasses over their shoulders – if they smash, that will bring good luck.

Christenings follow a similar pattern to weddings: following a ceremony in church, christening parties often move on to the local tavern, where the godparents are expected to pay for the guests to toast the baby's health with vodka. These celebrations often used to extend over several days, but in busy modern times they are more likely to take up only one day. The traditional gifts of linen robes and caps for the baby have also changed over the years into gifts of cash.

Hunting feasts

In the old days, when rich landowners owned large tracts of Polish countryside, they would organize communal hunting parties to spend the day on the trail of wild boar, game birds and other delicacies of the forest. The whole male population of the village would be co-opted to help in shooting or beating, bringing their hunting dogs with them.

After all this effort and fresh air, the hunters would return ready for some good hot food and drink. This appetite, in conjunction with the mixture of meats from the day's hunt, gave rise to the famous Polish hunter's stew *bigos*. This rich and satisfying mixture of different kinds of meat, sauerkraut, mushrooms and stock is well spiced with juniper berries and peppercorns. Today, both hunting and the stew are still popular, accompanied by a glass of chilled vodka.

Name days

Polish people celebrate their name days rather than their birthdays. Most people are called by biblical names, and the corresponding saint's day is usually the most important secular day of the year for each individual. The day is marked by a feast or party, involving a good spread of food, plus plenty of alcohol, chocolates and presents. The guests may also sing the traditional song 'Sto lat', wishing them 100 years of happy life.

Secular festivals

Although religious occasions are marked with the best feasts, Poles do celebrate other events throughout the year. Some follow the rhythm of the seasons, such as hunting feasts and the Midsummer festival on 24 June, others are political. These include Consitution Day on 3 May and Independence day on 11 November.

Left: A traditional Polish wedding in the mountains in the south of the country.

CLASSIC INGREDIENTS

For centuries the difficult terrain and climate caused most of Russia to be quite isolated, and the rural population survived exclusively on locally grown produce. Gradually, as communications were established with its neighbours, new ingredients such as wheat and green vegetables were introduced to the Russian diet. Poland, on the other hand, has had access to a greater variety of ingredients since medieval times, as well as a kinder climate with fewer extremes. The climate in Poland, with its humid summers and wet, cold winters, gives ideal growing conditions for many seasonal crops and supports the yearly cycle of rearing farm animals for food, resulting in a natural abundance of locally grown produce such as grain and many varieties of fruit and vegetables. In Russia, the western side of the country has a similar climate, but further east and north, agriculture is more restricted. The ingredients in Siberian recipes, for instance, tend to be more earthy – potatoes, cabbage, honey, fish and game.

Fish and Shellfish

Recipes using fish and seafood are very popular in both Russia and Poland, and there is a big variety of species caught and sold. Russian fishermen have access to three major oceans, a host of smaller seas and hundreds of large lakes and rivers. Polish fishermen, however, set out from only a relatively short section of the Baltic Sea coast, and are therefore more dependant on the abundance of freshwater rivers and lagoons in this low-lying land.

Freshwater fish

The rivers and lakes that thread their way through the countryside of both Russia and Poland contain a fantastic source of protein that has long been incorporated in family meals.

Pike, carp and perch live in the still, deep waters of huge lakes and slow-running waterways such as canals, while trout and salmon leap and flash their silvery scales in the shallow, fast-flowing rivers. Carp and pike are both cooked for celebration meals, roasted whole with a tasty herb or horseradish dressing, marinated in red wine, dressed with chopped hardboiled eggs or even jellied in aspic. These impressive large fish make a great centrepiece for a Christmas or Easter feast, particularly when meat is off the menu for religious reasons. The Poles say that a shiny scale from the Christmas Eve carp, hidden in your wallet, will guarantee wealth for the coming year. Perch is also very popular – it is a common river fish and easily caught, even by inexperienced anglers. It is served in all sorts of ways – marinated, fried or

Above: Dried fish, displayed at a fish market in Ukraine.

poached with a mushroom and dill sauce. Trout and salmon tend to be treated very gently and simply baked in the oven to let their fresh flavour shine through. Garlic and herbs make a splendid dressing for the delicate flesh. Salmon is also used in a tasty pie with puff pastry.

Sea fish

Many varieties of sea fish are cooked and eaten by the Poles and the Russians – and coastal fishing dates back to the very earliest days of settlements around the coastline. People who live on the northern shores of Russia, in particular, rely on fish as a major source of protein, since meat is scarce in these chilly latitudes.

The subtle flavour of a piece of fresh fish straight from the ocean is often combined with dill, the most commonly used herb of these regions, whose feathery fronds are sprinkled liberally over the finished dish. Fillets of haddock, cod, sole or halibut are usually simply fried in breadcrumbs, grilled (broiled) or poached and served with a tangy sauce seasoned with lemon or sour cream. Smaller fish such as sardines are grilled and served whole, fresh from the sea, with just some melted butter and parsley as a dressing. Fish soup made of halibut, turbot or any other firm white fish is another favourite dish, and the Russian twist is to cook it with chopped salted cucumbers and capers to sharpen the flavour.

Below: White fish steaks, such as cod, are usually served fried in breadcrumbs.

Below: River trout are eaten simply baked whole with butter and parsley.

Below: Both Poles and Russians enjoy pike, a fearsome-looking freshwater fish.

FISH AND SHELLFISH 29

Above: Herrings are caught in huge quantities, and so are often preserved.

Above: Caviar is still Russia's most popular and extravagant indulgence.

Above right: Blinis with salmon and caviar.

Shellfish

Although both Russians and Poles eat many different types of shellfish, such as lobster, oysters and crab, their main focus is on the larger fish to be found in the sea. One favourite dish, though, is crab salad. This creamy mixture dressed with parsley might grace the zakuski table as an appetizer, and will usually be made of ready-prepared or canned crab mixed with chopped cabbage and mayonnaise.

Caviar

The roe from cod or pike used to be the single most important dish on the Russian table. Over time, sturgeon caviar became the most popular variety, and in the 1800s a well-to-do family might present a bowl containing 20 kilos (45lb) of caviar on their zakuski table, with a large silver spoon so that their guests could help themselves to this salty treat. In the West, caviar has come to represent utter luxury, and is usually served in small portions or as a dressing on top of a plainer fish, for example in a special-occasion recipe for sole with vodka sauce and caviar. Today wild sturgeon are nearly extinct, and real, original Russian caviar is more expensive than ever. However, a lesser quality black sturgeon roe can still be found at a lower price and is almost equally delicious.

Preserved fish

Fish can be canned, salted, pickled, smoked or dried in Russia and Poland. The Russian tradition of zakuski, a table groaning with delightful mouthfuls of hot

and cold snacks arranged to please the eye as well as the tastebuds, relies heavily on mouthwatering preserved fish.

Salted herring is served quite plainly with golden mustard sauce or with smetana (sour cream). Sometimes it is covered in a dressing of chopped hardboiled eggs and vegetables, which is known as sjuba, meaning 'fur' – herring in a fur coat. Blinis are often topped with little pieces of smoked salmon, and chopped smoked or salted fish makes a frequent tasty addition to a salad of mixed vegetables.

Below: Fish is often smoked or salted to preserve it, but also because it tastes good. Russians especially adore smoked salmon.

Fish stock

Makes about 1 litre/2 pints/ 6 cups stock
1kg/2lb white fish bones, heads and trimmings
1 litre/2 pints/6 cups cold water
6 white peppercorns
a bouquet garni
3–4 mushrooms
1 leek, roughly chopped
1 onion, roughly chopped
1 celery stick, roughly chopped

1 Wash the fish heads and remove the gills. Chop heads and bones if necessary. Place in a large pan.

2 Add the other ingredients, bring to the boil, lower the heat and simmer for 20 minutes (no longer or the flavour will be unpleasant). Strain. Season to taste.

Meat and Poultry

The people of Poland and Russia love meat. It often forms the main course for lunch or supper, and always for large celebratory meals, when the religious calendar allows. On these important occasions the meat is often prepared whole, and roasted suckling pig, chicken or goose are characteristic dishes for Easter Sunday or New Year feasts. The lesser cuts need tenderizing, and this is achieved by simmering on a low heat for a long time in a covered pot.

Pork

A plump pig, carefully fattened through the summer and autumn and eaten during the cold winter months, is still found in many a backyard and smallholding. During the years of massive collective farms in Russia in the 20th century, pork meat and pork sausage was less easy to find, but in Poland, this tradition survived in the countryside throughout the Communist era. Pork is cooked in all kinds of delicious ways – fried in breadcrumbs, roasted as a large joint with prunes or apple stuffing, stewed with vegetables, minced (ground) as a filling for rolled cabbage leaves, or even combined with several other meats in a tasty hunter's stew.

Pork sausage and ham are the most common forms of cured pork. They, too, feature in hunter's stew, lending their smoky flavour to the dish. Ukrainian cooks make a particularly piquant form of sausage blended with peperivka, or spirits flavoured with cayenne pepper, which gives the meat a definite kick. Polish sausage (kielbasa) is such an important part of the diet that it was one of the

Above: A cow herder moves cattle to new pastures in a Russian Federation village.

essential ingredients to make its way abroad with emigrating families. It is added to stews and soups or simply eaten sliced, as a snack, with a glass of vodka.

Beef

There are many Russian and Polish recipes for delicious beef dishes, from beef stroganoff to steak tartare. It is said that the Tartars, who first brought beef cattle

to Poland, used to tenderize their beef steaks by placing them under the saddle – inspiring the recipe for raw steak tartare. Lesser cuts of beef are minced together and often mixed with pork to make succulent burgers, served with buckwheat or mashed potato, or to form the filling

Below: Pork chops make a frequent appearance on the Polish table.

Below: Smoked sausage can be served in slices with vodka or added to stews.

Below: Lamb or mutton is not such a favourite in Poland as it is in Russia.

Above: Smoked meat, especially chicken, is often eaten with salad in Russia.

for the little dumplings (pelmeni) so beloved of the Russians. Beef can also be simmered gently in a thick tomato, red wine and paprika sauce to make goulash, topped with a spoonful of sour cream for each portion.

Veal
Poles and Russians love veal, especially veal cutlets, which they eat in the same way as pork chops, simply fried in breadcrumbs. Veal liver, kidneys and brains, which make a luxurious savoury treat served on toast, are also popular.

Lamb
Although this is not quite such a popular meat as pork and beef, lamb features in many Polish and Russian recipes. It can be cooked as a whole roasted joint with

Below: Roast goose is served for special celebrations in both countries.

plenty of garlic and herbs, or as part of a meat soup, or a braised casserole, where its sweet taste blends well with aubergines (eggplants) and tomatoes.

Poultry
Many people still keep their own hens for fresh eggs and tasty meat. There are hundreds of recipes for using all parts of the chicken, from a whole roasted bird, stuffed with herbs and fruits, to a casserole or even a simple vegetable soup based on the stock from the carcase. However, the stronger flavours of goose and turkey are highly prized for special occasions, and potted goose, sealed and preserved in its own fat, is a winter favourite in Russia.

Game birds
Polish cuisine is full of recipes for partridge, pheasant, quail, pigeon and wild duck. The skill of plucking, dissecting, hanging, marinating and then cooking these wild birds is still one that is found in many kitchens. Juniper berries and other spices and herbs are often used to marinate the birds before cooking.

Game meat
Both Poland and Russia are full of wild places where hare, rabbit, deer and wild boar can be hunted. These strong-tasting meats are generally cooked in the oven to tenderize them and make the most of the fragrant gravy. Venison steaks are the exception; they are best pan-fried with strong wild mushrooms, and served with a red wine sauce.

Below: Partridges have less fat and a stronger taste than farm-reared birds.

Chicken stock

Makes about 1.5 litres/2½ pints/6½ cups
a whole chicken or 900g/2lb
  chicken wings and drumsticks
2 leeks, roughly chopped
1 large carrot, roughly chopped
1 celery stick, roughly chopped
2 bay leaves
2 sprigs fresh thyme
1.75 litres/3 pints/7½ cups water

1 Put all the ingredients into a large pan. Bring slowly to the boil, then use a spoon to skim.

2 Reduce the heat and simmer the stock very gently for 2–3 hours, skimming occasionally if necessary. Rapid boiling will make the stock cloudy.

Below: Venison is still hunted in both Russia and Poland.

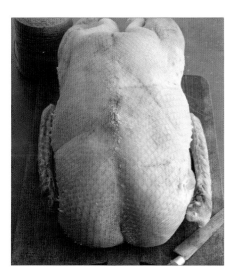

Dairy Produce and Eggs

The farmers of Poland and western Russia have always kept extensive sections of their land as pasture for cows, sheep and goats. The lush green fields of grass in the plains and on the lower mountain slopes, particularly in the Caucasus near Russia's south-western border, are watered by the plentiful rain and snow of these parts. Sheep and goats, as well as cows, are milked to make yogurt, cream, sour cream (smetana), butter and soft cheeses.

Fresh cream

The Russians and Poles are very fond of sweet food, in the form of gooey cakes and rich desserts. Fresh cream makes the perfect accompaniment, whether it is whisked to soft peaks and then spread between the layers of sponge cake, or heated with vanilla sugar to make a custard topping for Easter pastry.

Sour cream (smetana)

This tangy, smooth cream is a real feature of Russian and Polish cooking. Preserving food is a vital element of the cuisine, and sour cream tends to last a lot longer than the fresh variety. It is almost ubiquitous in Russian and Polish recipes, both sweet and savoury.

Sour cream is stirred into nearly every soup pan just as it is ready to serve, or added in spoonfuls on top of each individual portion. It is also a main ingredient in the sauce when cooking rabbit casserole or beef stroganoff. And there are yet more savoury uses for this delicious dairy product: as a dip for

Right: Sour cream is used in Russian cuisine in a huge variety of ways.

Above: Cows grazing on hillside pastures in the Tatra Mountains of Poland.

cheese dumplings, for instance, or a light dressing for salad, or forming the sauce for a panful of courgettes (zucchini).

Sour cream can also be used in a multitude of sweet dishes. It blends with soft cheese in a baked cheesecake, or with potato flour to make the succulent wrapping for a whole stuffed plum dumpling, or with butter, sugar and flour

Above: Whipped fresh cream accompanies desserts and cakes in Russia and Poland.

for the deep-fried little treats eaten at Christmas, known as angels' wings.

Sour cream is quite high in fat, but if calories are an issue, crème fraîche can be used instead. However, this does not give quite such a rich texture to the dish.

Below: Yogurt is sometimes used as an alternative to sour cream.

Above: Curd cheese is used to make dumplings and a range of desserts.

Above: Cottage cheese is a lighter alternative to curd cheese.

Above: Butter is used in cooking rather than spread on bread.

Yogurt

This is sometimes used as a lighter alternative to the sour cream (smetana) so beloved of both Russians and Poles. It can be stirred into soup in exactly the same way as sour cream, but does not blend quite so well and has a more astringent taste. It is often used in recipes from the Caucasus, for example in yogurt and barley soup, or as a topping for lamb dishes. It also has a longer shelf life so is more common in isolated areas.

Butter

Fresh country butter is most often used in baking. It lightens and enriches potato cakes and biscuits, and forms a major part of the creamy custard poured into a baked shell for the special Easter pastry.

Below: Eggs symbolize new life and spring in Polish and Russian traditions.

Cheese

While the favourite cheese for cooking in Poland and Russia is the soft variety, traditional types of harder cheese do exist. They are made of cow's, goat's or sheep's milk and tend to be quite smooth, yellow and creamy in texture. Mature varieties, such as Polish Tylzycki or Bursztyn, sometimes contain caraway seeds for a particularly zesty flavour. They are generally eaten with dark rye bread for breakfast or for a lunchtime snack.

The main form of cheese in Russia and Poland, however, is the soft kind, from the uneven texture of cottage cheese to smoother, richer curd cheeses. Like sour cream (smetana), it adds a velvety consistency to many dishes, and there are hundreds of recipes, both sweet and savoury, involving this useful ingredient with its bland flavour.

Soft cheese can be the main ingredient in baked cheesecake, a Russian favourite with a cup of tea in the afternoon, or form the filling for crêpes, blended with egg yolks and sugar. One of the traditional recipes eaten at Easter is a dome-shaped pudding called pashka, which is formed from a mixture of strained cottage cheese, eggs, butter and sugar, dotted with dried fruit.

In its savoury form, soft cheese appears in several Polish and Russian dumpling recipes, either as a filling mixed with onion and mashed potatoes, or as part of the dough.

Right: Hard-boiled eggs are used extensively in Russian cooking.

Eggs

'Round as an egg' was an old Russian saying to describe a beautiful young girl. This was a great compliment, as eggs were very precious. They are also an important part of the Russian Orthodox Church's Easter celebrations.

A perfect, cheap Russian dinner might consist of a couple of fried eggs, a piece of bread and two or three fried sausages or some tasty fried onions. Eggs are indispensable in baking as part of the pelmeni dough, and also in sweet cakes and gateaux, omelettes and pancakes.

Polish cooks also find a place for eggs in the form of baked goods such as cakes and desserts, but in Poland they are very often hard-boiled, sliced in two and served cold as part of a salad. Chopped hard-boiled eggs also make a great thickener for a creamy white sauce or mayonnaise, and add nutritional value.

Vegetables and Grains

The fertility of the black, humus-rich soil in the most populated parts of Russia and Poland, and the culture of maintaining a kitchen garden, have led to an emphasis on vegetables of all kinds in Russian and Polish cuisine. Before trading links were forged with the rest of the world in the 16th century, both countries tended to rely on the sturdy root vegetables, wild mushrooms and nourishing grains that were the only crops that grew reliably in the difficult climate. More delicate salad vegetables, grown in hothouses, appeared in the 17th and 18th centuries.

Beetroot (beets)
This ruby-red vegetable is much loved by both Poles and Russians for its sweet taste and nutritional qualities, not to mention its reputation as an aphrodisiac! It was first mentioned as being cultivated in Poland and the Ukraine as far back as the 11th century. Beetroot makes a lovely rich and satisfying hot soup with sour cream (borscht), and it also blends beautifully with sour cream and hard-boiled eggs to make a fragrant cold soup. Chopped beetroot is a favourite ingredient in salads, and seems to offset the texture of oily fish particularly well. Russians mix it with chopped hard-boiled eggs, apples and strips of salted herring and pile it into a dome shape for the famous dish, Russian salad. They also use finely diced beetroot as a tasty topping for blinis, when it is known as beetroot caviar.

Potatoes
It is quite surprising that the potato, now found in so many Polish and Russian recipes, was unknown in both countries until the 17th century. Peter the Great introduced it to Russia and it has become ubiquitous in Russian cooking, whether as

Above: Seasonal vegetables and fruits piled high on a market stall in Krakow, Poland.

a separate vegetable accompaniment, in a stew, or cooked and cooled as part of a salad. Cold boiled potatoes with a sour cream dressing and plenty of feathery dill are a favourite part of the zakuski table.

Polish cooks tend to use potatoes in all sorts of ways too – as a thickener in soups, as a main course with mushrooms, mashed and made into pancakes and dumplings – all of which are substantial and filling dishes suitable for the cold weather. Potato pies, pirojki, consist of a yeast pastry encircling a filling of mashed potatoes and fried onion. Soup is sometimes poured into a hole at the top of these little baked or fried treats.

Left: Beetroot is one of the main ingredients of the world-famous borscht.

Right: Red and green cabbage keep well through the long winter months.

Other root vegetables
Many of these feature in Russian and Polish recipes, usually as a basic ingredient of soups and stews, where they blend into the liquid and add flavour and health-giving qualities. Carrots, kohlrabi, swede (rutabaga), celeriac, black radish and turnips are ideal crops for growing in a smallholding and also are stored away to last through the winter.

Onions are found in most savoury dishes. They can be chopped small and blended with meat to make a juicy burger or a stuffing for roast meat, or sliced into stock for soups and stews.

Cabbage
The aroma of cabbage soup simmering on the stove must have filled many a Russian or Polish house over the last few centuries. Cabbage is a nutritious vegetable that grows through the winter and keeps well once cut. The traditional cabbage soup is a peasant dish that can contain a variety of ingredients depending on what is available: carrots, potatoes, celeriac and herbs. Like most Russian and Polish soups, it is served topped with a spoonful of sour cream.

Above: Potatoes were introduced to Polish and Russian kitchens in the 17th century.

The large outer leaves of green cabbage are rolled around minced (ground) meat or fish mixtures and baked in the oven, and the more delicate inner leaves are popular served raw, shredded and dressed with creamy mayonnaise in a salad. Red cabbage has its own distinctive flavour, and also looks stunning as an accompaniment to roast meat when braised with apples, herbs, honey and spices, and even a dash of red wine.

Sauerkraut

The best way to preserve cabbage if there is a glut is to pickle it in brine, after which it can be kept for up to seven months. Sauerkraut is made by slicing the cabbage

Below: White cabbage is grown in huge quantities and preserved in brine.

Above: Swedes are an important part of the winter diet in both countries.

finely, seasoning it with salt and then letting it mature in an oak barrel or a glass jar. Nowadays sauerkraut is more often bought ready prepared from the market, in a jar or a can.

This pungent mixture is used in all sorts of ways in Polish and Russian kitchens, helping to preserve health and enliven the taste of blander ingredients. It can be served as a side dish with sausages or poultry, stirred into a bubbling hunter's stew, blended with the stuffing for dumplings or mixed with other cold ingredients to make a tasty salad. Its strong flavour is an acquired taste for anyone not brought up to eat this typical Eastern European delicacy.

Below: Green cabbage is prized for its ability to grow through the winter.

Cooking with sauerkraut

Although often eaten cold, gentle simmering in a stew is a simple and delicious way to use sauerkraut. These casseroles become even tastier when left to stew overnight. As with all kinds of slow home cooking, the results vary according to the taste of the cook and the ingredients that are available. Sauerkraut can also be fried with onions and then cooked in wine or water. Some Russians cook sauerkraut in champagne.

Salted cucumbers

This is a Russian speciality. Salted cucumbers are made by preserving them with salt, spices, herbs and sometimes

Below: Russians are very fond of salted cucumbers dipped in honey and smetana.

Above: Cultivated mushrooms may not involve the thrill of the hunt but are almost as popular a cooking ingredient.

garlic or horseradish. They are set in layers in oak casks, interleaved with oak and cherry tree leaves. These strongly flavoured ingredients have many uses in Russian cuisine. They can be eaten quite plain, dipped in honey or sour cream, as part of a zakuski spread, or added to soups such as soljanka or rassoljnik. They are also sometimes even added to hot or cold sauces to spice up the mixture and add some texture.

Mushrooms

A staple of the kitchen, mushrooms grow wild and abundant in the forests of Poland and Russia. Many families still make expeditions to the countryside in autumn to pick mushrooms, using the knowledge of which varieties are good and safe to eat that has been handed down through the generations. Mushrooms are earthy, rich vegetables, which form an integral part of many savoury recipes. The flavour goes so well with robust dishes, for instance in a wild boar casserole or a sturdy, filling soup with pasta.

The best-loved mushrooms in Russia are porcini and ceps. They are delicious accompaniments to most food, and of all wild mushrooms they are the easiest to dry, making them available all year round. Their flavour seems to become even more

intense after drying, and once hydrated, they can be added in small quantities to enliven soups, sauces and pie fillings.

Salad vegetables

The Italian Queen Bona Sforza brought her retinue to Poland in the 16th century when she married King Sigismund I. Among her servants were several chefs, who delighted the court with their light, airy dishes and their talent for making refreshing salads from tender vegetables such as lettuce, spinach and leeks, previously unknown in the chilly, damp

Below: Wild mushrooms, such as chanterelles, are hand picked and added to stews or served as a side dish.

Above: Apple and leek salad is said to be one of the dishes that was introduced to Poland by their queen, Bona Sforza, who came from Italy.

Polish climate. These ingredients are still known in Poland as wloszczyzna, or 'Italian vegetables'.

Russians tend to use the sturdier vegetables such as carrots and cabbage in their salads, rather than delicate lettuce. Both Polish and Russian recipes for appetizers and side dishes are often based on cold salads and mixtures of fruit and vegetables, such as apple and leek salad, which makes the perfect accompaniment to cold meat and fish.

Wheat

Like potatoes, wheat made a late appearance in this corner of Eastern Europe, but has since become an absolute favourite. Half of the wheat crop of the world is now grown in Russian fields and used for home and export markets.

Poles love to use refined wheat flour in their white bread, which is eaten for breakfast and is also made into breadcrumbs, used in many dishes as a topping or a coating for pan-fried meat or fish. Plain (all-purpose) white wheat flour is often used in pastry and cakes, and makes superb Polish dumplings.

Russians also make kvass, a sweet low-alcohol drink, from wheat. It can be drunk as a refreshing pick-me-up or added to a cold soup for a little extra kick.

Above: Although the grain was introduced relatively recently, wheat crops now take up a very large proportion of Russian and Polish farmland.

Buckwheat

The grains originally grown in Russia and Poland were the earthier, stronger ones such as buckwheat. In its milled form it has a slightly grey colour that is not so appealing to the eye as white wheat flour or dark rye flour. However, it has a distinctive taste that Russians love in pancakes, and Poles know best in the form of kasha, a porridge-like side dish.

Below: The distinctive, almost triangular, shape of grains of buckwheat.

Rye

The word 'bread' in Russia and Poland often means a dark, dense rye loaf. The Russian obsession with rye bread is so all-consuming that in the past, people tended to eat as much as 1 kilogram (2lb) of it every day. It was also discovered that rye bread made with a sourdough mixture remained fresh for a long time.

Black rye bread is still the most popular kind of bread in Russia and Poland, even today, and no meal, at any time of day, is complete without it. Rye bread is an excellent accompaniment to smoked and pickled fish.

Like wheat, rye can be fermented and turned into a mixture that forms the base of a special soup. White borscht is made with fermented rye flour stirred into a vegetable stock. Its sharp, tangy taste is quite distinctive.

Barley

This grain has traditionally been grown in the wide, flat pastures of rural Poland and Russia, and in fact, Russia is the world's largest producer of barley.

As pearl barley it often adds welcome carbohydrates to soups. Pearl barley is barley that has been polished, or processed, to remove the nutritious hull and bran. It doesn't need pre-cooking, just simmering gently in the stock.

Below right: Barley is the perfect ingredient to add to soups and stews. Some of the best vodka in Poland is made from barley.

Below: Rye flour is used for making bread and white borscht in Poland.

How to cook buckwheat

Despite its name, buckwheat is not related to wheat and is often sought as a gluten-free alternative to wheat. High in manganese, iron, magnesium, phosphorus, copper and zinc, buckwheat is eaten as a side dish or added to soups and stews.

1 To cook buckwheat as a side dish, first measure how much you need, then wash it in several changes of cold water.

2 Put the buckwheat in a pan and add twice as much water, bring to the boil, cover, and simmer for 10–15 minutes until all the water has been absorbed. Season and serve immediately.

Fruit and Nuts

One of the great blessings of the Russian and Polish climate is its suitability for growing fruit and nuts. The temperate zones of Poland and south-western Russia contain orchards full of apples, grapes, plums and almonds; the woods and forests further north overflow with juicy berries and nuts in the autumn. Even in the colder areas of both countries, some low-growing berry bushes have become used to the frost and snow and in fact cannot tolerate any hot sun in the summer.

Left: A fruit farm in Russia, growing orchard fruits such as apples and pears.

Orchard fruits

Polish orchards are full of apple, pear and plum trees covered in blossom in the spring. So long as a cold April wind or a sudden frost does not destroy the crop, these will produce a huge number of delicious fruits in the autumn. Poles and Russians are particularly fond of blending sweet fruits with savoury meats, for instance in a fruity stuffing for roast goose, pork or duck, or as a tart plum sauce for beef kebabs. Polish fruit soup is a particular speciality, made of mixed plums, pears and cherries with water, sugar and sour cream. It is served cold as a summer treat, with potato dumplings.

Some of the most traditional recipes are for fruit desserts and cakes, such as an apple pie studded with raisins and enclosed in puff pastry, or simple baked apples. Plum dumplings contain a hidden treasure – a whole plum is encased in potato and sour cream pastry, with a spoonful of cinnamon and sugar tucked inside the fruit. At harvest time in Poland, cooks make a cake with a sweetened yeast dough topped with halved plums, which is often served as a dessert with cream or ice cream.

Berries

Russians and Poles are very diligent at finding and cooking what nature provides, and berry picking is one of their great pleasures in the autumn. Some of the more delicate fruits, such as strawberries and raspberries, are only found in the warmer areas of the country. Tiny wild strawberries, which do grow in the cooler forests, are quite tart, and need plenty of sugar to make them palatable.

Perhaps the best known fruits of the berry crop are dark red cranberries, with their astringent flavour. Russians love to make their own cranberry juice mixed with sugar and served with ice on the zakuski table, alongside the vodka. Cranberries also add a sharp note to a

Below: Strawberries are often grown in Polish gardens and made into jam.

Below: Apple pie is a favourite dessert in both Poland and Russia.

Below: Plums are often dried to become prunes, and enjoyed through winter.

Summer berry jam

675g/1½lb/6 cups raspberries
675g/1½lb/6 cups strawberries
300ml/½ pint/1¼ cups water
1.3kg/3lb/6½ cups granulated
  (white) sugar, warmed
juice of 2 lemons

Use whichever summer berries are
in season: strawberries and raspberries as here, or red currants,
blackberries, or blueberries.

1 Put the berries and water in a
large pan on a low heat, cover and
cook gently for about 15 minutes.

2 Add the sugar and lemon juice
to the pan and cook over a low
heat, stirring frequently, until the
sugar has dissolved. Bring to the
boil and cook for 5–10 minutes, or
until the jam reaches setting point
(105°C/220°F).

3 Remove the pan from the heat
and skim using a slotted spoon.
Leave to cool for 5 minutes, then
stir gently and pour into warmed
sterilized jars. Seal and label.

strongly flavoured sauerkraut salad. For a
change of colour, purple blueberries are a
favourite filling for sweet pies, topped
with a sour cream and icing sugar glaze.

Dried fruits
Raisins and prunes, thriftily made from the
autumn crop of grapes and plums, are
used in both sweet and savoury recipes,
particularly those that mark the religious

Above: The intense red of cranberries
makes them a Christmas favourite.

high points of the year. Polish Easter
pastries and Christmas poppy seed cake,
as well as the Russian Easter dessert,
pashka, contain raisins – not too many,
but just enough to add a background
sweetness and a deliciously different
texture. Prunes are a favourite with
savoury recipes such as roasted pork or
sauerkraut stew, where the strong
flavours blend so well. All kinds of dried
fruits are used in a compote for dessert,
mixed together with cinnamon and
reconstituted in citrus-flavoured juice.

Nuts
The subtle flavour of nuts is part of many
Russian and Polish dishes. Like dried fruit,
nuts are used in celebration dishes such as
Christmas Eve almond soup, a sweet and
sour mixture containing ground almonds,
currants for sweetness and egg yolks as a

Below: Almonds are often ground and
used in baking recipes.

Above: Prunes, raisins and dried apricots
are often poached for dessert.

thickening agent. Whole or chopped nuts
are also sprinkled on top of Easter pastries
alongside the dried fruits. A delicious
mixture of chopped almonds and
cinnamon works well as a stuffing for
baked apples, and a single halved almond
makes a crunchy topping for honey and
cinnamon cookies. Nut rolls, or kolachi,
are well known in Russia to accompany a
cup of tea or coffee. They are made with
a sweet yeast dough wrapped round
ground nuts, sugar, milk and butter.

Nuts can also be found in savoury
recipes, particularly those from Georgia
and the south-west of Russia. Chicken
with walnut sauce uses the nuts as the
main thickening ingredient in a sauce
made fragrant with onion, garlic,
coriander (cilantro) and spicy cayenne
pepper. This kind of nut sauce can
accompany chicken fillets or pork chops.

Below: Walnuts are grown in Georgia and
feature in local dishes.

Condiments and Flavourings

Russian and Polish food relies on good-quality basic ingredients – fresh fish, meat, mushrooms, root vegetables and berries – and dishes are not highly spiced or seasoned. A selection of herbs and other flavourings are used judiciously to enhance rather than hide the main ingredients and to enliven the meal: a delicate sprinkling of parsley or some fronds of dill, for example, alongside more piquant flavours such as garlic, capers, horseradish and juniper berries.

Dill

This is the favourite herb in Poland and Russia. It grows well in the cool climate of both countries. Its slightly aniseed flavour adds a tart accent to blander foods such as plain white fish or boiled potatoes, where it really shines and is used in great abundance. But dill also has an important role to play as a garnish, with its feathery leaves decorating anything from cold Russian salad to hot cabbage soup.

Parsley

Although dill has the reputation of being the Eastern European herb par excellence, parsley is the flavouring automatically added to every hotpot, soup, vegetable, meat and fish dish. It almost goes without saying that a few sprigs or chopped sprinklings of this gently peppery herb will be needed every day in the kitchen. The flat leaf kind is most often used, with its slightly stronger flavour, and this is also ideal as a garnish for cold dishes such as veal brawn or crab salad.

Other green herbs

Many other herbs have their place in Russian and Polish cuisine. Coriander (cilantro) has a particular affinity with the spicier dishes of the south-west of Russia,

Flavoured vodkas

Both Russian and Polish vodkas are famous for their taste and strength, and in each country they are thought of almost as a national drink, with rituals and traditions of their own. Many flavoured vodkas are produced, including red pepper, ginger, fruit flavours, vanilla, chocolate (without sugar), and cinnamon. In Russia and Ukraine, vodka flavoured with honey and pepper is also popular.

such as Georgian bean salad or Georgian chicken with walnut sauce. Marjoram, thyme, sage and bay leaves blend well with the meaty braised dishes such as hunter's stew or anything containing wild mushrooms. Chives have a rich onion flavour and as such they are best suited to the well-defined flavour of a whole roasted carp.

Garlic

Western Russian cooks from the areas around the Caucasus mountains use lots of garlic. While it is not such a feature of recipes that come from the eastern side of Russia, nor of Polish recipes, where the flavourings tend to be a little more subtle, garlic makes a real impact in dishes such as Georgian pressed fried chicken with garlic sauce. The distinctively aromatic flavour is also an integral part of lamb dishes such as Uzbekistani pilaff or a roasted lamb joint brushed with garlic butter and studded with rosemary.

Horseradish

The horseradish root has a very tangy, almost bitter flavour. It is freshly grated and mixed with stock or sour cream for a robust sauce that goes well with game or one of the more meaty fish dishes, such

Below: Dill is a favourite herb with most types of fish dish.

Below: Coriander is a popular cooking ingredient in the south-west area of Russia.

Below: Garlic is one of the ingredients that Uzbekistan has introduced to Russia.

Above: The knobbly horseradish root, when grated, gives a powerful flavour.

Above: The distinctive taste of juniper berries flavours many savoury stews.

Spiced honey drink

This spiced drink, sbitenj, is one of Russia's oldest drinks.

as roasted carp. It can also be used to flavour pickled vegetables, such as beetroot (beets). A very little grated horseradish goes a long way.

Juniper berries

Traditionally the main flavouring in marinades for game such as hare, pheasant or wild boar, these small dried berries have a pungent, spicy taste that lends a distinctive note to meat and sauces. They are used widely in both Poland and Russia. The berries need to be gently crushed before adding to a stew or marinade to release their full flavour.

Poppy seeds

These aromatic little black seeds are added to many baked goods such as breads, sweet cakes and puddings. In Russia they are often sprinkled over the top of cakes and breads, and their fragrant taste is mixed with wheat kernels, nuts and honey in a Polish dish known as kutia, part of the traditional Christmas Eve feast.

Below: Black poppy seeds are used to flavour cakes and breads.

Other spices

Cinnamon and cloves are often used in both savoury and sweet dishes, including flavouring marinades or compotes of dried fruit. Vanilla is added to many desserts and cakes, especially traditional festive baked goods such as Polish Easter cake. Savoury spices include allspice, with its peppery flavour, which is ideal for enlivening a marinade for game and blends very well with juniper berries. Capers add a tangy, vinegary note to fish dishes, including fish soup.

Honey

In the past, honey was used as a preservative as well as a sweetener. In Poland, honey is particularly associated with Christmas, in the form of honey and almond cookies and angels' wings biscuits. It is also added to vodka with cloves and cinnamon for a Polish Christmas drink and for the Russian sbitenj (see box).

Below right: Versatile and delicious, honey is used in baking and to make drinks.

Below: Inside the dried husks of the vanilla pod lie the fragrant, pungent seeds.

Serves 4–6
150g/5oz/generous ½ cup honey
100g/3¾oz/generous ½ cup sugar
500ml/17fl 2 cups water

For the spice mixture
10ml/2 tsp St John's wort
2 cloves
5–6 black peppercorns
1.5ml/¼ tsp ground ginger
5ml/1 tsp ground cinnamon
10ml/2 tsp dried mint
1 litre/1¾ pints/4 cups water

1 Put all the ingredients for the spice mixture in a pan. Bring to the boil, simmer for 5 minutes, then remove from the heat.

2 Mix the honey and sugar and water in a separate pan. Bring to the boil, stirring. Lower the heat and simmer for 10 minutes. Strain the spiced water into the pan and heat gently, without boiling. Serve warm.

SOUPS

Both Russians and Poles have a passion for soups, whether hot or cold. Piping hot, filling soups are served during the harsh winter months, when there is a special need for sustaining food that warms from the inside out. Borscht, the famous beetroot (beet) soup with its splendid ruby-red colour, is perhaps the best known and has several variations, including White Borscht from Poland, but Cabbage Soup is also very popular, especially in Russia. Even Catherine the Great enjoyed cabbage soup, and developed a ritual for serving it to her guests. Poland enjoys hearty main course soups too, such as Chicken Noodle Soup, which is an entire meal in a bowl. There are also recipes for cold soups, and two Russian favourites are okroshka, made with the nation's favourite beer, and svekoljnik, made from beetroot. Both of these are popular as a refreshing appetizer during the summer.

Fish Soup with Salted Cucumber and Capers

This fish soup is considered to be the queen of Russian soups. Its lovely, rich flavour is accentuated by the addition of salted cucumbers, capers and olives. If you can find sturgeon, use that instead.

Serves 4

2 onions
2–3 carrots
1 parsnip
200g/7oz Salted Cucumbers (page 79)
30–45ml/2–3 tbsp rapeseed
  (canola) oil
15ml/1 tbsp tomato purée (paste)
1 bay leaf
4–5 black peppercorns
1 litre/1¾ pints/4 cups home-made or
  good-quality fish stock
400–500g/14oz–1¼lb salmon, halibut
  and turbot fillets, skinned
8 green olives
8 black olives
30ml/2 tbsp capers plus 5ml/1 tsp juice
  from the jar
4 thin lemon slices
60ml/4 tbsp smetana or crème fraîche
45ml/3 tbsp chopped fresh dill,
  to garnish

1 Finely chop the onions. Dice the carrots, parsnip and finely dice the cucumbers.

2 Heat the oil in a large pan, add the onions and fry over a medium heat for 2–3 minutes, until softened.

3 Add the carrots and parsnip to the onions, and fry over a medium heat, stirring all the time, for a further 5 minutes until softened.

4 Add the cucumbers, tomato purée, bay leaf and peppercorns to the pan and fry for a further 2–3 minutes. Add half of the stock, cover and bring to the boil. Reduce the heat and simmer for 10 minutes.

5 Meanwhile, cut the fish into 2cm/¾in cubes. Add the remaining stock, green and black olives, the capers and the caper juice to the pan.

6 Return to the boil and add the fish. Reduce the heat and simmer for 5 minutes, until the fish is just tender, being careful not to overcook the fish.

7 To serve, spoon the soup into warmed bowls, add a slice of lemon, a spoonful of smetana or crème fraîche and dill.

VARIATION Soups with salted cucumbers as an ingredient are often called soljanka. Soljankas can also contain cooked meat. Just substitute the fish with a mixture of boiled beef, ham and cooked sausages.

Energy 389kcal/1613kJ; Protein 24.5g; Carbohydrate 9.1g, of which sugars 7.2g; Fat 28.5g, of which saturates 7.7g; Cholesterol 73mg; Calcium 74mg; Fibre 3.1g; Sodium 361mg.

Chicken Noodle Soup

The Russians are masters at making excellent stock and this recipe is a good example. It is said that the stock should be translucent and as clear as a teardrop. This clarity is achieved by keeping the heat low when cooking the chicken – you need to aim for a very gentle simmer.

3 Transfer the chicken to a plate and leave to cool. Pass the stock through a sieve (strainer) and pour back into the pan. When the chicken is cool, cut into bitesize pieces.

4 To make the noodles, put the flour, egg, water and salt in a food processor and blend to a smooth dough.

5 Put the dough on a floured surface and knead for 2–3 minutes. Wrap in clear film (plastic wrap) and leave to rest in the refrigerator for 30 minutes.

6 Divide the dough into four even pieces. Using a rolling pin or pasta machine, roll out one piece at a time until very thin, and then cut into 5–6cm/2–2½in strips. Leave the strips to dry for 5 minutes.

7 Place a few strips on top of each other and shred them diagonally into very thin strips. Toss in flour and allow them to dry.

8 To serve the soup, put the chicken pieces into four individual serving bowls. Bring the stock to the boil, add half the noodles and cook for 5 minutes. Pour into the soup bowls, garnish with chopped parsley and accompany with smetana or crème fraîche.

COOK'S TIP Only half the noodles are required for this recipe. Keep the remaining noodles in an airtight container for up to a week in the refrigerator, or freeze. Substitute ready-made noodles if you are short of time.

Serves 4

1 small chicken
1.5 litres/2½ pints/6¼ cups water
1 onion, cut into wedges
1 carrot, peeled and sliced
1 parsnip, peeled and sliced
1 leek, white parts only, cut into chunks
5ml/1 tsp salt
45ml/3 tbsp finely chopped parsley, to garnish
60ml/4 tbsp smetana or crème fraîche, to serve

For the noodles
150g/5oz/1¼ cups plain white (all-purpose) flour
1 egg
30–45ml/2–3 tbsp cold water
1.5ml/¼ tsp salt

1 Put the chicken in a large pan, add the water and bring to a slow boil. Reduce the heat and simmer. Skim the surface.

2 Add the onion, carrot, parsnip, leek and salt to the pan, cover and simmer very gently for 45 minutes, or until the chicken is tender. Using a slotted spoon, remove the vegetables from the pan and discard.

Energy 427kcal/1805kJ; Protein 54.5g; Carbohydrate 40.2g, of which sugars 7.8g; Fat 6.4g, of which saturates 1.7g; Cholesterol 152mg; Calcium 76mg; Fibre 5.3g; Sodium 237mg.

Georgian Meat Soup

With its lovely aroma of garlic, and its smooth, creamy texture, this is the king of soups in the Russian province of Georgia. It is one of the most popular dishes served in Russian restaurants and is served on both festive occasions and weekdays.

Serves 4

- 1.2kg/2½lb chunky pieces breast or shoulder lamb, on the bone
- 1.5 litres/2½ pints/6¼ cups water
- 3 large onions
- ½ mild chilli
- 5 garlic cloves
- 2 tomatoes
- 45–60ml/4–5 tbsp olive oil
- 15ml/1 tbsp tomato purée (paste)
- 45–60ml/4–5 tbsp chopped fresh parsley
- 45–60ml/4–5 tbsp long grain rice
- salt
- 60ml/4 tbsp Plum Sauce (page 143), to serve

VARIATION Instead of serving the soup with Plum Sauce, try adding 3–4 chopped fresh plums to the soup at the same time as the rice is added.

1 Put the meat in a large pan, add the water and bring to the boil. Reduce the heat and simmer for 5 minutes. Skim the surface, cover with a lid and simmer for 50–60 minutes, until the meat is tender.

2 Meanwhile, roughly chop the onions. Remove the seeds from the chilli. Finely chop the garlic. Slice the tomatoes into rough wedges.

3 Heat the oil in a large frying pan. Add the onions and fry for about 5 minutes, until golden brown.

4 Add the tomatoes and tomato purée to the pan and fry, stirring all the time, for a further 1 minute. Add the onion and tomato mixture to the pan containing the meat and stock. Then add the parsley, chilli and garlic.

5 Add the rice to the pan. Season with salt to taste and cook for 20–25 minutes.

6 To serve, divide the meat between four soup bowls, pour the soup on top, and accompany with the Plum Sauce.

Energy 433kcal/1801kJ; Protein 27.6g; Carbohydrate 24g, of which sugars 12g; Fat 25.5g, of which saturates 8.1g; Cholesterol 95mg; Calcium 72mg; Fibre 2.6g; Sodium 369mg.

Veal Kidney and Cucumber Soup

Many Russians prefer this soup to be as thick as porridge (kasha), but a thinner consistency may be more to your taste. It is important that you don't bring the soup back to a boil after the Lezjen sauce has been added, otherwise it may curdle.

Serves 4

1.5 litres/2½ pints/6¼ beef stock
50g/2oz/generous ¼ cup pearl barley
4–5 potatoes
1 onion
1 small leek
2 carrots
50g/2oz celeriac
3–4 Salted Cucumbers plus
  30ml–45ml/2–3 tbsp juice
600g/1lb 6oz calf's kidney
45ml/3 tbsp rapeseed (canola) oil
2 bay leaves
5 black peppercorns
2 allspice berries
25g/1oz chopped fresh dill

For the Lezjen sauce
15g/½oz/1 tbsp butter
1 egg yolk
75ml/5 tbsp double (heavy) cream

1 Heat half of the stock in a large pan. Add the barley and cook for 35–50 minutes until soft.

2 Meanwhile, cut the potatoes into small wedges and add to the barley for the last 10 minutes of cooking.

3 Meanwhile, chop the onion, slice the leek, finely slice the carrots and celeriac, and dice the Salted Cucumbers.

4 Cut the calf's kidney into small chunks, trimming away and discarding any fat.

5 Heat the oil in a large frying pan. Add the onion, leek, carrots and celeriac and fry over a medium heat, stirring occasionally, for about 10 minutes, until the onions and leeks are softened.

6 Add the Salted Cucumbers, bay leaves, peppercorns and allspice to the pan, and fry for a further 1–2 minutes, stirring.

7 Add the vegetable and cucumber mixture to the pan together with the cooked barley and potatoes. Add the kidney and the remaining stock. Bring to the boil, then reduce the heat and simmer for 20 minutes.

8 Just before serving the soup, make the Lezjen sauce. Melt the butter in a pan. Remove the pan from the heat and mix in the egg yolk and cream.

9 Alternatively, make the sauce in advance and keep warm in a bowl, uncovered, standing over a pan of hot water at a maximum of 55°C/130°F, until ready to serve.

10 Add the dill or parsley to the soup and season with the Salted Cucumber juice, according to taste.

11 Bring the soup back to the boil, stirring all the time. Remove from the heat and serve immediately, topped with a spoonful of Lezjen sauce.

COOK'S TIP Do not boil the soup after the sauce has been added as it might curdle.

VARIATION As a quick alternative to making the Lezjen sauce, you can also top the soup with a spoonful of smetana or crème fraîche.

Energy 515kcal/2152kJ; Protein 29.7g; Carbohydrate 38.5g, of which sugars 8.6g; Fat 27.9g, of which saturates 11.4g; Cholesterol 684mg; Calcium 107mg; Fibre 4.7g; Sodium 340mg.

Tripe Soup

Firm and white ox tripe can be used to make an economical and nourishing meal. In Poland, it is usually prepared with spices and served as a soup. Although it takes some time to prepare, it is a great delicacy and is well worth the effort.

3 Cut the cooked tripe into slices. Pour the cooking liquid into a measuring jug (cup) and add enough water make up the volume to 1.75 litres/3 pints/7½ cups. Return the tripe and liquid to the pan.

4 Add the carrots, celeriac and leeks to the pan and cook for 15 minutes, or until tender. Add the chopped onions.

Serves 4–6

1.3kg/3lb scalded and cleaned ox tripe
pinch of salt
2 carrots, cut into matchsticks
½ medium celeriac, cut into
  matchsticks
2 large leeks, cut into matchsticks
2 small onions, chopped
75g/3oz/6 tbsp butter
40g/1½oz/⅓ cup flour
2.5ml/½ tsp ground ginger
1.5ml/¼ tsp freshly grated nutmeg
1.5ml/¼ tsp ground black pepper
8 allspice berries
5ml/1 tsp sweet paprika
10ml–15ml/2–3 tsp dried marjoram
rye bread and shots of vodka, to serve

1 Rinse the tripe several times in cold water, draining well each time. Put in a pan and add enough water to cover the tripe. Bring to the boil and cook for 20 minutes, then drain.

2 Cover the tripe with fresh boiling water, add a pinch of salt, and cook again over a low heat for about 3 hours, or until the tripe is tender.

COOK'S TIP There are two types of tripe: the smooth type, known as 'blanket' tripe, which comes from the first stomach, and 'honeycomb' tripe, which comes from the second. Both types should be thick, firm and white in appearance; avoid any that is grey or slimy.

5 Make a roux by melting the butter in a small pan over a low heat, then add the flour and mix to a smooth paste. Stir a small amount of the broth into the roux, then add to the pan containing the tripe and the vegetables.

6 Add the ginger, nutmeg, pepper, allspice, paprika and dried marjoram, and cook over a low heat for 20 minutes.

7 Serve the soup immediately with rye bread and some ice-cold vodka.

VARIATION Some cooks like to add a glass of dry white wine to the broth at step 5.

Energy 234kcal/977kJ; Protein 18.3g; Carbohydrate 13.5g, of which sugars 5.8g; Fat 12.3g, of which saturates 7.1g; Cholesterol 165mg; Calcium 168mg; Fibre 3g; Sodium 202mg

Barley Soup

This tasty soup, which has many variations all over Eastern Europe, is ideal for keeping out the chill on bitterly cold winter days. Combining economical cuts of meat and staple winter vegetables, this version is a favourite in Poland and is eaten all over the country.

Serves 4–6

800g/1¾lb pork ribs
2.25 litres/4 pints/10 cups water
2 bay leaves
2.5ml/½ tsp dried marjoram
2.5ml/½ tsp salt
6 peppercorns
2 carrots, chopped
2 celery sticks, chopped
2 parsnips, chopped
2 leeks or 1 large onion, chopped
4 small dried boletus mushrooms, soaked and sliced into thin strips
75ml/5 tbsp pearl barley
25g/1oz/2 tbsp butter
2 potatoes, peeled and diced (optional)
chopped fresh parsley, to garnish

VARIATION You can use beef ribs in place of the pork, if you like.

1 Put the pork ribs in a large pan and pour in the water. Add the bay leaves, marjoram, salt and peppercorns, then cover the pan and cook on a low heat for about 1 hour.

2 Lift the ribs out of the liquid, remove the meat and discard the bones. Cube the meat, then return it to the pan and add the carrots, celery, parsnips, leeks or onion and mushrooms. Cover and simmer for 30 minutes, until the vegetables are tender.

3 Add the pearl barley, butter and potatoes (if using) to the pan and cook over a gentle heat for a further 15–20 minutes, or until the barley is tender. Serve the soup immediately, garnished with chopped parsley.

Energy 282kcal/1184kJ; Protein 31.3g; Carbohydrate 18.3g, of which sugars 5.5g; Fat 9.7g, of which saturates 4.2g; Cholesterol 93mg; Calcium 51mg; Fibre 3.5g; Sodium 137mg.

Fresh Cabbage Soup

Soups play an important part in both Russian and Polish cuisine and this simple cabbage-based vegetarian soup is one of the most popular everyday soups in Russia. Every housewife has her own recipe and the variations and adaptations are endless.

Serves 4

40g/1½oz/3 tbsp butter
1 onion, sliced
1 head white cabbage, total weight 750g/1lb 10oz, shredded
1 carrot, shredded or grated
1 piece celeriac, total weight 50g/2oz, shredded and grated
2 bay leaves
5 black peppercorns
1.5 litres/2½ pints/6¼ cups vegetable stock
5 new potatoes, diced
15ml/1 tbsp sunflower oil
1 (bell) pepper, cored and sliced
2 tomatoes, chopped
salt and ground black pepper
45ml/3 tbsp chopped fresh dill, to garnish
smetana or crème fraîche and rye bread, to serve

1 Melt the butter in a large pan over a medium heat. Add the sliced onion and cook, stirring, for 3 minutes, until softened but not browned. Add the shredded cabbage, carrot and celeriac and cook for 3 minutes.

2 Add the bay leaves, peppercorns and 200ml/7fl oz/scant 1 cup of stock to the cabbage. Bring to the boil, then reduce the heat, cover and simmer for 15 minutes, stirring occasionally.

3 Add the remaining stock and the potatoes and simmer for a further 10 minutes until the potatoes are soft.

4 Heat the oil in a frying pan over medium heat. Add the pepper and tomatoes and fry for 2–3 minutes, until softened. Transfer to the soup and simmer for 5 minutes. Season to taste.

5 Spoon the soup into bowls and sprinkle with the chopped dill. Top with smetana or crème fraîche and serve with rye bread.

Energy 273kcal/1141kJ; Protein 6g; Carbohydrate 36.7g, of which sugars 17.4g; Fat 12.2g, of which saturates 5.8g; Cholesterol 21mg; Calcium 122mg; Fibre 7.2g; Sodium 106mg.

Mushroom Soup

In the damp, dark woods of Russia, there are plenty of wild mushrooms. The best time to pick them is early autumn, and these are then often marinated, pickled or dried to make sure that there is an ample supply throughout the year. This soup is made with dried porcini mushrooms.

Serves 4

30g/1¼oz dried sliced porcini
  mushrooms
1.5 litres/2¼ pints/6¼ cups water
75–90ml/5–6 tbsp pearl barley
1 onion, finely chopped
1 large carrot, diced
1 parsnip, diced
4 potatoes, diced
45ml/3 tbsp rapeseed (canola) oil
2 bay leaves
5 peppercorns
salt and ground black pepper
60ml/4 tbsp smetana or crème fraîche,
  and 45–60ml/3–4 tbsp dill, to serve

1 Put the mushrooms in a pan, add the water and soak for 3 hours or overnight. Bring the liquid to the boil, reduce the heat and simmer for about 10 minutes. Then remove the mushrooms from the pan, reserving the cooking liquid. If using whole mushrooms, slice them.

2 Add the barley to the stock, season and cook for 30 minutes or until soft.

3 Heat the oil in a frying pan, add the onion, carrot, parsnip and fry, stirring, over a medium heat, until golden brown.

4 Add the fried vegetables to the mushrooms, stock and pearl barley. Add the potatoes, bay leaves and peppercorns, bring to the boil and cook for 15 minutes. Season with salt and pepper to taste.

5 To serve, pour the soup into individual soup bowls, and top each with a spoonful of smetana or crème fraîche. Sprinkle with chopped dill to garnish.

VARIATION Instead of pearl barley, use small pasta, such as orzo or conchiglie, and add to the soup towards the end of the cooking time.

Energy 196kcal/828kJ; Protein 4.1g; Carbohydrate 37g, of which sugars 1.8g; Fat 4.5g, of which saturates 0.6g; Cholesterol 0mg; Calcium 20mg; Fibre 1.4g; Sodium 11mg

Mushroom Soup with Pasta

This fragrant Polish soup is served with sour cream, chopped fresh herbs and delicate flakes of home-made pasta, making it both sustaining and delicious.

Serves 4

50g/2oz/1 cup dried ceps
1.5 litres/2½ pints/6¼ cups water
1 carrot, roughly chopped
1 parsnip, roughly chopped
½ celeriac, roughly chopped
1 large onion, roughly chopped
15g/½oz/1 tbsp butter
6–8 black peppercorns
juice of 1 lemon
salt, to taste
sour cream and chopped fresh
    parsley or dill, to garnish

For the pasta

115g/4oz/1 cup plain (all-purpose)
    flour, plus extra for sprinkling
1 egg, beaten
2.5ml/½ tsp salt
15–30ml/1–2 tbsp water

1 Rinse the dried mushrooms, then place in a large pan with the water, heat until warm and leave to soak for 30 minutes.

2 Bring to the boil. Cover and simmer for 25–30 minutes, or until the mushrooms are soft. Strain the stock into a clean pan, reserving the mushrooms.

3 To make the pasta, sift the flour into a bowl, make a well in the centre and add the egg, salt and 15ml/1 tbsp water. Mix to a dough, adding more water if needed.

4 Transfer the dough to a lightly floured surface and knead for about 5 minutes, or until the dough is firm.

5 Roll out the dough as thinly as possible, then sprinkle the surface with flour and leave to dry out.

6 Add the carrot, parsnip, celeriac, onion, butter, peppercorns and salt to taste to the pan containing the mushroom stock. Simmer gently over a low heat for a further 20 minutes.

7 Strain the stock into a clean pan, discarding the other vegetables. Slice the reserved mushrooms into thin strips. Cut the pasta dough into 1cm/½in squares.

8 Bring a large pan of lightly salted water to the boil, add the pasta squares and cook for about 4 minutes. Drain, rinse in cold water, then drain again.

9 Bring the pan of stock back to the boil, then add the lemon juice, the sliced mushrooms and cooked pasta, and heat through. To serve, ladle the soup into warm bowls, then swirl a little sour cream in the centre of each and garnish with chopped parsley or dill.

Energy 265kcal/1111kJ; Protein 7.4g; Carbohydrate 31.3g, of which sugars 0.9g; Fat 13.2g, of which saturates 7.4g; Cholesterol 75mg; Calcium 72mg; Fibre 2.4g; Sodium 343mg.

Polish Easter Beetroot Soup

Two versions of borscht have formed an intrinsic part of Polish cuisine for centuries, with the oldest-known recipe dating back to the 16th century. One is made specially for the Christmas Eve feast, while this one is for eating at Easter, and is made with fermented juice.

Serves 4–6

1kg/2¼ lb beef bones
1 leek, roughly chopped
1 large onion, roughly chopped
2 slices of celeriac or parsnip
2 carrots, roughly chopped
5ml/1 tsp salt
5–6 dried wild mushrooms, rinsed
  and soaked in warm water for
  30 minutes
juice of ½ lemon (optional)
pinch of sugar (optional)
175ml/16fl oz/¾ cup dry red wine
  (optional)
1 garlic clove, crushed (optional)
chopped fresh dill, to garnish
Dumplings Stuffed with Mushrooms
  (page 184), to serve

For the fermented beetroot juice
1.8kg/4lb raw red beetroot (beets)
1.5 litres/2½ pints/6¼ cups boiled
  water, allowed to cool until just
  lukewarm
1 slice wholegrain (whole-wheat)
  bread
4–5 garlic cloves, peeled
10 black peppercorns
4–5 allspice berries
2–3 bay leaves

1 To make the fermented beetroot juice, carefully wash the beetroot, then peel and slice them thinly.

2 Place the beetroot slices in a large glass jar or a bowl and cover completely with the lukewarm water.

3 Place the bread on top, then add the garlic, peppercorns, allspice and bay leaves. Cover the jar or bowl with a piece of muslin (cheesecloth) and put in a warm place. Leave to ferment for 3 days.

4 Skim off the foam that will have risen to the surface and strain the ruby-red juice into a bowl, then transfer to clean bottles or jars. Cork and keep in a cool place until required. (It will keep for several months, if stored in a cool place.)

5 Put the bones in a large pan, pour over 600ml/1 pint/2½ cups of water and add the chopped vegetables and salt. Bring to the boil and simmer for 15 minutes, or until the vegetables are cooked.

6 Put the dried mushrooms and 475ml/ 16fl oz/2 cups water in a separate pan, bring to the boil and simmer for 5 minutes, until the mushrooms are cooked.

COOK'S TIP Red borscht is sometimes served in a cup as a drink at a wedding, or as a hangover cure after a party.

7 Strain the meat stock and the mushroom cooking liquid into a measuring jug (cup) to measure the final quantity. Pour into a large, clean pan, and add 600ml/1 pint/2½ cups of fermented beetroot juice for every 300ml/½ pint/1¼ cups stock. Heat gently until the borscht just boils, then remove from the heat.

8 Taste the borscht and add lemon juice or sugar, as you prefer. To enhance the acidity, add a glass of red wine, or for extra flavour and aroma, add crushed garlic about 15 minutes before serving.

9 Serve in warmed bowls with Dumplings Stuffed with Mushrooms, garnished with chopped fresh dill.

Energy 84kcal/348kJ; Protein 0.5g; Carbohydrate 0.5g, of which sugars 0.1g; Fat 9g, of which saturates 3.4g; Cholesterol 8mg; Calcium 2mg; Fibre 0g; Sodium 672mg.

Russian Beetroot Soup

This famous soup is the centre and highlight of the Russian meal. There are many versions of the recipe. The secret behind a good borscht is the home-made stock and the high quality of the root vegetables.

Serves 4–6

5–6 beetroot (beets), total weight 500g/1¼lb
3 carrots, total weight 250g/9oz
1 cabbage wedge, total weight 300g/11oz, shredded
3 potatoes, diced
2 onions, sliced
45ml/3 tbsp tomato purée (paste)
15ml/1 tbsp sugar
5ml/1 tsp salt
60–90ml/4–6 tbsp smetana or crème fraîche
chopped fresh dill, to garnish
4–6 lemon wedges, to serve

For the stock
1kg/2¼lb beef on the bone
2 litres/3½ pints/8 cups water
1 carrot
1 parsnip
1 piece celeriac
1 onion
2 bay leaves
4–5 black peppercorns
2–3 fresh parsley stalks
5ml/1 tsp salt

COOK'S TIP It is a good idea to make double the quantity of this recipe and freeze what you don't need. The soup is easy to heat up for a quick meal.

1 To make the stock, put the beef and bones in a large pan, add the water and bring to the boil. Lower the heat and simmer for 10 minutes, skimming the surface of any residue.

2 Add the carrot, parsnip, celeriac, onion, bay leaves, peppercorns, parsley and salt to the pan. Cover and simmer gently for 1 hour. Remove the vegetables and herbs from the pan and discard. Remove the meat from the pan and dice.

3 To make the soup, add the beetroot and carrots to the stock, bring to the boil then simmer for about 40 minutes, until the vegetables are tender. Remove the beetroot and carrots from the pan.

4 Add the shredded cabbage, potatoes and onions to the stock, bring it back to the boil then simmer for 15–20 minutes.

5 Grate the cooled beetroot and carrots. When the cabbage and potatoes are tender, add the beetroot, carrots and meat to the stock with the tomato purée, sugar and salt. Simmer for 10 minutes.

6 To serve, pour the soup into warmed bowls. Top each serving with 15ml/1 tbsp smetana or crème fraîche and dill. Accompany with a lemon wedge.

Energy 127kcal/535kJ; Protein 4g; Carbohydrate 20.2g, of which sugars 17.7g; Fat 4g, of which saturates 2.3g; Cholesterol 9mg; Calcium 60mg; Fibre 5g; Sodium 143mg.

White Borscht Soup

This light, sour soup from Poland is made from a fermented rye flour, water and bread mixture, which needs to be prepared several days before you want to make the soup.

2 Transfer to a large, sterile glass jar, cover with muslin (cheesecloth), then close the lid and leave to ferment in a warm place for at least 3 days.

3 To make the stock, put the celeriac, carrots, leek, onion, parsley, garlic, bay leaves and water in a large pan.

4 Bring to the boil, then simmer for 20 minutes, or until the vegetables are tender. Strain, discarding the vegetables.

5 Add the dried, soaked mushrooms and 600ml/1 pint/2½ cups of the white borscht to the hot stock. Bring to the boil, then season to taste.

6 Add the potatoes and hard-boiled eggs. Serve immediately, garnished with fresh marjoram or dill.

Serves 4

50g/2oz/2 cups rye flour
1 rye bread crust
1 celeriac, roughly chopped
3 carrots, roughly chopped
1 leek, roughly chopped
1 onion
2 parsley sprigs
4 garlic cloves, crushed
4 bay leaves
1.2 litres/2 pints/5 cups water
5–6 dried mushrooms, soaked in warm water for 30 minutes
4 small boiled potatoes, cubed
2 hard-boiled eggs, cut into quarters
salt and ground black pepper, to taste
marjoram or dill, to garnish

1 To make the white borscht, put the rye flour in a large, heatproof bowl and stir in enough boiling water until the flour forms a thin paste. Leave it to cool, then add 1.2 litres/2 pints/5 cups lukewarm water and the bread crust.

Energy 133kcal/561kJ; Protein 6g; Carbohydrate 19.1g, of which sugars 1.5g; Fat 4.2g, of which saturates 0.9g; Cholesterol 95mg; Calcium 26mg; Fibre 1.1g; Sodium 1109mg.

Ukrainian Borscht

This borscht is flavoured with salo, salted pig's lard. If you can't find genuine Ukrainian salo, use Italian lardo, often sold in delicatessens, or other cured pork fat, instead.

Serves 4

2 potatoes
1 red (bell) pepper
juice of ½ lemon
300g/11oz cooked boiled beef
60–75ml/4–5 tbsp rapeseed
  (canola) oil
4–5 medium beetroot (beets), grated
1 carrot grated
1 small piece celeriac, grated
1 small onion
1 small wedge cabbage, finely sliced
30ml/2 tbsp tomato purée (paste)
1.5 litres/2½ pints/6¼ cups beef stock
3–4 garlic cloves
50g/2oz salo or lardo
15ml/1 tbsp sugar
salt

1 Peel and cut the potatoes into wedges and finely slice the pepper, discarding the core and seeds. Cut the boiled beef into small chunks.

2 Heat the oil in a large frying pan. Add the grated beetroot, carrot and celeriac, the onion and cabbage, then stir-fry for 10 minutes, until softened.

3 Add the potatoes, tomato purée and half of the stock to the beetroot mixture. Bring to the boil, then reduce the heat and simmer for 15 minutes.

4 Add the remaining stock and the slices of red pepper to the pan and simmer for a further 5–10 minutes, until all the vegetables are tender.

5 Meanwhile, chop the garlic. Put in a mortar with the salo or lardo and grind together with a pestle.

6 Add the meat to the soup, bring to the boil, then turn off the heat. Stir in the lemon juice, sugar and garlic mixture, and season to taste.

Energy 483kcal/2015kJ; Protein 22.4g; Carbohydrate 36.5g, of which sugars 20.8g; Fat 28.4g, of which saturates 9g; Cholesterol 55mg; Calcium 75mg; Fibre 5.7g; Sodium 169mg.

Christmas Eve Almond Soup

A traditional part of the Christmas Eve feast in Poland, this nourishing, slightly sweet almond soup is made with rice and currants and is often served with an egg yolk. It makes a hearty appetizer for a winter meal, or can be eaten on its own as a snack.

Serves 4

500ml/17fl oz/generous 2 cups milk
225g/8oz/2 cups ground almonds
115g/4oz/1 cup cooked rice
    (50g/2oz/¼ cup raw weight)
a drop of almond extract
50g/2oz/¼cup currants
    or raisins
15ml/1 tbsp sugar (optional)
4 egg yolks (optional)

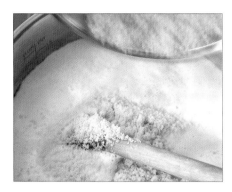

VARIATION You may find that the dried fruit gives the soup enough sweetness for your taste, in which case omit the sugar.

COOK'S TIP Only use the freshest free range eggs for this recipe, as they are served raw.

1 Bring the milk to the boil in a large, heavy pan. Add the ground almonds and cook gently, stirring often, over a low heat for 15–20 minutes, or until slightly thick.

2 Mix together the rice, almond extract, currants or raisins and sugar, if using.

3 Place a heaped tablespoon of the rice and currant mixture in the base of each of four bowls.

4 Ladle the soup into the bowls. If you like, place a raw egg yolk into each one before serving immediately.

Energy 480kcal/1999kJ; Protein 17.3g; Carbohydrate 28.2g, of which sugars 16.7g; Fat 33.6g, of which saturates 3.8g; Cholesterol 7mg; Calcium 299mg; Fibre 4.4g; Sodium 64mg.

Sorrel Soup with Eggs

Sorrel grows wild in grassy areas in Poland, but it is also cultivated commercially for use in a range of dishes, including soups, sauces and salads. It has a pleasant, slightly sour taste, which is complemented by the richness of the sour cream and hard-boiled eggs in this dish.

Serves 4

15ml/1 tbsp butter
400g/14oz fresh sorrel leaves,
  chopped
15ml/1 tbsp plain (all-purpose) flour
1 litre/1¾ pints/4 cups beef or
  vegetable stock
45–60ml/3–4 tbsp sour cream
4 hard-boiled eggs, chopped
salt and ground black pepper,
  to taste

1 Melt the butter in a large pan, then add the chopped sorrel leaves and a pinch of salt. Stir well so that all the leaves are coated in the melted butter.

2 Cook the sorrel over a low heat for 5–7 minutes, until the leaves have just wilted.

3 Put the flour in a small bowl and gradually add 60ml/4 tbsp stock, mixing constantly to make a paste.

4 Add the flour mixture to the pan and stir to combine with the sorrel. Stir in the remaining stock, bring to the boil and simmer for 10 minutes.

5 Season the soup to taste with salt and ground black pepper, then gradually add the sour cream, whisking well between each addition.

6 Transfer the soup to warmed soup bowls and top with a spoonful of chopped hard-boiled egg.

VARIATION If you are unable to find sorrel leaves, you could use rocket (arugula) or large basil leaves, although this will alter the flavour.

Energy 162kcal/673kJ; Protein 9.8g; Carbohydrate 5g, of which sugars 2g; Fat 11.7g, of which saturates 5g; Cholesterol 205mg; Calcium 215mg; Fibre 2.2g; Sodium 238mg.

Cold Beetroot Soup

All year round, soup is the heart of every Russian meal. In the summer the soups are often served chilled, as in this recipe, to be enjoyed in the summer heat. You will need to leave plenty of time between making this soup and serving it so it has time to chill properly.

2 Put the eggs in a pan, cover with cold water and bring to the boil. Reduce the heat and simmer for 10 minutes. Drain and put under cold running water. Remove the shells and chop the eggs.

3 When the beetroot are cold, pour the beetroot stock into a jug (pitcher) or bowl and put in the refrigerator. Remove the skin from the beetroot, and coarsely grate it into a large serving bowl.

4 Dice the cold potatoes and add them to the grated beetroot together with the cucumbers, eggs, spring onions and the mustard. Mix together.

5 To serve, pour the beetroot stock over the beetroot in the serving bowl, add the smetana or crème fraîche and mix gently together. Season with the lemon juice, sugar and salt to taste. Sprinkle the chopped dill on top to garnish.

COOK'S TIP

This soup can be prepared in advance up to step 5 until ready to serve.

Serves 4

800g/1¾lb small raw beetroot (beets)
1.2 litres/2 pints/5 cups water
3 eggs
4 medium potatoes, cooked
2–3 cucumbers, total weight
   300g/11oz, cut into thin strips
1 bunch spring onions (scallions),
   finely chopped
15ml/1 tbsp mustard
60ml/4 tbsp smetana or crème fraîche
15–30ml/1–2 tbsp fresh lemon juice
5–15ml/2–3 tsp sugar
salt
60–75ml/4–5 tbsp fresh dill, chopped

1 Put the beetroot and water in a pan, add 5ml/1 tsp salt and boil for about 50 minutes. Leave to cool in the stock.

Energy 215kcal/908kJ; Protein 11.8g; Carbohydrate 28.9g, of which sugars 19.9g; Fat 6.8g, of which saturates 2.3g; Cholesterol 147mg; Calcium 122mg; Fibre 6.3g; Sodium 311mg.

Cold Kvass Soup

Kvass is a fermented low-alcohol drink enjoyed in Russia. It is also used as a base for this soup, known as okroshka. The soup is very easy to make and is perfect for a light lunch on a lazy summer day. When chilled, tasty okroshka will cool you even in the hottest weather.

Serves 4

2 eggs
15ml/1 tbsp mustard
100ml/3½fl oz/scant ½ cup smetana
  or crème fraîche plus 60ml/4 tbsp,
  to serve
1 litre/1¾ pints/4 cups kvass or
  buttermilk (see Cook's tip)
250g/9oz cooked meat, such as
  unsmoked ham or roast pork, or
  cooked sausages, diced
1 cucumber, total weight 250g/9oz,
  very finely sliced
1 bunch spring onions (scallions),
  finely sliced
15ml/1 tbsp sugar
45ml/3 tbsp finely chopped fresh dill
salt

COOK'S TIP If you cannot find kvass, which is a sweet, wheat-based Russian drink, buttermilk will give a different but equally good flavour.

1 Put the eggs in a pan, cover with cold water and bring to the boil. Reduce the heat and simmer for 10 minutes. Drain and put under cold running water. Shell the eggs and separate the yolks from the whites. Reserve the whites.

2 Put the egg yolks in a soup tureen or bowl and mash until smooth. Add the mustard and the 100ml/3½fl oz/scant ½ cup smetana or crème fraîche and mix together. Slowly add the kvass or buttermilk, and blend.

3 Finely chop the reserved egg whites. Add the diced meat, sliced cucumber, spring onions and chopped egg to the egg yolk and kvass mixture and mix together. Finally add the sugar and dill and season with salt to taste.

4 To serve, pour the soup into soup bowls and top with the remaining smetana or crème fraîche.

Energy 353kcal/1473kJ; Protein 27.6g; Carbohydrate 17.6g, of which sugars 17.3g; Fat 19.8g, of which saturates 10.3g; Cholesterol 169mg; Calcium 363mg; Fibre 0.8g; Sodium 305mg.

Fruit Soup with Sour Cream

The wealth of forests and gardens provides an abundance of summer fruits in Poland, and this has greatly influenced the cuisine. Made with a mixture of fresh, seasonal fruit, this delicious soup is ideal for a summer meal. Serve it cold with Grated Potato Dumplings or sweet rolls.

Serves 4

4 cups mixed fresh fruit, such as
    pears, plums and cherries
1 litre/1¾ pints/4 cups water
5 cloves
1 cinnamon stick
45ml/3 tbsp plain (all-purpose) flour
250ml/8fl oz/1 cup sour cream
90g/3½oz/½ cup sugar, or to taste
175ml cherry vodka (optional)
Grated Potato Dumplings (page 173),
    or sweet bread rolls to serve

VARIATION You can also serve this refreshing soup with some noodles or crispy croûtons.

1 Wash and peel the fruit, remove the cores and stones (pits) and cut larger fruits into even-sized pieces. Put in a pan, add the water, cloves and cinnamon, and simmer for about 10 minutes.

2 When the fruit is tender, strain the liquid into a large bowl and reserve. Push the fruit in the sieve (strainer) so that all the juice is squeezed out. Then return the pulp together with the liquid to the pan and bring to the boil.

3 In a small jug (pitcher), mix the flour with the sour cream. Pour the mixture into the pan, gradually, and stir to mix. Bring back to the boil, stirring constantly.

4 Remove from the heat and add sugar to taste. Add the cherry vodka, if using. Serve immediately with Potato Dumplings or sweet rolls.

COOK'S TIP If the soup tastes a little too sweet, squeeze some lemon juice into the mixture before serving.

Energy 299kcal/1258kJ; Protein 3.4g; Carbohydrate 45.8g, of which sugars 37.2g; Fat 12.7g, of which saturates 7.8g; Cholesterol 38mg; Calcium 91mg; Fibre 2.4g; Sodium 30mg

Mini Bread Rolls with Garlic Sauce

These soft little rolls are called pampushki in Russian. They are small, sweet and fluffy and are delicious served warm, dipped into an aromatic garlic sauce. They are often served with soups or to accompany main-course dishes, and are traditionally eaten with Ukrainian borscht.

Makes 60 rolls

25g/1oz/2 tbsp butter
250ml/8fl oz/1 cup milk
420–480g/14½–1lb 1oz/heaped 1⅔–2
 cups plain white (all-purpose) flour
5g/⅛oz easy-blend (rapid-rise)
 dried yeast
2.5ml/½ tsp salt
5ml/1 tsp sugar
1 egg

For the garlic sauce
3 garlic cloves
pinch of salt
30ml/2 tbsp rapeseed oil
75ml/5 tbsp lukewarm water

1 Melt the butter in a small pan. Pour in the milk and warm until it reaches blood temperature. Remove from heat.

2 Put 420g/14½oz/heaped 1⅔ cups of the flour, yeast, salt and sugar in a large bowl. Add the warmed milk mixture and mix well together, then knead for about 5 minutes, until the dough is smooth, adding more flour if necessary. Cover the bowl with a clean dish towel and leave in a warm place for about 40 minutes, until doubled in size.

3 Preheat the oven to 230°C/450°F/Gas 8. Line a large baking tray with baking parchment. Transfer the dough to a lightly floured surface and knead lightly. Divide the dough into four pieces then roll out each piece between your fingers, into a long thin roll.

4 Cut each roll into 15 small pieces and form each piece into a small ball. Put the rolls on the prepared baking tray. Brush the tops with beaten egg. Bake in the oven for 10-15 minutes until golden brown. Transfer to a wire rack, cover with a clean dish towel and leave to cool.

5 To make the garlic sauce, crush the garlic into a bowl and mix with the salt, oil and water.

6 Serve the warm rolls with the Garlic Sauce as a dip.

Energy 34kcal/143kJ; Protein 0.9g; Carbohydrate 5.8g, of which sugars 0.4g; Fat 1g, of which saturates 0.4g; Cholesterol 4mg; Calcium 15mg; Fibre 0.2g; Sodium 7mg

APPETIZERS

The tasty appetizers, known in Russia as zakuski, are served at the beginning of most Russian meals. For an everyday meal, zakuski will not be too filling or very numerous, perhaps just two or three different little dishes, but for parties and celebrations, zakuski become much more elaborate and can consist of ten or more different recipes, both hot and cold. Often they contain a salty fish or shellfish, such as herring or crab, or a selection of vegetable 'caviars', and they are carefully chosen to complement the main course. However, these delicate dishes are also ideal for a light lunch or supper in their own right, and are sometimes used for the whole meal. Favourite Polish appetizers are more like the first course to a meal, rather than a buffet of several dishes. They also often include fish, especially herring – frequently marinated in spices and sour cream – and potato pancakes. The Poles also enjoy game pâtés and terrines.

Chopped Herring Salad

Although the ingredients for this Russian dish are simple, it is usually served at festive occasions. The herring fillets must be soaked overnight, so allow time to do this. You can buy ready-made forshmak in Russian delicatessens. It is delicious served with ice cold vodka.

3 When the eggs are cooked, drain and put under cold running water. Remove the shell and separate yolks from whites.

4 Peel, core and chop the apple and put in a food processor. Add the salted or pickled herring fillets, egg yolks and the butter and process briefly. Transfer to a bowl and mix in the fried onion.

5 Finely chop the reserved egg whites and finely slice the spring onions. Put the salad on a serving plate and serve garnished with the egg whites and spring onions.

Serves 6

250g/9oz salted or pickled
   herring fillets
2 eggs
45ml/3 tbsp rapeseed (canola) oil
1 onion, finely chopped
1 Granny Smith apple
40g/1½oz/3 tbsp butter, at
   room temperature
1–2 spring onions (scallions),
   to garnish

1 If using salted herrings, soak the fillets in cold water overnight. The next day, rinse the herring fillets under running water and then drain.

2 Put the eggs in a pan, cover with cold water and bring to the boil. Reduce the heat and simmer for 10 minutes. Meanwhile, heat the oil in a frying pan, add the chopped onion and fry for about 5 minutes, until softened but not browned. Set aside.

Energy 212kcal/875kJ; Protein 7.6g; Carbohydrate 3.2g, of which sugars 2.8g; Fat 18.9g, of which saturates 4.6g; Cholesterol 97mg; Calcium 32mg; Fibre 0.3g; Sodium 223mg.

Polish-style Herrings

Herrings, prepared in many different ways, are a firm favourite in Poland. They are particularly popular during Lent, on Christmas Eve and on Ash Wednesday, when meat is not allowed. This dish of herrings marinated with spices can be made in advance and kept for a week.

Serves 4

4 medium herrings, cleaned, or 8
  boneless fillets
2 large onions, thinly sliced
2 lemons, cut into thin slices
10 black peppercorns
5 allspice berries
4 bay leaves, broken into pieces
juice of 3 lemons
150ml/¼ pint/⅔ cup sour cream
2.5ml/½ tsp sugar
4 large potatoes, peeled and sliced
¼ tsp caraway seeds
90ml/6 tbsp vegetable oil
salt and ground black pepper, to taste
chopped fresh parsley, to garnish
lemon wedges, to serve

1 Soak the herrings in cold water for at least 24 hours and up to 36 hours, changing the water several times.

2 Drain the water and carefully remove the skin by sliding a sharp knife between skin and flesh.

3 If using whole herrings, cut off the head and tail. Divide the fish into fillets and remove all the bones, using tweezers or your fingers.

4 Place a layer of fillets in the base of a large glass jar with a lid, then add a thin layer of onions and lemon slices, some peppercorns, allspice berries and bay leaf. Add another layer of herring and repeat the layers until all the ingredients have been used.

5 In a small bowl or a jug (pitcher), mix together the lemon juice, sour cream and sugar, then pour the mixture into the jar, giving it a little shake as you pour.

6 Screw on the lid and turn upside down a few times to make sure the sour cream mixture covers the fillets evenly. Leave to marinate in a cool place for 24–36 hours.

7 Preheat the oven to 200°C/400°F/ Gas 6. Layer the potatoes in a greased ovenproof dish, sprinkle over the caraway seeds, drizzle with vegetable oil and season to taste. Bake for 35–40 minutes, until the potatoes are tender and golden.

8 Spoon the herrings on to four serving plates and garnish with chopped parsley. Serve with the hot potatoes and lemon wedges for squeezing.

Energy 508kcal/2098kJ; Protein 19.5g; Carbohydrate 5.4g, of which sugars 4.2g; Fat 45.5g, of which saturates 10.9g; Cholesterol 73mg; Calcium 108mg; Fibre 0.7g; Sodium 137mg.

Russian Salad with Herring

This salad looks like a cake, and is internationally called herring à la Russe. The cover under which the herrings dwell is made from several layers of vegetables and mayonnaise, and is always topped with grated hard-boiled eggs. Every Russian cook has their own recipe. This herring dish is served both on the zakuski table and as a main course. Many Russians would also gladly eat what is left for breakfast.

**Serves 8 as an appetizer,
4 as a main course**

- 250g/9oz salted herring fillets
- 3 carrots, total weight 250g/9oz
- 4 eggs
- 1 small red onion, finely chopped
- 200g/7oz/scant 1 cup mayonnaise
- 5–6 cooked beetroot (beets), total weight 300g/11oz
- 2 Granny Smith apples
- 45ml/3 tbsp chopped fresh dill

VARIATION Replace the cooked beetroot with pickled beetroot if you want to add the tang of vinegar to this dish.

1 Soak the herring fillets in water overnight. The next day, rinse the herring under running water and then drain. Cut into small pieces and put in a bowl.

2 Put the whole carrots in a pan of cold water, bring to the boil, then reduce the heat, cover and simmer for 10–15 minutes, until just tender. Drain and put under cold running water. Set aside.

3 Meanwhile, put the eggs in a pan, cover with cold water and bring to the boil. Reduce the heat and simmer for 10 minutes. When the eggs are cooked, immediately drain and put under cold running water. Set aside.

4 Add the chopped onion to the herrings with 15ml/1 tbsp of the mayonnaise. Spread the mixture over a serving dish measuring about 25cm/10in in diameter.

5 Coarsely grate the carrots, beetroot and apples into small piles or bowls. Add a layer of grated beetroot over the herring mixture and spread 45–60ml/3–4 tbsp mayonnaise on top. Repeat with a layer of grated carrots and mayonnaise and then a layer of grated apple.

6 Spread a thin layer of mayonnaise to cover the salad. Cover with clear film (plastic wrap) and chill in the refrigerator overnight, or for at least 1 hour.

7 Just before serving remove the shell from the eggs and grate coarsely. Sprinkle the grated egg all over the salad so that it covers it completely and creates a final layer, then garnish with chopped dill.

Energy 130kcal/544kJ; Protein 12.1g; Carbohydrate 9.3g, of which sugars 8.7g; Fat 5.3g, of which saturates 0.8g; Cholesterol 95mg; Calcium 96mg; Fibre 2.2g; Sodium 1697mg.

Cold Cod Salad

This salad, with its golden top, was created during Russia's Soviet era when there was a shortage of food. If nothing else, cod, carrots and onions were always to be found in the supermarket 'Gastronom'. The salad is best if chilled overnight, so make it in advance.

Serves 6–8

600g/1lb 6oz cod fillets, skinned
5ml/1 tsp salt
4–5 black peppercorns
1 bay leaf
200ml/7fl oz/scant 1 cup rapeseed (canola) oil
3 large onions, diced
3 large carrots, grated
45ml/3 tbsp water
200g/7oz/scant 1 cup mayonnaise

1 Put the cod fillets in a pan and add the salt, peppercorns and bay leaf.

2 Just cover the cod with water, bring to the boil, then reduce the heat and simmer for 5–10 minutes. Drain and leave to cool.

3 Heat half of the oil in a large frying pan. Add the onions and fry, stirring, until golden brown. Remove from the pan and set aside to cool.

4 Grate the carrots. Heat the remaining oil in the frying pan, add the carrots and stir-fry over medium heat for 10 minutes.

5 Add the water to the carrots and continue cooking for 5–10 minutes, stirring, until the water has completely evaporated. Set aside.

6 Use your fingers to divide the cooled fish into small chunks, removing all bones as you do so, and spread in a shallow serving dish.

7 Cover the fish with the onions and then spread the carrots on top. Cover the top with mayonnaise.

8 Chill the salad overnight, or for at least 2–3 hours before serving with bread.

VARIATION As an alternative, you can substitute the cod with perch, pike or other white fish.

Energy 528kcal/2179kJ; Protein 15.3g; Carbohydrate 9.5g, of which sugars 7.5g; Fat 47.9g, of which saturates 6.6g; Cholesterol 63mg; Calcium 38mg; Fibre 2g; Sodium 225mg.

Crab Salad

The famous Russian crab meat, charka, is sold in food shops all over the world. The high quality merits the price. However, inventive Russian housewives found a way to supplement the expensive crab meat by adding finely cut, fresh white cabbage. The result is surprisingly good.

Serves 4–8

1 wedge white cabbage, about
  250g/9oz total weight
250g/9oz can crab meat, preferably
  Russian charka crab meat in its
  own juice
100g/3¾oz/scant ½ cup mayonnaise
salt
30ml/2 tbsp finely chopped fresh
  parsley, to garnish
French bread, to serve

VARIATION This salad can also be served on pieces of very thin, crispy toast, which makes a perfect snack to hand round with drinks.

1 Finely shred the cabbage, discarding the thick stalk. Put in a large bowl and cover with just boiled water from the kettle.

2 Leave the cabbage to soak for 2–3 minutes. Drain off the water and squeeze the cabbage dry with your hands, transferring the handfuls to a dry bowl as you do so. Set aside and leave to cool.

3 When the cabbage is cool, add the crab meat and mayonnaise to the bowl and stir until mixed together. Season and transfer to a serving plate. Garnish with chopped parsley and serve with French bread.

Energy 121kcal/501kJ; Protein 6.4g; Carbohydrate 1.9g, of which sugars 1.8g; Fat 9.8g, of which saturates 1.5g; Cholesterol 32mg; Calcium 66mg; Fibre 1g; Sodium 232mg.

Chicken Liver Pâté

This easy-to-make pâté, with fried onion, melts in your mouth and is one of the most popular dishes on the Russian zakuski table. In restaurants the mousse is often served in shells made out of frozen butter.

Serves 4–6

2 eggs
400g/14oz chicken livers, rinsed
2.5ml/½ tsp salt
1 onion, chopped
45ml/3 tbsp rapeseed (canola) oil
100g/3¾oz/7½ tbsp butter,
  softened
salt and ground black pepper
bread slices, to serve

For the garnish
2 onions
45ml/3 tbsp rapeseed oil
4–6 sprigs flat leaf parsley

1 Put the eggs in a pan, cover with cold water and bring to the boil. Reduce the heat to low and simmer for 10 minutes. When the eggs are cooked, drain and put under cold running water. Remove the shell from the eggs, then cut them in half.

2 Put the livers in a pan and cover with boiling water from the kettle. Simmer for 5–8 minutes, until the livers are cooked.

3 Heat the oil in a small frying pan, add the chopped onion and fry over medium heat, stirring constantly, for 5 minutes until softened and golden brown.

4 Using a slotted spoon, put the livers in a food processor. Add the fried onion, egg halves and butter and process to form a smooth paste. Season the mixture with salt and pepper to taste.

5 Spoon the mixture into a serving bowl, cover and chill in the refrigerator for at least 3–4 hours or overnight.

6 When ready to serve, make the garnish. Finely chop the onions. Heat the oil in a small frying pan, add the onions and fry, stirring occasionally, for about 5 minutes until softened and golden brown. Remove the onions from the pan and leave to cool.

7 Remove the pâté from the refrigerator, garnish with the fried onions and parsley sprigs and serve with slices of crusty bread or hot toast.

Energy 263kcal/1088kJ; Protein 14.1g; Carbohydrate 0.9g, of which sugars 0.7g; Fat 22.6g, of which saturates 10.3g; Cholesterol 352mg; Calcium 20mg; Fibre 0.1g; Sodium 175mg.

Russian Salad with Chicken

The creamy Russian salad was devised in the 1880s by Lucien Olivjer, French chef of the Hermitage Restaurant, in Moscow. The dish has since travelled the world under the name Salade Russe. To serve it as they would in Russia, try heaping the salad into a pyramid shape.

Serves 4

3 potatoes
4 carrots
400g/14oz/3½ cups frozen peas
3 eggs
150g/5oz Salted Cucumbers
175g/6oz/¾ cup mayonnaise
200g/7oz cooked or smoked game, wild poultry, turkey or chicken, thinly sliced
2 spring onions (scallions)
salt and ground black pepper
5–6 fresh dill sprigs, to garnish

COOK'S TIP Do not peel the vegetables before cooking as, if you do, they will lose some of their valuable vitamins. Save some slices of carrot, egg and some peas to garnish the salad.

1 Put the potatoes in a pan of salted water, bring to the boil, then cook for about 20 minutes until tender. Drain and leave to cool.

2 Put the carrots in a separate pan of salted water, bring to the boil and cook for 25 minutes.

3 One minute before the end of the cooking time, add the peas to the carrots, return to the boil and continue cooking. Drain and leave to cool.

4 Put the eggs in a pan, cover with cold water, and bring to the boil. Reduce the heat to low and simmer for 10 minutes. When the eggs are cooked, drain and put under cold running water.

5 Cut the cooled potatoes, carrots and the Salted Cucumbers into small dice and place in a large bowl with the cooked peas. Mix together. Shell and chop the hard-boiled eggs and fold these into the potato mixture.

6 Add the mayonnaise to the vegetables, season with salt and pepper to taste and stir gently together. Turn the salad on to a serving dish.

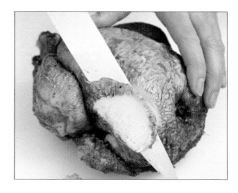

7 Thinly slice the meat of your choice and place on top of the salad. Thinly slice the spring onions and sprinkle over the top. Serve garnished with dill sprigs.

Energy 455kcal/1890kJ; Protein 28.1g; Carbohydrate 12.8g, of which sugars 5g; Fat 32.8g, of which saturates 5.7g; Cholesterol 387mg; Calcium 162mg; Fibre 4.3g; Sodium 963mg.

Salted Cucumbers

Salted cucumbers are the most popular zakuski dish and a cherished ingredient in Russian cooking. This way of serving them, prepared in just a few minutes, arouses all the taste buds, especially when they are served with shot glasses of ice cold Russian vodka.

Makes 1kg/2¼lb

1kg/2¼lb mini cucumbers or medium, fresh gherkins, or regular cucumbers
10 blackberry leaves
10 garlic cloves
3–4 dill sprigs with flowers
1–2 bay leaves
50g/2oz fresh horseradish, finely diced
20 black peppercorns

For the marinade
1 litre/1¾ pints/4 cups water
2.5ml/½ tsp red or white wine vinegar
45ml/3 tbsp salt

To serve 2 as an appetizer
4–6 salted cucumbers
5ml/1 tsp lemon juice
60ml/4 tbsp smetana or crème fraîche
60ml/4 tbsp clear honey
Russian vodka

1 To prepare the marinade for the cucumbers, put all the ingredients in a pan, bring to the boil, then remove from the heat and leave to cool.

2 If you can find mini cucumbers or fresh gerkins, prick all over with a fork; if you are using a large cucumber, cut it into thick fingers.

3 Put the cucumbers into one or several clean, dry glass jars, layering them with blackberry leaves, garlic cloves, dill sprigs, bay leaves, horseradish and peppercorns.

4 Pour in the marinade to cover and seal the jars. Leave to marinate for 5–6 hours. Then store the jars in the refrigerator for at least 2–3 weeks.

5 To serve, place the cucumbers in a serving bowl, cutting into fingers if they were salted whole. Mix the lemon juice with the smetana or crème fraîche. Put the honey in a separate small serving bowl. To eat, dip the cucumbers in honey or smetana or crème fraîche. Serve with ice-cold vodka.

COOK'S TIP These days the use of blackberry leaves as a herb has almost disappeared. In fact, the young leaves have a pronounced blackberry flavour and can be useful for flavouring syrups and jams. They can also be dried to make a country tea.

Energy 503kcal/2086kJ; Protein 8.8g; Carbohydrate 62.7g, of which sugars 61.6g; Fat 25.1g, of which saturates 16.3g; Cholesterol 68mg; Calcium 238mg; Fibre 6.5g; Sodium 80mg.

Hare and Calf's Liver Terrine

Hare and other furred game is popular all over Poland, where it has been hunted and cooked for centuries. For tender meat and a good flavour, use young hare that has been hung. However, you can use slightly older animals for this terrine, as the meat is minced finely.

Serves 4

5 dried mushrooms, rinsed and
   soaked in warm water for 30
   minutes
saddle, thighs, liver, heart and lungs
   of 1 hare
2 onions, cut into wedges
1 carrot, chopped
1 parsnip, chopped
4 bay leaves
10 allspice berries
300g/11oz calf's liver
165g/5½oz unsmoked streaky (fatty)
   bacon rashers (strips)
75g/3oz/1½ cups soft white
   breadcrumbs
4 eggs
105ml/7 tbsp 95 per cent proof Polish
   spirit or vodka
5ml/1 tsp freshly grated nutmeg
10ml/2 tsp dried marjoram
10g/¼oz juniper berries
4 garlic cloves, crushed
150g/5oz smoked streaky (fatty)
   bacon rashers (strips)
salt and ground black pepper,
   to taste
redcurrant jelly and salad, to serve

1 Drain the mushrooms and slice into strips. Put the pieces of hare in a large pan and pour in enough water to just cover. Add the onions, carrot, parsnip, mushrooms, bay leaves and allspice. Bring to the boil, then cover and simmer gently for 1 hour. Add a pinch of salt and allow the meat to cool in the stock.

2 Slice the liver and 50g/2oz unsmoked bacon into small pieces and put in a medium pan. Add a ladleful of the stock and simmer for 15 minutes.

3 Preheat the oven to 180°C/350°F/Gas 4. Put two ladlefuls of the stock in a bowl, add the breadcrumbs and leave to soak.

4 Remove the hare pieces, liver and bacon from the stock and chop finely with a large knife. Transfer to a large bowl, then add the soaked breadcrumbs, eggs, Polish spirit or vodka, nutmeg, marjoram, juniper berries and crushed garlic. Season to taste and mix well to combine thoroughly.

5 Line a 1.2 litre/2 pint/5 cup ovenproof dish with the smoked and remaining unsmoked bacon rashers, making sure they overhang the edges.

6 Spoon the meat mixture into the dish and fold the overhanging bacon over the top. Cover with buttered baking parchment, then cover with a lid or foil.

7 Place the dish in a roasting pan containing boiling water, then put in the oven and bake for 1½ hours, or until a skewer pushed into the centre comes out clean and the juices run clear. Remove the baking parchment and lid or foil about 15 minutes before the end of cooking to allow the terrine to brown.

8 Remove from the oven, and take the dish out of the roasting pan. Cover the terrine with baking parchment and a board and weight down with a 900g/2lb weight (such as two cans).

9 Leave the dish until it is completely cool, then turn the terrine out on to a serving dish. Serve in slices with redcurrant jelly and a green salad.

Energy 370kcal/1544kJ; Protein 25g; Carbohydrate 14.1g, of which sugars 2.5g; Fat 18.1g, of which saturates 6.4g; Cholesterol 291mg; Calcium 52mg; Fibre 1.3g; Sodium 851mg.

Veal Brawn

On the Russian zakuski table, brawn – cooked meat set in jelly – is much enjoyed. Pig's trotters are vital, as they provide the jelly in which the veal sets. Brawn should be served with hot mustard or horseradish.

Serves 8–12

700g/1lb 10oz veal pieces, such as leg, on the bone,
3 pig's trotters (feet), split lengthways
1 onion, cut into wedges
2 carrots
6 white peppercorns
6 black peppercorns
1 bay leaf
about 1 litre/1¾ pints/4 cups water
2 eggs
salt
3–4 fresh parsley sprigs, to garnish
hot mustard or finely grated fresh horseradish, to serve

1 Put the meat, trotters, onion, 1 carrot, sliced, 10ml/2 tsp salt, white and black peppercorns and bay leaf in a large pan and add enough water to cover the meat. Bring to the boil and cook for 2–3 minutes. Skim the surface, cover with a lid and cook over a medium heat for 2 hours, until the meat begins to fall off the bones.

2 Using a slotted spoon, remove the meat from the pan. Separate the bones and gristle and return to the pan, putting the meat on a chopping board.

3 Boil the stock with the bone and gristle for a further 1 hour. (This will extract more flavour from the bones and also produce more jelly for the brawn.)

4 Put the remaining carrot in a pan of salted water, bring to the boil and cook for 15 minutes. Drain and leave to cool.

5 Meanwhile, cut the cooled meat into very fine pieces. When cool enough to handle, thinly slice the cooked carrot.

6 Put the eggs in a pan, cover with cold water and bring to the boil. Reduce the heat to low, cover and simmer for 10 minutes. When the eggs are cooked, immediately drain them and place under cold running water. Remove the shell and slice the egg.

7 Pour the stock through a sieve (strainer) into a measuring jug (cup). Measure the stock, then pour into a bowl. Measure the same quantity of meat and add to the stock. Season with salt to taste.

8 You are now ready to assemble the brawn. Arrange the slices of carrot and egg in an attractive pattern in the bottom of individual soup plates. Gently pour the meat and stock into the plates, trying to preserve the pattern. Place the plates in the refrigerator for at least 4 hours until the brawn is firm and set.

9 Serve from the bowl or turn out on to plates. Garnish with parsley and accompany with mustard or grated horseradish on the side.

VARIATION As an alternative to veal, you could use either beef or chicken. Pig's trotters are the traditional way to make the jelly set, and they give extra flavour. However, if you can't get hold of them, gelatine can be used, in which case you may need to increase the seasoning.

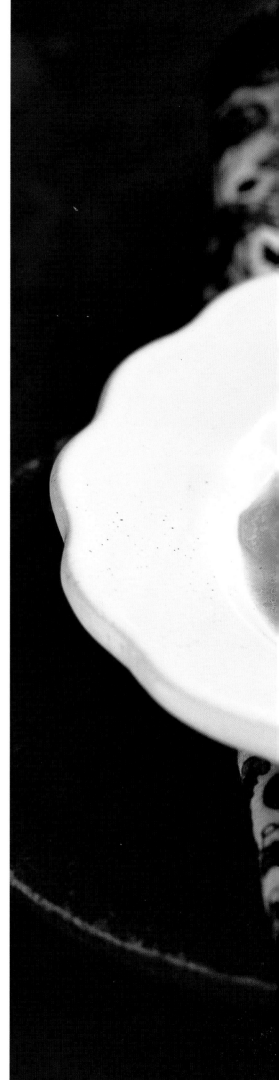

Energy 101kcal/423kJ; Protein 10.6g; Carbohydrate 1.1g, of which sugars 0.9g; Fat 6.1g, of which saturates 2.2g; Cholesterol 51mg; Calcium 9mg; Fibre 0.3g; Sodium 52mg.

Potato Pancakes

This dish was especially popular in Russia during World War II, when there was little to buy in the shops, and it was served as a treat for children. These pancakes are still enjoyed today, and taste delicious with sugar, apple sauce, or sour cream and a dash of paprika.

3 Put the bacon fat or oil in a large, heavy frying pan and heat over a high heat until it is almost smoking.

4 Carefully put a large spoonful of the potato mixture into the pan and flatten it slightly with a fork. Repeat until you have about four pancakes in the pan.

5 Fry each pancake until it is golden brown on both sides, then remove from the pan with a slotted spoon and drain on kitchen paper.

6 Keep the cooked pancakes warm in a low oven while you cook the rest of the mixture in the same way.

7 Serve the pancakes warm, with a topping of your choice.

Serves 4–6

4–5 large potatoes, peeled and grated
1 large onion, grated
2 eggs
60ml/4 tbsp plain (all-purpose) flour
120ml/4fl oz/½ cup melted bacon fat
  or oil
salt and ground black pepper
  (optional)
sour cream and paprika, or sugar, or
  apple sauce to serve

1 Rinse the grated potatoes and onion, then squeeze in your hands to remove the excess liquid.

2 Put the potatoes and onion in a large bowl with the eggs, flour, and salt and pepper if serving with a savoury topping. Mix to combine thoroughly.

Energy 291kcal/1221kJ; Protein 6g; Carbohydrate 35.4g, of which sugars 2.9g; Fat 15g, of which saturates 2.2g; Cholesterol 63mg; Calcium 36mg; Fibre 2.1g; Sodium 42mg.

Russian Pancakes

These little pancakes are called blinis. Often served with caviar or smoked salmon, or with smetana, soused herring and chopped onion, blinis can be served with a topping already added, or in a pile – with toppings provided separately – so people can make their own.

Makes 20

25g/1oz fresh yeast
5ml/1 tsp caster (superfine) sugar
50ml/2fl oz/¼ cup warm (37°C/98°F)
  water
2 egg yolks
250ml/8fl oz/1 cup warm
  (37°C/98°F) milk
2.5ml/½ tsp salt
175g/6oz/1½ cups plain white
  (all-purpose) flour
3 egg whites
150ml/¼ pint/⅔ cup rapeseed
  (canola) oil

For the toppings
slices of smoked salmon
pickled herring, chopped
chopped onion
smetana or crème fraîche
caviar
lemon wedges and dill, to garnish

1 Put the yeast, sugar and warm water in a small bowl and blend until smooth. Leave in a warm place for 20 minutes until frothy.

2 Mix together the egg yolks, 200ml/ 6fl oz/¾ cup of the warm milk and the salt in a large bowl. Stir in the yeast mixture and the flour, a little at a time, to form a smooth batter. Leave the batter to rise in a warm place for 4–5 hours, stirring three or four times during that time.

3 Stir the remaining 50ml/2fl oz/¼ cup of the milk into the batter.

4 Whisk the egg whites in a dry bowl until they form soft peaks. Fold into the batter and set aside for 30 minutes.

5 Heat the oil in a frying pan and add 25–30ml/1½–2 tbsp of batter for each blini. Fry over a medium heat until set, then flip and cook the other side. Continue to make 20 blinis.

6 Serve with a selection of toppings. Your guests can choose their own or you can assemble the blinis yourself.

COOK'S TIP Russians would never serve onion with caviar on the same blini. If you have real Russian black caviar, serve it by itself on the blini, with a spoonful of smetana or crème fraîche on the side.

Energy 89kcal/372kJ; Protein 2g; Carbohydrate 7.6g, of which sugars 0.7g; Fat 5.9g, of which saturates 0.9g; Cholesterol 21mg; Calcium 30mg; Fibre 0.3g; Sodium 16mg.

Aubergine Bake

This Russian aubergine dish comes from Samarkand, Taskjent and Bochara – ancient cities in the Central Asian part of the former Soviet Union. It is as filling and satisfying as a meat dish. Serve at room temperature, spread on bread or warm as a main course with potatoes.

Serves 8

1 onion
2 (bell) peppers, preferably
   different colours
3 tomatoes
1 bunch fresh dill
2 aubergines (eggplants)
100ml/3½fl oz/scant ½ cup rapeseed
   (canola) or olive oil
salt and ground black pepper
45ml/3 tbsp chopped fresh parsley
   and 4 lemon wedges, to garnish

1 Preheat the oven to 200°C/400°F/Gas 6. Slice the onion, peppers and tomatoes. Chop the dill. Cut the aubergines into 1cm/½in thick slices and brush with half of the oil.

2 Heat a large frying pan, add the aubergine slices and fry over medium heat, covered with a lid, for 1 minute on both sides, until golden brown. Alternatively, grill (broil) the slices on each side until golden brown. Season with salt and pepper and set aside.

3 Heat the remaining oil in the frying pan, add the onion slices and fry until softened but not browned. Using a slotted spoon, remove from the pan and set aside. Add the peppers to the pan and cook in the same way, then cook the tomatoes, keeping each vegetable separate.

4 Starting with half of the aubergines, layer the vegetables in an ovenproof dish, so that you have two layers of each vegetable. Season each layer with salt, pepper and the chopped dill. Cover the dish with foil.

5 Bake the vegetables in the oven for 10 minutes. Leave to cool, before serving garnished with chopped parsley and lemon wedges.

COOK'S TIP The dish can be cooked on top of the stove instead of in the oven. When all the vegetables have been fried, return them to the pan, in layers. Add 30-45ml/2–3 tbsp water and simmer the vegetables, covered, over a low heat, making sure that they do not burn.

Energy 118kcal/486kJ; Protein 1.4g; Carbohydrate 5.5g, of which sugars 5.1g; Fat 10.2g, of which saturates 1.5g; Cholesterol 0mg; Calcium 25mg; Fibre 2.4g; Sodium 7mg

Beetroot and Vegetable Salad

A ruby-red beetroot salad is a must on the table at any Russian dinner party, forming part of the traditional zakuski. Every hostess has her own variation of the recipe and sometimes the salad is garnished with pieces of pickled herring and surrounded by little mounds of sauerkraut.

Serves 4–6

2 potatoes
2 carrots
4–5 cooked beetroot (beets)
2–3 Salted Cucumbers (page 79)
1 red onion
30–45ml/2–3 tbsp sunflower oil
30–45ml/2–3 tbsp sauerkraut
salt and ground black pepper

VARIATION For a creamier salad, replace the oil with150g/5oz/⅝ cup mayonnaise.

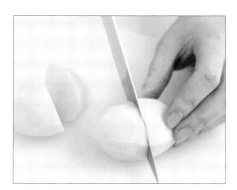

1 Halve the potatoes, put in a pan of cold water, bring to the boil, then simmer for about 15 minutes. Put the whole carrots in a separate pan of cold water, bring to the boil, then reduce the heat, cover and simmer for 10-15 minutes. When the potatoes and carrots are cooked, drain and put under cold running water.

2 Dice the beetroot, potatoes and carrots. Chop the Salted Cucumbers and thinly slice the onion. Put all the vegetables in a large serving dish and mix together.

3 Add the oil and sauerkraut to the vegetables. Season with salt and pepper and stir together.

Energy 130kcal/546kJ; Protein 3g; Carbohydrate 21.5g, of which sugars 10.7g; Fat 4.1g, of which saturates 0.6g; Cholesterol 0mg; Calcium 40mg; Fibre 3.6g; Sodium 100mg.

Marinated Mushrooms

With the possible exception of Italians, Russians are the most enthusiastic mushroom pickers in the world. In the mushroom season the best-looking mushrooms are preserved in a spicy marinade to be served on the zakuski table during winter.

3 Add the remaining salt, the vinegar, sugar, allspice, peppercorns, bay leaves, cinnamon stick and whole garlic clove to the mushrooms. Simmer for 10 minutes.

4 Put the dill and the blackcurrant leaves, if using, in the bottom of clean, sterilized glass jars. When the spiced mushrooms are completely cool, pour into the jars and seal tightly. Store in a cool, dark place or in the refrigerator.

Makes 1 litre/1³/₄ pints/4 cups

500g/1¼lb mixed wild mushrooms, such as porcini
500ml/17fl oz/generous 2 cups water
25ml/1½ tbsp salt
30ml/2 tbsp red or white wine vinegar
15–30ml/1–2 tbsp sugar
5–6 allspice berries
5–6 black peppercorns
2 bay leaves
1 small piece cinnamon stick
5–6 cloves
1 garlic clove
2–3 stems fresh dill
2 blackcurrant leaves (optional)

1 Wipe the mushrooms with kitchen paper to remove any dirt or traces of soil. If the mushrooms are large, cut them in half, but leave small mushrooms whole.

2 Put the mushrooms in a large pan, add the water and 15ml/1 tbsp salt. Bring to the boil, then reduce the heat and simmer for 30 minutes, stirring occasionally and skimming the surface.

COOK'S TIP Serve these aromatic sweet-sour mushrooms on your zakuski table or as an accompaniment to meat dishes, such as roast beef. The mushrooms will keep for 2–3 months but once opened should be eaten in 3–4 days.

Energy 183kcal/779kJ; Protein 9.2g; Carbohydrate 33.4g, of which sugars 32.4g; Fat 2.5g, of which saturates 0.5g; Cholesterol 0mg; Calcium 48mg; Fibre 5.5g; Sodium 8673mg.

Beetroot Caviar

The delicacies of the sea or Russian inland waters, such as caviar, are often a part of the zakuski table, but chopped vegetable dishes, known as 'poor man's caviars', are also popular alternatives. As with other vegetable caviars, this beetroot caviar is served on rye bread.

Serves 4–8

1 onion, total weight 150g/5oz
4 medium beetroot (beets), cooked
  and peeled
45ml/3 tbsp rapeseed (canola) oil
30ml/2 tbsp tomato purée (paste)
salt and ground black pepper
rye bread, to serve
finely chopped fresh parsley,
  to garnish

VARIATION Add 1–2 crushed garlic cloves to the caviar, either cooked with the onion or, if you prefer it, raw, added with the salt and pepper in step 4. You can also use fresh dill instead of parsley.

1 Chop the onion and coarsely grate the cooked beetroot. Heat the oil in a medium pan, add the onion and fry gently for 5–8 minutes, until softened and golden brown.

2 Add the grated beetroot to the onion and fry, stirring all the time, for a further 5 minutes.

3 Add the tomato purée to the pan and stir into the onion and beetroot mixture. Cover the pan and simmer gently for about 10 minutes.

4 Season the mixture with salt and pepper to taste. Transfer to a bowl and leave to cool completely.

5 Cut the rye bread into slices, and then cut each slice into squares.

6 To serve, pile the beetroot caviar on to the squares of rye bread and sprinkle with chopped parsley to garnish. Add another little sprinkle of black pepper, if liked.

Energy 60kcal/251kJ; Protein 1.1g; Carbohydrate 4.9g, of which sugars 4.2g; Fat 4.2g, of which saturates 0.5g; Cholesterol 0mg; Calcium 14mg; Fibre 1.1g; Sodium 34mg.

Aubergine Caviar

This is one of several Russian recipes for so-called vegetable caviars. The tastiest aubergines (eggplants) are imported to Russia from the Middle East and Georgia and the recipes for vegetable caviars also stem from these regions. Serve with rye bread in the traditional way.

Serves 4–8

2 aubergines (eggplants)
1 red onion
30–45ml/2–3 tbsp rapeseed oil
salt and ground black pepper
rye bread, to serve

COOK'S TIP If preferred, you can mix the ingredients in a blender or food processor to make the caviar into a smooth paste.

1 Preheat the oven to 180°C/350°F/Gas 4. Pierce the aubergines with a fork to prevent them from bursting when baked. Put them in a roasting pan and bake in the oven for 20–30 minutes, until completely soft. Leave to cool.

2 When the aubergines are cool enough to handle, cut them in half lengthways and with a metal spoon scrape out the soft insides. Discard the skins. Chop the flesh into very small dice and put in a large bowl.

3 Finely chop the onion and add to the aubergine. Add the oil and mix well.

4 Season well with salt and pepper to taste and turn into a serving dish. Serve with rye bread.

Energy 35kcal/145kJ; Protein 0.5g; Carbohydrate 1.7g, of which sugars 1.4g; Fat 3g, of which saturates 0.4g; Cholesterol 0mg; Calcium 7mg; Fibre 1.1g; Sodium 1mg

Georgian Bean Salad

A delicious fresh bean salad, with a touch of spice, is an excellent contribution to the zakuski table. This Georgian-style bean salad is also a very good accompaniment to many meat dishes, especially roast lamb, or one of the many burger recipes that the Russians enjoy making.

Serves 4–6

500g/1¼lb/3 cups broad (fava) beans
1–2 large onions
45ml/3 tbsp olive oil
45ml/3 tbsp red wine vinegar
15g/½oz/¼ cup finely chopped fresh
   coriander (cilantro) or parsley
1 small red onion

1 Put the broad beans in a pan, cover with water and bring to the boil. Reduce the heat and simmer for 3 minutes. Drain.

2 Chop the onions. Heat the oil in a frying pan, add the onions and fry, stirring all the time, for about 5 minutes until softened. Add the cooked beans and mix together. Remove the pan from the heat and leave to rest for 5 minutes.

3 Turn the bean mixture into a bowl. Add the vinegar and chopped herbs and stir together. Put the bowl in the refrigerator to chill overnight.

4 To serve, finely slice the red onion. Add to the bean salad shortly before serving and mix together.

VARIATION You can combine several types of beans for this salad, such as flageolet or cannellini beans.

Energy 145kcal/609kJ; Protein 7.6g; Carbohydrate 15.9g, of which sugars 5.4g; Fat 6.2g, of which saturates 0.9g; Cholesterol 0mg; Calcium 71mg; Fibre 6.6g; Sodium 10mg

FISH

Fish has always played an important role in Russian cooking. It has been a staple food ever since people first settled along the many rivers and lakes in its extensive rural landscape. Today fish is still a very popular element of the lunch or dinner table and is prepared in many different and interesting ways. Fish dishes are often accompanied by boiled potatoes sprinkled with dill, and served with a sharp and spicy tartare sauce or with a rich creamy sauce such as Sole with Vodka Sauce and Caviar.

Polish cuisine is more dependent on freshwater fish than seafood, and although it will never supersede meat as the favourite choice for Polish main courses, fish such as carp or pike come into their own for Christmas and Easter celebrations, and during times when meat is forbidden by the Catholic Church. During the rest of the year, most fish is simply fried or grilled and served with butter and herbs, or simmered in a robust sauce such as in the recipe for Haddock and Beer Casserole.

Marinated Perch in Tomato Sauce

In Russia it is quite common to eat cold main course dishes with really hot accompaniments. This fish dish, cooked in advance and garnished with lots of fresh herbs, is often served chilled or at room temperature with some freshly cooked, hot boiled potatoes. Making it a day in advance means that the flavours develop beautifully.

Serves 4–6

2 onions
3–4 carrots
600–700g/1lb 6oz–1lb 10oz perch fillets, skinned
45–60ml/3–4 tbsp plain white (all-purpose) flour
100ml/3½fl oz/scant ½ cup rapeseed (canola) oil
30ml/2 tbsp tomato purée (paste)
2 bay leaves
5–6 black peppercorns
200–300ml/7–10fl oz/scant 1–1¼ cups water
salt
chopped fresh parsley to garnish
hot boiled potatoes, and 4–6 lemon wedges, to serve

1 Chop the onions and coarsely grate the carrots. Cut the fish fillets into large chunks, allowing about three pieces per serving. Season the fish pieces with salt and then coat each side in the flour.

2 Heat half of the oil in a large frying pan. Add the fish and fry for about 1 minute on each side until golden brown. Transfer the fish to a large pan.

3 Add the remaining oil to the frying pan, heat until hot, then add the onions. Fry for 1–2 minutes.

4 Add the carrots to the onions and fry for a further 3–5 minutes, stirring all the time, until soft and golden brown.

5 Add the tomato purée, bay leaves and peppercorns to the onion and carrot mixture and fry for 1 minute. Add 200ml/7fl oz/scant 1 cup of the water and cook the sauce, over a medium heat, for 5 minutes.

6 Add the sauce to the fish, cover the pan and simmer, over a low heat, for 5–10 minutes, adding the remaining water if the sauce is too thick. Leave to cool.

7 Turn the fish and sauce into a serving dish and garnish with parsley. Serve with hot boiled potatoes and lemon wedges.

VARIATION Russians use pike for this dish, but if perch or pike are not available you can substitute any firm-fleshed white fish.

Energy 212kcal/881kJ; Protein 19.9g; Carbohydrate 3.9g, of which sugars 0.1g; Fat 13g, of which saturates 1g; Cholesterol 0mg; Calcium 16mg; Fibre 0.2g; Sodium 56mg

Fried Fish with Tartare Sauce

Deep-fried fish – most often perch or pike – served with a tartare sauce is a favourite in
Russian restaurants. Here a delicious light beer batter is used to coat the fish, but Russians often
use smetana as a coating for fried food, which you might like to try instead.

Serves 4

700g/1lb 10oz perch fillet, skinned
  and boned
5ml/1 tsp salt
15ml/1 tbsp fresh lemon juice
115g/4oz/1 cup plain white
  (all-purpose) flour
150ml/¼ pint/⅔ cup light beer
1 egg white
about 1 litre/1¾ pints/4 cups rapeseed
  (canola) oil
lemon wedges, to serve

For the tartare sauce
3 large pickled gherkins
200g/7fl oz/scant 1 cup mayonnaise
15ml/1 tbsp capers
5ml/1 tsp finely chopped fresh dill
15ml/1 tbsp finely chopped fresh
  parsley
2.5ml/½ tsp mustard
1.5ml/¼ tsp salt
1.5ml/¼ tsp ground black pepper

COOK'S TIP Try garlic mayonnaise instead
of tartare sauce to accompany the fried
fish. Simply crush half a clove of garlic
into 200g/7fl oz/scant 1 cup mayonnaise.

1 To make the tartare sauce, peel and
finely chop the gerkins. Put in a bowl with
the mayonnaise, capers, dill, parsley and
mustard. Mix together. Add salt and
pepper to taste, and transfer the sauce to
a serving bowl.

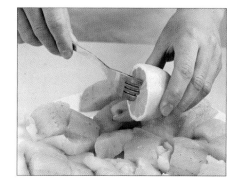

2 Cut the fish fillets into pieces measuring
about 3cm/1¼in and put on a plate.
Sprinkle the fish pieces with the salt and
lemon juice.

3 Put the flour and beer in a bowl and
whisk together until it forms a smooth
batter. In a separate bowl, whisk the egg
white until it stands in soft peaks, then
fold into the batter.

4 Heat the oil in a deep fryer to
180°C/350°F or until a cube of bread
browns in 1 minute. Dip and turn the fish
pieces in the batter and then drop into
the hot oil. Fry for 1–2 minutes, until
golden. Using a slotted spoon, remove
from the pan and drain on kitchen paper.

5 Serve the fish hot with lemon wedges
and the tartare sauce.

Energy 719kcal/2986kJ; Protein 36.7g; Carbohydrate 24.3g, of which sugars 2.1g; Fat 53.4g, of which saturates 7.6g; Cholesterol 118mg; Calcium 95mg; Fibre 1.8g; Sodium 352mg.

Fried Carp in Breadcrumbs

This farmhouse dish is often served as the main course of the 12-course Christmas Eve feast in Poland, but it makes a delicious meal at any time of the year. Chunks of carp are coated in breadcrumbs and fried in oil, and served simply with lemon wedges.

Serves 4

1 carp, about 900g/2lb, cleaned
 and filleted
2.5ml/½ tsp salt
50g/2oz/½ cup plain (all-purpose)
 flour
pinch ground black pepper
1–2 eggs, lightly beaten
115g/4oz/1¾ cups dry breadcrumbs
90ml/6 tbsp vegetable oil, for frying
lemon wedges, to serve

1 First scald the carp by putting it into a large heatproof dish or roasting pan and pouring boiling water over it. Turn and repeat on the other side. Drain.

2 Cut the cleaned and scalded carp into even portions and sprinkle lightly with salt. Leave to stand for about 30 minutes. Remove the skin, if you like.

3 Mix together the flour and pepper in a medium bowl. Put the beaten egg in another, and the breadcrumbs on a plate.

4 Dip the fish pieces first into the bowl of flour, then into the beaten egg, and then into the breadcrumbs, coating them evenly at each stage.

5 Heat the oil in a large, heavy pan, until very hot. Carefully add the coated fish pieces and cook for about 5 minutes on each side, until golden brown all over.

6 Remove the fish pieces using a slotted spoon and drain on kitchen paper. Serve hot with lemon wedges.

Energy 479kcal/2008kJ; Protein 32.3g; Carbohydrate 32g, of which sugars 0.9g; Fat 25.6g, of which saturates 4.1g; Cholesterol 148mg; Calcium 133mg; Fibre 1g; Sodium 301mg.

Grilled Sardines with Parsley

Sardines are easy to cook, nutritious, good value for money and extremely tasty, so it is little wonder that they are very popular in Poland. Here, they are simply grilled and served with lemon wedges to squeeze over. This recipe also works well on a barbecue.

Serves 4–6

900g/2lb fresh sardines,
   gutted and scaled
30ml/2 tbsp melted butter
salt and ground black pepper,
   to taste
60ml/4 tbsp chopped fresh parsley,
   to garnish
lemon wedges, to serve

1 Preheat the grill (broiler) to high. Wash the prepared sardines under cold running water and dry with kitchen paper.

COOK'S TIP To butterfly sardines, place the sardines, belly side down, on a board. Run a thumb along the spine to press out. Turn over and pull out the backbone.

2 Brush the fish with melted butter or oil, then season to taste with salt and pepper.

3 Place the sardines on the grill pan and put under the preheated grill. Cook for about 3–4 minutes on each side, until the skin begins to brown.

4 Transfer the sardines to warmed plates, sprinkle with parsley, and serve immediately with lemon wedges.

Energy 327kcal/1362kJ; Protein 35g; Carbohydrate 0.3g, of which sugars 0.3g; Fat 20.5g, of which saturates 8g; Cholesterol 16mg; Calcium 192mg; Fibre 0.5g; Sodium 240mg.

Fish Kebabs

To cook fish outside on skewers over coals or a wood fire and then serve with squeezed lemon and fresh tomato, is an ancient Russian tradition. Although incredibly simple to prepare, this dish is a popular choice in many Caucasian restaurants in Russia.

Serves 4

30ml/2 tbsp fresh lemon juice
60ml/4 tbsp smetana or crème fraîche
1kg/2¼lb firm white fish fillets, such
  as halibut or monkfish
25g/1oz/2 tbsp butter
salt

For the garnish
25g/1oz/2 tbsp butter
4 spring onions (scallions), sliced
1 lemon, cut into wedges
4 tomatoes, cut into wedges
30ml/2 tbsp finely chopped
  fresh parsley

VARIATION In Russia, sturgeon is often used for this dish but any firm, white fish is suitable. You can also use salmon.

1 Heat a barbecue or preheat the oven to 240°C/475°F/Gas 9.

2 Put the lemon juice and smetana or crème fraîche in a large bowl and mix. Cut the fish into small chunks, season with salt, add to the marinade and stir to coat all over. Leave for 10–15 minutes for the fish to absorb the flavours.

3 Melt the butter. Thread the fish chunks tightly on to four metal skewers or wooden skewers that have been soaked in water. Heat the grill (broiler) if using.

4 Cook the skewers on the barbecue, or under the grill for about 10 minutes, turning every few minutes. Baste occasionally with the melted butter and the remaining marinade.

5 To serve, put the skewers on a large serving dish and sprinkle over the sliced spring onions and chopped parsley. Arrange the lemon and tomato wedges around the fish skewers.

Energy 303kcal/1267kJ; Protein 46.1g; Carbohydrate 0.4g, of which sugars 0.4g; Fat 12.9g, of which saturates 7.6g; Cholesterol 145mg; Calcium 32mg; Fibre 0g; Sodium 191mg.

Roasted Carp with Smetana

Roasting a whole fish in the oven, covered with smetana to stop the fish from drying as it cooks, is an old Russian method. A more modern way is to use fish fillets, instead of a whole fish, and bake them in ramekin dishes on top of a base of boiled buckwheat.

Serves 4–6

40g/1½oz/3 tbsp butter, plus extra
   for greasing
1 whole carp, bream or trout, gutted,
   total weight 1–1.5kg/2¼–3¼lb
45ml/3 tbsp plain white
   (all-purpose) flour
300ml/½ pint/1¼ cups smetana or
   crème fraîche
100ml/3½fl oz/scant ½ cup water
salt and ground black pepper
5–6 fresh parsley sprigs, to garnish
salad leaves and hot boiled potatoes,
   to serve

VARIATION In Russia, mayonnaise is sometimes used instead of the smetana.

1 Preheat the oven to 230°C/450°F/ Gas 8. Generously grease an ovenproof dish with butter. Season the whole fish on the inside and outside with salt and pepper, then coat both sides in the flour. Place the fish in the prepared dish.

2 Melt the butter in a small pan. Spread the smetana or crème fraîche over the prepared fish, making sure that it is covered completely.

3 Pour the melted butter over the fish and pour the water around it.

4 Bake in the preheated oven. A 40–50cm/16–20in thick fish will need around 20 minutes and a 60cm/24in thick fish will need 30 minutes.

5 The fish is cooked when the flesh is white and not translucent. Test by inserting a fork in the backbone of the fish where it is thickest.

6 Serve the fish in portions straight from the dish, garnished with parsley and accompanied by salad leaves and boiled potatoes tossed in oil and salt.

Energy 395kcal/1640kJ; Protein 22.3g; Carbohydrate 7.1g, of which sugars 1.2g; Fat 31.1g, of which saturates 18.1g; Cholesterol 149mg; Calcium 96mg; Fibre 0.2g; Sodium 102mg.

Baked Trout with Garlic Butter

The rivers in Poland abound with trout, making them a popular choice in a country with only one seaboard. In this delicious recipe they are simply baked in the oven, drizzled with hot garlic butter and served with sprigs of parsley and wedges of lemon.

Serves 4

2 garlic cloves, crushed
50g/2oz/¹⁄₄ cup butter, softened,
  plus extra, for greasing
4 medium-sized trout, about
  300g/11oz each, cleaned and gutted
1 lemon
salt and ground black pepper, to taste
fresh parsley sprigs, to garnish
lemon wedges, to serve

1 Mix together the garlic and butter in a bowl. Set aside until required.

2 Preheat the oven to 200°C/400°F/ Gas 6. Grease a large baking dish.

3 Place the fish in the baking dish. Squeeze lemon juice all over and inside the trout, then season with salt and pepper and put in the oven.

4 Bake the trout for 15–20 minutes, or until the flesh flakes easily when you insert the point of a sharp knife. Place on warm serving plates.

5 Melt the garlic butter in a pan, then pour over the fish. Garnish with parsley and serve with lemon wedges.

Energy 205kcal/853kJ; Protein 19.5g; Carbohydrate 0.1g, of which sugars 0.1g; Fat 14.1g, of which saturates 6.5g; Cholesterol 27mg; Calcium 11mg; Fibre 0g; Sodium 132mg.

Foil-baked Salmon

Baking the whole salmon in a foil package ensures that the flesh remains wonderfully moist, and is a favourite cooking method in both Russia and Poland. It can be served hot, with new potatoes and cucumber salad, or cold with a salad, for a summer lunch.

3 Spread the mixture inside the cavity of the fish, and all over the outside. Put the peppercorns and bay leaves inside the cavity, then season the skin with salt and pepper, to taste.

4 Bring the edges of the foil up and seal to make a loose parcel. Put the fish in the preheated oven and cook for about 30–40 minutes, or until the fish is tender and cooked.

5 Remove from the oven, lift out of the foil and divide the fish into six portions. Transfer to warmed plates.

6 Pour over any juices caught in the foil, and serve immediately with lemon wedges, boiled new potatoes and Polish-style Cucumber Salad.

Serves 6

1 salmon, about 1kg/2¼lb,
    cleaned and trimmed
1 small bunch fresh dill, roughly
    chopped
4 garlic cloves, finely chopped
115g/4oz/½ cup unsalted butter
50ml/2fl oz/¼ cup dry white wine
juice of ½ lemon
10–12 black peppercorns
4–5 fresh bay leaves
salt and ground black pepper, to taste
lemon wedges, boiled new potatoes
    and Polish-style Cucumber Salad
    (page 193), to serve

1 Preheat the oven to 200°C/400°F/ Gas 6. Place the salmon in the centre of a large piece of foil.

2 In a bowl, mix together the dill, garlic and butter, to form a smooth paste. Add the wine and lemon juice, and combine.

Energy 242kcal/1005kJ; Protein 20.3g; Carbohydrate 0.1g, of which sugars 0.1g; Fat 17.9g, of which saturates 6.2g; Cholesterol 68mg; Calcium 23mg; Fibre 0g; Sodium 96mg.

Sole with Vodka Sauce and Caviar

In Russia, caviar was once served only with silver spoons to protect the taste. Today, caviar is served on white buttered toast or blinis, or as a luxurious garnish to a delicious fish. Sole is traditionally used for this recipe, but you can substitute any other flat fish.

Serves 4

500–600g/1lb 4oz–1lb 6oz sole, flounder or plaice fillets
200ml/7fl oz/scant 1 cup fish stock
60ml/4 tbsp caviar
salt
fresh dill, to garnish
lemon wedges and hot boiled potatoes, to serve

For the vodka sauce
25–40g/1–1½oz/2–3 tbsp butter
5–6 shallots, finely diced
5ml/1 tsp plain white (all-purpose) flour
200ml/7fl oz/scant 1 cup double (heavy) cream
200ml/7fl oz/scant 1 cup fish stock
100ml/3½fl oz/scant ½ cup dry white wine
30ml/2 tbsp vodka
salt and ground black pepper

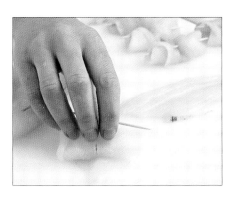

1 Season the fish fillets with salt. Roll up and secure each fillet with a cocktail stick (toothpick).

2 Heat the stock in a small pan. Place the fish rolls in the pan, cover and simmer for 5–8 minutes, until the fish is tender. Remove from the pan and keep warm.

3 Meanwhile, make the sauce. Melt the butter in a pan, add the shallots and fry gently for 3–5 minutes, until softened but not browned. Add the flour and stir until well mixed.

4 Gradually add the cream and stock until smooth. Slowly bring to the boil, stirring, until the sauce bubbles. Reduce the heat and simmer for 3–5 minutes, until the sauce thickens. Remove the shallots with a slotted spoon. Add the wine and vodka and bring to the boil. Season to taste.

5 Pour the sauce over the base of four warmed plates. Place the fish rolls on top and add a spoonful of caviar to each. Garnish with dill and serve with the lemon wedges and potatoes.

Energy 470kcal/1952kJ; Protein 27.9g; Carbohydrate 3.2g, of which sugars 1.9g; Fat 35g, of which saturates 20.4g; Cholesterol 188mg; Calcium 103mg; Fibre 0.3g; Sodium 548mg.

Halibut Steaks with Lemon Butter

Poles often simply grill or fry fresh fish, and this elegant dish is a good example. Spreading the steaks with parsley, lemon and butter before cooking ensures the flesh is moist and enables the flavours to permeate the fish without overpowering its delicate flavour.

2 Soften the butter in a bowl with a fork or wooden spoon, then add the parsley and lemon juice, mix together, then spread over both sides of each fish steak.

3 Line a grill pan with foil, then put the steaks on the foil. Place under the hot grill and cook for 3–4 minutes.

4 Turn the fish over and cook for a further 3–4 minutes on the other side. Check with the point of a sharp knife that the fish is cooked but still tender.

5 Transfer to warmed plates. Serve immediately, with lemon wedges for squeezing over, and garnished with parsley sprigs if using.

Serves 4

    4 halibut steaks, weighing about
        185g/6½oz each
    150g/5oz/10 tbsp butter
    30ml/2 tbsp chopped fresh parsley
    30ml/2 tbsp lemon juice
    salt and ground black pepper,
        to taste
    lemon wedges, to serve
    parsley sprigs, to garnish (optional)

VARIATION This butter and lemon sauce can be used for all white fish. Use hake or cod steaks if halibut is not available.

1 Season the fish with a generous amount of salt and pepper on both sides. Preheat the grill (broiler) to medium.

Energy 464kcal/1928kJ; Protein 38.2g; Carbohydrate 0.6g, of which sugars 0.5g; Fat 34.3g, of which saturates 20.1g; Cholesterol 141mg; Calcium 83mg; Fibre 0.6g; Sodium 337mg.

Haddock with Dill Sauce

Dill is Poland's favourite herb, especially when it is served with fish dishes. Here it is used to lift the simple cream sauce that accompanies the moist fillets of poached haddock. Serve the fish on its own, or accompanied by seasonal vegetables.

Serves 4

50g/2oz/¼ cup butter
4 haddock fillets, about
    185g/6½oz each
200ml/7fl oz/scant 1 cup full fat
    (whole) milk
200ml/7fl oz/scant 1 cup fish stock
3–4 bay leaves
75ml/5 tbsp plain (all-purpose) flour
150ml/¼ pint/⅔ cup double
    (heavy) cream
1 egg yolk
30ml–45ml/2–3 tbsp chopped
    fresh dill
salt and ground black pepper,
    to taste
dill fronds and slices of lemon,
    to garnish

5 Stir the egg yolk and chopped dill into the cream and butter mixture, then return to the heat and simmer for 4 minutes, or until the sauce has thickened. Do not boil.

6 Remove the haddock fillets to a serving dish or warmed plates.

7 Taste the sauce and add salt and pepper if needed, then pour it over the fish.

8 Garnish the fish with dill fronds and slices of lemon and serve immediately on warmed plates.

COOK'S TIP A member of the cod family, silver-skinned haddock is sold whole, as steaks or as fillets. It is suitable for grilling (broiling), frying or smoking. This sauce can also be used for any other type of white fish.

1 Melt half of the butter in a large frying pan, then add the haddock fillets, milk, fish stock, bay leaves, and a generous amount of salt and pepper.

2 Bring the liquid to a simmer, then poach the fish gently, uncovered, over a low heat for 10–15 minutes until tender.

3 Meanwhile, melt the remaining butter in a small pan, add the flour and cook, stirring, for 2 minutes.

4 Remove the pan from the heat and add a spoonful of double cream. Beat the cream into the flour and butter, then slowly add the rest of the cream, whisking constantly, so that no lumps form.

Energy 503kcal/2097kJ; Protein 36.6g; Carbohydrate 15.5g, of which sugars 1.2g; Fat 33.2g, of which saturates 19.6g; Cholesterol 191mg; Calcium 92mg; Fibre 1g; Sodium 207mg.

Fish with Mushroom and Dill Sauce

Dill and flat leaf parsley are the herbs most commonly used in Russian cuisine, and both go superbly with most fish dishes. In this recipe the fish is accompanied by a creamy mushroom sauce with a rich taste of dill.

Serves 4

4 perch fillets, total weight
    500–600g/1lb 4oz–1lb 6oz, skinned
5ml/1 tsp salt
plain white (all-purpose) flour, to coat
35–50g/1½–2oz/3–4 tbsp butter
hot boiled new potatoes, to serve

For the dill sauce
2 onions, finely chopped
20 fresh mushrooms, thinly sliced
45ml/3 tbsp rapeseed (canola) oil
15ml/1 tbsp plain white
    (all-purpose) flour
200ml/7fl oz/scant 1 cup fish stock
250ml/8fl oz/1 cup double
    (heavy) cream
100ml/3½fl oz/scant ½ cup smetana or
    crème fraîche
100ml/3½fl oz/scant ½ cup dry
    white wine
1 large bunch fresh dill, chopped
1–2 dashes mushroom or soy sauce
salt and white pepper

3 Stir the cream and smetana or crème fraîche into the sauce. Reduce the heat and simmer for 3 minutes. Add the white wine, soy sauce, salt and pepper and dill.

4 Meanwhile, season the fish fillets with the salt and coat with the flour. Heat the butter in a large non-stick frying pan over a medium heat. Add the fish and fry for 3 minutes on each side or until golden brown and crisp.

1 First make the sauce. Heat the oil in a large frying pan, add the onions and fry, over a medium high heat, for 3–5 minutes until softened but not browned. Add the sliced mushrooms and fry for a further 5–10 minutes.

2 Sprinkle the flour into the onions and mushrooms and stir until mixed. Gradually stir in the stock until smooth. Slowly bring to the boil, stirring all the time, until the sauce boils and thickens.

5 Spoon the sauce over the fish in the pan, reheat gently and serve with hot boiled new potatoes.

Energy 706kcal/2924kJ; Protein 31.2g; Carbohydrate 15.6g, of which sugars 7.5g; Fat 56.3g, of which saturates 30.7g; Cholesterol 191mg; Calcium 98mg; Fibre 1.8g; Sodium 137mg.

Carp with Horseradish Sauce

Carp is a traditional fish on both Russian and Polish menus, and has been farmed in Poland since the 13th century. There are several varieties, the best being the mirror or king carp. The horseradish sauce in this recipe complements the fish perfectly.

Serves 4

750ml/1¼ pints/3 cups cold water
120ml/4fl oz/½ cup vinegar
1 medium carp, about 400g/14oz,
   cut into 4 fillets
115g/4oz/1 cup plain (all-purpose)
   flour
115g/4oz/½ cup butter
250ml/8fl oz/1 cup dry white wine
30ml/2 tbsp fresh horseradish
2 egg yolks, beaten
30ml/2 tbsp chopped fresh chives
salt and ground black pepper,
   to taste

1 Mix the water and vinegar in a large bowl or platter, place the carp fillets in the liquid, turning so each side is coated, and then leave to soak for 1 hour.

2 After an hour, remove the fish from the liquid and pat them dry on kitchen paper.

3 Coat the fillets in seasoned flour. Melt the butter in a frying pan over a high heat, and when foaming add the fish. Fry the fillets for 3–4 minutes on each side, until golden brown.

4 Add the wine to the frying pan and season with salt and pepper. Cover and simmer for 10–15 minutes.

5 When the fish is cooked, transfer it to a serving dish and keep warm.

6 Peel and grate the horseradish. Return the pan to the heat, add the horseradish and egg yolks to the juices and simmer for 5 minutes, or until thickened.

7 Pour the hot sauce over the warm fish and garnish with chopped chives. Serve immediately.

COOK'S TIP Soaking the carp in water and vinegar takes away the muddy taste that river-caught fish sometimes has.

VARIATION If you are unable to buy carp, use river trout instead.

Energy 500kcal/2083kJ; Protein 22.3g; Carbohydrate 23.2g, of which sugars 1.3g; Fat 31.6g, of which saturates 16.7g; Cholesterol 229mg; Calcium 135mg; Fibre 1.5g; Sodium 229mg.

Carp in Wine Sauce

This old Polish carp dish from Krakow forms part of the Christmas Eve meal. Traditionally, the carp was killed and the blood collected in a cup containing lemon juice. This was then added to the sauce. The following version does not require you to do this!

Serves 4–6

400g/14oz carp, cut into thick steaks
750ml/1¼ pints/3 cups water
350ml/12fl oz/1½ cups red wine
30ml/2 tbsp lemon juice
1 small celeriac, sliced
2 onions, sliced
6–8 black peppercorns
2.5ml/½ tsp ground ginger
grated rind of 1 lemon
salt and ground black pepper, to taste

For the sauce
15ml/1 tbsp butter
15ml/1 tbsp plain (all-purpose) flour
45ml/3 tbsp lemon juice
15ml/1 tbsp redcurrant jelly
15ml/1 tbsp clear honey
120ml/4fl oz/½ cup red wine
30ml/2 tbsp currants
30ml/2 tbsp chopped blanched
  almonds

1 Rinse the fish pieces under cold running water, then sprinkle with salt and leave in a cool place for 20 minutes.

2 Meanwhile, make the stock. Put the water, wine, lemon juice, celeriac, onions, peppercorns, ginger, seasoning and lemon rind in a large pan. Bring to the boil and simmer, uncovered, for 15 minutes.

3 Place the fish in a shallow pan and pour over the stock and vegetables. Simmer, uncovered, over a low heat for about 15 minutes, or until the fish flakes easily.

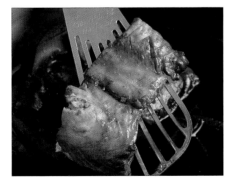

4 Remove the fish to a serving plate using a slotted spoon, and keep warm.

5 Skim out the vegetables and press through a fine sieve (strainer) to form a purée. Add the purée to the stock in the pan. You should have 500ml/17fl oz/2¼ cups stock. Add more water to make up the volume if necessary.

6 To make the sauce, melt the butter in a pan over a medium heat, then add the flour and cook, stirring, for 2 minutes. Stir in the stock. Add the lemon juice, redcurrant jelly, honey and red wine, and cook for 7 minutes.

7 Stir in the currants and almonds, then bring to the boil. Pour the sauce over the carp and serve immediately.

Energy 213kcal/891kJ; Protein 13.2g; Carbohydrate 9.5g, of which sugars 7.5g; Fat 8g, of which saturates 2.1g; Cholesterol 50mg; Calcium 58mg; Fibre 0.6g; Sodium 52mg.

Pike with Hard-boiled Eggs

This dish of poached pike with hard-boiled eggs and parsley is a traditional part of the Polish Christmas Eve meal, although it is eaten at other times of the year, too. Like carp, pike is another very popular freshwater fish in both Poland and Russia.

1 Put the carrots in a large pan and add the parsnips, celery, leek, onion, peppercorns, bay leaves and fish.

2 Pour over enough cold water to just cover. Bring to the boil and simmer, uncovered, for 15–20 minutes, or until the fish flakes easily.

3 Meanwhile, melt the butter in a small pan, then add the chopped hard-boiled eggs and parsley, and heat through.

4 Remove the fish from the pan with a slotted spoon and transfer to a warm serving plate.

5 Liberally sprinkle the fish with the lemon juice, top with the hot egg and parsley mixture and serve immediately.

VARIATION If you are unable to buy carp, use river trout instead.

COOK'S TIP The addition of egg makes this a nourishing and sustaining dish, perfect for the cold Polish winter.

Serves 4

2 carrots, roughly chopped
2 parsnips, roughly chopped
¼ celery stick, roughly chopped
1 leek, roughly chopped
1 large onion, roughly chopped
4–5 black peppercorns
2–3 bay leaves
1.8kg/4lb pike, cleaned, scaled and
    cut into 4 steaks
25g/1oz/2 tbsp butter
3 hard-boiled eggs, chopped
15ml/1 tbsp chopped fresh parsley
juice of 2 lemons

Energy 327kcal/1368kJ; Protein 39.8g; Carbohydrate 0.2g, of which sugars 0.1g; Fat 18.8g, of which saturates 6.2g; Cholesterol 290mg; Calcium 124mg; Fibre 0.2g; Sodium 178mg.

Haddock and Beer Casserole

The earthy flavour of wild mushrooms perfectly complements the delicate taste of the haddock steaks and creamy sauce in this satisfying dish. This Polish recipe, using beer, ensures that the flesh is moist and makes a distinctive and delicious addition to the sauce.

Serves 4

150g/5oz/2 cups wild mushrooms
50g/2oz/¼ cup butter
2 large onions, roughly chopped
2 celery sticks, sliced
2 carrots, sliced
4 haddock steaks, about
    185g/6½oz each
300ml/½ pint/1¼ cups light lager
4 bay leaves
25g/1oz/¼ cup plain (all-purpose)
    flour
200ml/7fl oz/scant 1 cup double
    (heavy) cream
salt and ground black pepper, to taste
dill sprigs, to garnish

1 Preheat the oven to 190°C/375°F/ Gas 5. Brush the wild mushrooms to remove any grit and only wash the caps briefly if necessary. Dry with kitchen paper and chop them.

2 Melt half the butter in a flameproof casserole, then add the onions, mushrooms, celery and carrots. Fry for about 8 minutes, or until golden brown.

3 Place the haddock steaks on top of the vegetables, then slowly pour over the lager so it doesn't fizz.

4 Add the bay leaves to the casserole and season well with salt and pepper.

5 Put the casserole in the preheated oven and cook for 20–25 minutes, or until the fish flakes easily when tested.

6 Remove the fish and vegetables from the casserole with a slotted spoon and transfer to a serving dish. Cover and keep warm while you make the sauce.

7 Melt the remaining butter in a medium pan, then stir in the flour and cook, stirring constantly, for 2 minutes.

8 Gradually pour in the liquid from the casserole, a little at a time, blending in well each time. Simmer, stirring, for 2–3 minutes until the sauce has thickened.

VARIATION You can replace the beer with the same amount of white wine, if you prefer.

9 Add the double cream to the sauce and reheat briefly, without boiling. Serve the fish and vegetables on warmed plates, accompanied by the sauce and garnished with sprigs of dill.

Energy 564kcal/2346kJ; Protein 37g; Carbohydrate 17.9g, of which sugars 10.5g; Fat 38.8g, of which saturates 23.5g; Cholesterol 158mg; Calcium 106mg; Fibre 3.4g; Sodium 231mg.

Salmon Pie

This Russian speciality is a puff-pastry pie filled with cured salmon, hard-boiled eggs and rice. Pastry of all kinds is very popular in Eastern Europe and it is especially enjoyed in Russia. In the times of the tsar, elaborate pastries were sent as party invitations.

Serves 4

4 eggs
50g/2oz/¼ cup long grain rice, cooked
300g/11oz gravlax or smoked salmon
15g/2oz/¼ cup chopped fresh dill
45ml/3 tbsp smetana or crème fraîche
1 sheet ready-made puff pastry,
   measuring about 40x20cm/16x8in
salt and ground black pepper
1 egg yolk
5ml/1 tsp water
15ml/1 tbsp fresh white breadcrumbs

1 Put the eggs in a pan, cover with cold water and bring to the boil. Reduce the heat to low and simmer for 10 minutes. When the eggs are cooked, drain and put under cold running water. Remove the shell, and chop the eggs into small pieces.

2 Cut the gravlax or smoked salmon into strips and put in a large bowl. Add the eggs, rice, dill and smetana or crème fraîche and mix together. Season with salt and pepper to taste.

3 Preheat the oven to 220°C/425°F/Gas 7. Put the sheet of pastry on a dampened baking tray. Spread the filling lengthways on one half of the pastry sheet.

4 Brush the edges with water and fold the other side over to enclose the filling. Seal together by pressing with a fork along the join. It should be like a tightly packed loaf.

5 Whisk together the egg yolk and water. Brush the pastry with the glaze and make some small holes in the top with a fork. Sprinkle the breadcrumbs over the top.

6 Bake the pie in the oven for 12–15 minutes, until golden brown. Leave the baked pie to rest for 5–10 minutes, then cut into slices and serve.

VARIATION Instead of mixing the filling ingredients, place them in layers. Start with rice, then salmon, then smetana or crème fraîche, then eggs and finally dill.

Energy 624kcal/2606kJ; Protein 32.7g; Carbohydrate 45.6g, of which sugars 1.6g; Fat 36.4g, of which saturates 5.6g; Cholesterol 280mg; Calcium 121mg; Fibre 0.3g; Sodium 1786mg.

POULTRY AND GAME

Poland is a superb hunting country. Its relatively sparsely populated countryside is covered with forests and fields, where hare, deer, wild boar and many game birds flourish, and hunting for the pot is still a popular pastime. Many traditional ingredients of Polish cooking feature in their recipes for game, from juniper berries and herbs to sour cream and mushrooms. Poultry also has a good flavour in Poland, where intensive farming methods are rare, and chicken, geese and ducks are reared on rural smallholdings, eating their natural diet. Russia also enjoys poultry and game recipes, although its hunting traditions are less universal. Venison and rabbit are probably the most common game. Chickens, however, are still often kept in country homes, for eggs as well as for the pot, and there are some typically Russian signature dishes such as Chicken Kiev and Chicken with Walnut Sauce in this chapter.

Chicken Kiev

These classic Ukrainian chicken breasts, filled with garlic butter and then deep-fried, are often accompanied with mushroom sauce. Prepare the chicken parcels well in advance to allow them to chill in the refrigerator before frying. You can also freeze them and cook from frozen.

Serves 4

4 skinless chicken breast fillets
65g/2½oz/5 tbsp cold butter
1.5ml/¼ tsp ground white pepper
4 cloves garlic, peeled and crushed
150g/5oz/3 cups fresh white
   breadcrumbs
2–3 eggs
750ml/1¼ pints/3 cups rapeseed
   (canola) oil
salt
cooked rice and sugarsnap peas,
   to serve

For the mushroom sauce
250g/9oz fresh porcini, chopped
25g/1oz/2 tbsp butter
15ml/1 tbsp plain white (all-purpose)
   flour
300ml/½ pint/1¼ cups whipping cream
salt and ground black pepper

1 Separate the small finger-thick chicken fillets from the larger fillets. Put one fillet at a time between sheets of oiled clear film (plastic wrap) and beat with a rolling pin until the large fillets are 5mm/¼in thick and the smaller fillets 3mm/⅛in thick. When flat, remove from the clear film and put on a board.

2 Cut the butter into four sticks. Put the white pepper, crushed garlic and 1.5ml/ ¼ tsp salt on a plate and mix together.

3 Roll the butter sticks in the mixture and then place one stick in the centre of each large fillet.

4 Cover the butter with a small fillet and fold the edges of the large fillet up to form a tight parcel. If necessary, secure with a cocktail stick (toothpick). Sprinkle with salt. Chill until ready to cook.

5 To make the sauce, melt the butter in a frying pan, add the mushrooms and cook over a medium heat, stirring frequently. Add the flour and stir until mixed.

6 Gradually stir the cream into the mushroom and flour mixture, a little at a time, until smooth.

7 Slowly bring the sauce to the boil, stirring. Reduce the heat and simmer for 10 minutes. Season to taste.

8 Preheat the oven to 220°C/425°F/Gas 7. Line a baking sheet with foil. Spread the breadcrumbs on a plate.

9 Lightly beat the eggs in a small bowl. Brush the chicken parcels with the beaten eggs, then roll in the breadcrumbs to coat on all sides. Brush again with the beaten eggs, and roll again in the breadcrumbs until thickly and evenly coated.

10 Heat the oil in a deep fryer to 180°C/350°F or until a cube of bread browns in 1 minute. Add the chicken parcels to the hot oil and deep-fry for 3–4 minutes, until golden brown.

11 Remove from the pan and place on the prepared baking sheet. Fold in the foil to cover. Bake in the oven for 5–10 minutes (20 minutes if cooking from frozen). Serve with the mushroom sauce.

Energy 938kcal/3901kJ; Protein 46.2g; Carbohydrate 31.5g, of which sugars 3.3g; Fat 70.7g, of which saturates 33.9g; Cholesterol 327mg; Calcium 122mg; Fibre 1.5g; Sodium 568mg.

Pressed Fried Chicken with Garlic Sauce

This famous dish from Georgia is truly delicious. Whole chickens are flattened, seasoned and fried under a weight so that they are evenly browned. The meat is then crisp on the outside, and juicy inside. Anything you have to hand will do as a weight, from a full jar to a brick.

Serves 4

2 small chickens, each weighing about
 750g/1lb 10 oz
5ml/1 tsp salt
2.5ml/½ tsp ground black pepper
10 garlic cloves
50–65g/2–2½ oz/4–5 tbsp butter

For the garlic sauce
200ml/7fl oz/scant 1 cup smetana or
 crème fraîche
2 garlic cloves
3–4 dashes Tabasco sauce

1 Put the chickens breast-side down on a chopping board and cut open lengthways, through the back. Prise open, turn skin-side up and press down firmly to flatten. Season with the salt and pepper and tuck the chopped garlic under the skin.

2 Melt the butter in two frying pans. Add a chicken to each pan, skin-side down, and fry for about 10 minutes, until lightly browned. Place a weighted plate on top of the chicken. Fry over a low-medium heat for 20 minutes. Turn the chickens, replace the weights and fry the other side for a further 20 minutes, until cooked. If necessary, lower the heat.

3 Meanwhile, make the garlic sauce. Put the smetana or crème fraîche into a bowl. Crush the garlic cloves, add to the bowl with the Tabasco sauce and mix together.

4 Place the fried chickens on a warmed serving dish, allow to rest for 5–10 minutes, then serve with a spoonful of garlic sauce.

Energy 826kcal/3417kJ; Protein 47.9g; Carbohydrate 3.2g, of which sugars 1.3g; Fat 68.9g, of which saturates 31.6g; Cholesterol 325mg; Calcium 52mg; Fibre 0.5g; Sodium 293mg

Chicken Casserole

Warming and nourishing, this casserole consisting of plenty of vegetables as well as chicken, and enriched with egg yolk and cream, is ideal comfort food during cold weather. Served with Buckwheat Kasha it makes a delicious and sustaining main meal.

Serves 4

50g/2oz dried mushrooms, rinsed and
  soaked in warm water for 30
  minutes
800g/1¾lb chicken pieces
550ml/18fl oz/2½ cups water
2 celery stalks, chopped
1 carrot, chopped
30ml/2 tbsp chopped fresh parsley
25g/1oz/2 tbsp butter
25g/1oz/2 tbsp plain (all-purpose)
  flour
120ml/4fl oz/½ cup dry white wine
2 egg yolks
salt and ground black pepper, to taste
Buckwheat Kasha (page 192), to serve

1 Strain the mushrooms, reserving the juices, then chop finely.

2 Put the chicken in a flameproof casserole, add the water and bring to the boil. Simmer for 10 minutes.

3 Add the mushrooms, celery, carrot, parsley and reserved mushroom juices to the casserole. Season, then cover and simmer for 30–45 minutes.

4 Meanwhile, make the roux. Melt the butter in a small pan, add the flour and cook, stirring, for 1 minute.

5 Remove the chicken from the casserole with a slotted spoon and set aside on a warm plate.

6 Add the roux to the casserole and stir. Add the wine and bring to the boil. Remove the casserole from the heat.

7 Put the egg yolks in a small bowl and add a ladleful of the hot juices, stirring constantly. Add to the casserole and stir to combine.

8 Return the chicken to the sauce and heat gently to warm through. Serve with Buckwheat Kasha.

Energy 285kcal/1196kJ; Protein 38.3g; Carbohydrate 6.7g, of which sugars 1.8g; Fat 9.7g, of which saturates 4.5g; Cholesterol 219mg; Calcium 43mg; Fibre 0.8g; Sodium 148mg.

Chicken Burgers with Mushroom Sauce

Burgers made with minced meat, fish or vegetables, are popular everyday food in Russia.
Chicken burgers are served in restaurants coated with crisp snippets of toasted bread rather
than breadcrumbs, and are delicious eaten with puréed potatoes.

Serves 4

600g/1lb 6oz minced (ground)
  chicken breast
1 egg
75g/3oz/1½ cups fresh white
  breadcrumbs
40g/1½oz/3 tbsp butter
salt and ground black pepper

For the mushroom sauce
25g/1oz dried sliced mushrooms, such
  as porcini, soaked for 2–3 hours
700ml/1 pint 3½fl oz/scant 3 cups
  water
30ml/2 tbsp rapeseed (canola) oil
1 onion, chopped
15ml/1 tbsp plain white (all-purpose)
  flour
45ml/3 tbsp smetana or crème fraîche
salt and ground black pepper

For the puréed potatoes
1kg/2¼lb floury potatoes
200–250ml/7–8fl oz/scant 1–1 cup
  milk, warmed
15g/½oz/1 tbsp butter
salt

COOK'S TIP Turkey breast can be
substituted for chicken in this recipe.

1 For the mushroom sauce, put the
soaked mushrooms and the water
in a pan and simmer for 40 minutes.
Using a slotted spoon, remove the
mushrooms from the pan, reserving
the water.

2 Heat the oil in a large frying pan, add
the onion and fry, stirring frequently, for
3 minutes until golden brown. Add the
mushrooms and fry, stirring all the time,
for a further 5 minutes. Sprinkle the flour
over the mushrooms and stir until mixed.

3 Gradually stir all the reserved water into
the mushrooms and flour mixture, a little
at a time, until smooth. Slowly bring to
the boil, stirring all the time, until the
sauce boils and thickens.

VARIATION For garlic mash, steep a clove
of garlic, peeled and cut in half, in the
milk as you slowly warm it on a low heat.
Leave the milk to stand for 5–10 minutes,
then reheat when you are ready to add it
to the mashed potatoes.

4 Reduce the heat and simmer the sauce
for 10 minutes. Add the smetana or
crème fraîche and simmer for a further
5 minutes. Season with plenty of salt
and pepper to taste.

5 Meanwhile, prepare the potato purée.
Peel and cut the potatoes into chunks. Put
in a pan of salted cold water, bring to the
boil, then reduce the heat and simmer for
15–20 minutes, or until soft.

6 Drain the potatoes, return to the pan
and mash with a potato masher or a fork.
Add the warm milk and butter, beating
with a wooden spoon all the time, until
the butter is melted and the purée is
smooth. Season with salt.

7 Put the minced chicken, egg, salt and
pepper into a bowl and mix well. Form
the mixture into eight to ten burgers.

8 Spread the breadcrumbs on to a plate.
Turn the burgers in the breadcrumbs until
coated and then place them on a plate.

9 Heat the butter in a large frying pan
until melted. Add the burgers and fry, in
batches if necessary, for about 3 minutes
on each side.

10 When all the burgers are cooked,
return them to the pan, cover with a lid
or folded aluminium foil, and cook over
low heat for a further 5 minutes. Serve
the burgers hot with the mushroom sauce
and potato purée.

Energy 588kcal/2479kJ; Protein 46.6g; Carbohydrate 61.6g, of which sugars 7.3g; Fat 19g, of which saturates 7.8g; Cholesterol 178mg; Calcium 131mg; Fibre 3.3g; Sodium 331mg.

Chicken with Walnut Sauce

Sacivi is a Georgian dish that is popular at the end of the summer, when walnuts are ready to be picked. You need to make the dish a day in advance to give the chicken time to chill.

Serves 4–6

> 4 chicken breast fillets, total weight 500g/1¼lb
> 500ml/17fl oz/generous 2 cups water
> 5ml/1 tsp salt
> 45ml/3 tbsp rapeseed (canola) oil
> 2 onions, chopped
> 2 garlic cloves, finely chopped
> 100g/3¾oz/1 cup walnut halves, plus 5–6 halves, to garnish
> 5ml/1 tsp ground coriander
> pinch of cayenne pepper
> 45ml/3 tbsp finely chopped fresh coriander (cilantro), to garnish

1 Put the chicken in a medium pan and pour over enough cold water to cover. Bring to the boil, reduce the heat and simmer for 5 minutes. Skim the surface if necessary and add the salt. Cook for a further 15 minutes then remove the chicken from the pan, reserving the stock.

2 Heat the oil in a small frying pan. Add the chopped onions and garlic and fry for 5 minutes, until they are softened, but not browned.

3 Transfer the onions and garlic to a food processor. Add the walnuts, coriander and cayenne pepper and half of the stock from the chicken.

4 Process until a smooth paste is formed. Add the remaining stock, a little at a time, until it reaches the consistency of a thick sauce. Transfer to a large bowl.

5 Cut the cooked chicken into 3cm/ 1¼in chunks. Add to the sauce and stir until the chicken is coated in the sauce. Cover and chill overnight.

6 To serve, turn the chicken into a serving dish. Garnish with walnut halves and chopped coriander.

VARIATION Sacivi can also be made with a firm white fish such as halibut.

Energy 285kcal/1187kJ; Protein 23.7g; Carbohydrate 7.4g, of which sugars 5.3g; Fat 18.1g, of which saturates 1.8g; Cholesterol 58mg; Calcium 58mg; Fibre 2.2g; Sodium 384mg.

Stuffed Roast Turkey

Turkey is one of the cheaper types of poultry in Poland and is often used to replace more expensive goose. It is best to buy birds that are between seven and nine months old. In this recipe the bird is stuffed with a rich herb stuffing and served with cranberry jelly.

Serves 6

1 turkey, about 4.5–5.5kg/10–12lb, washed and patted dry with kitchen paper
25g/1oz/2 tbsp butter, melted
salt and ground black pepper, to taste
cranberry jelly, to serve

For the stuffing
200g/7oz/3½ cups fresh white breadcrumbs
175ml/6fl oz/¾ cup milk
25g/1oz/2 tbsp butter
1 egg, separated
1 calf's liver, about 600g/1lb 6oz, finely chopped
2 onions, finely chopped
90ml/6 tbsp chopped fresh dill
10ml/2 tsp clear honey
salt and ground black pepper, to taste

1 To make the stuffing, put the breadcrumbs and milk in a large bowl and soak until swollen and soft. Melt the butter in a frying pan and mix 5ml/1 tsp with the egg yolk.

2 Heat the remaining butter in a frying pan and add the liver and onions. Fry gently for 5 minutes, until the onions are golden brown. Remove from the heat and leave to cool.

3 Preheat the oven to 180°C/350°F/Gas 4. Add the cooled liver mixture to the bowl of soaked breadcrumbs.

4 Add the butter and egg yolk mixture to the stuffing together with the dill, honey and seasoning. Mix well.

5 Whisk the egg white to soft peaks, then fold into the stuffing mixture.

6 Stuff the turkey cavity, then weigh to calculate the cooking time. Allow 20 minutes per 500g/1¼lb, plus an additional 20 minutes. Brush the outside with melted butter, season with salt and pepper and transfer to a roasting pan. Place in the oven and roast for the calculated time.

7 Baste the turkey regularly during cooking, and cover with foil for the final 30 minutes. To test if the turkey is done, pierce the thickest part of the thigh with a knife; the juices should run clear.

8 Remove the turkey from the oven, cover with foil and leave to rest for about 15 minutes. Carve, spoon over the juices and serve with stuffing and cranberry jelly.

Energy 740kcal/3126kJ; Protein 112.3g; Carbohydrate 35.9g, of which sugars 7.3g; Fat 13.5g, of which saturates 6.6g; Cholesterol 507mg; Calcium 122mg; Fibre 1.7g; Sodium 517mg.

Roast Goose with Apples

In Russia the goose is viewed as the king of poultry, and it is traditional to serve your guests roast goose with apples on New Year's Eve. The goose will be served with much excitement and flourish, often on a silver platter, and certainly carved with much ceremony at the table.

Serves 4–6

65g/2½oz/5 tbsp butter
1 goose
8–10 Granny Smith apples, peeled,
  cored and cut into wedges
200ml/7fl oz/scant 1 cup water
salt and ground black pepper
boiled or roasted potatoes with fresh
  dill, Sauerkraut Stew (page 188) or
  boiled buckwheat, to serve

1 Preheat the oven to 180°C/350°F/ Gas 4. Grease a roasting pan with 25g/1oz/ 2 tbsp of the butter, then season the goose inside and out with plenty of salt and black pepper.

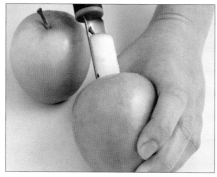

2 Peel, core and quarter four of the apples and stuff them inside the neck end of the goose. Fold the neck skin over, then truss the goose, making sure that the legs are close to the body.

3 Weigh the goose to work out cooking time, and calculate 15 minutes per 450g/1lb, plus a further 15 minutes.

4 Melt the rest of the butter. Put the goose in the pan and brush with the butter. Pour the water around the goose.

5 Roast for 1½ hours. Core the remaining apples and place in the pan. Return to the oven for the rest of the cooking time.

6 When cooked, rest the goose for 20 minutes, then carve into slices and serve with the apples and accompaniments.

Energy 822kcal/3437kJ; Protein 54.8g; Carbohydrate 44.1g, of which sugars 21.8g; Fat 48.7g, of which saturates 0.9g; Cholesterol 0mg; Calcium 87mg; Fibre 3.1g; Sodium 486mg.

Potted Goose

The season for shooting wild geese starts in autumn. If a Polish housewife is lucky enough to have more birds than she can roast, she will probably pot one of them. Sealing goose meat in fat is a traditional way of preserving, and is an incredibly delicious treat on hot toast.

Serves 6

5kg/11lb goose, boned and fat
   reserved (see Cook's Tip)
5ml/1 tsp salt
5ml/1 tsp fresh thyme leaves
5ml/1 tsp chopped fresh dill
4 bay leaves
5ml/1 tsp ground allspice
toasted rye bread, to serve

1 Cut the goose into large pieces and place in a large bowl.

2 Sprinkle over the salt, thyme, dill, bay leaves and allspice. Toss to coat the meat, then cover, place in the refrigerator and leave to marinate for 48 hours.

3 Place the goose fat in a large pan with a lid and melt gently. Add the goose portions to the pan, cover and simmer very gently for 2–3 hours.

4 Remove the meat from the pan. Pour a layer of fat into the bottom of a 2 litre/3½ pint/8 cup stoneware pot or preserving jar.

5 Place the goose portions on top of the fat, slice or shred first if you prefer. Pour in enough fat to fill the jar to the top.

6 Seal and keep in a cool, dark place for up to 2 months, until required.

7 Remove the goose from the jar and scrape off any excess fat. Serve cold, or heat through slowly if you prefer, before serving with toasted rye bread.

COOK'S TIPS It is very easy to remove the bones from the goose yourself, if you prefer. Once the goose portions have been marinated, drain them and pick out the bones with your fingers.

   The potted goose will keep for a couple of months if stored in a dark, cool place.

Energy 903kcal/3735kJ; Protein 41.3g; Carbohydrate 0g, of which sugars 0g; Fat 82g, of which saturates 23.8g; Cholesterol 200mg; Calcium 18mg; Fibre 0g; Sodium 153mg.

Roast Partridges with Sage, Thyme and Garlic

It is important that you select young birds for this simple Polish recipe. Basting the meat regularly during the cooking time prevents the flesh from drying out and adds a lovely buttery flavour, and the herbs and garlic add a subtle yet distinctive note.

Serves 2

2 small partridges, cleaned
  and gutted
4 slices pork fat or streaky
  (fatty) bacon
50g/2oz/¼ cup butter, softened, plus
  5ml/3 tbsp melted butter, for basting
6 fresh sage leaves, roughly chopped
1 bunch fresh thyme
4 garlic cloves, roughly chopped
salt and ground black pepper, to taste
cranberry preserve, to serve (optional)

1 Preheat the oven to 190°C/375°F/ Gas 5. Wash the cavities of the partridges, then dry with kitchen paper. Season the birds well, inside and out, then place in a roasting pan.

2 Lay the slices of pork fat or bacon over the birds, making sure the breasts are completely covered.

3 Shred the leaves of thyme from the stalks and discard the stalks. Mix together the softened butter, herbs and garlic, and use to stuff the cavities of the birds.

4 Place in the oven and roast for about 1½ hours, until cooked through, basting often with the melted butter.

5 Remove from the oven, cover with foil and allow to rest for 15 minutes.

6 Serve with cranberry preserve, if you like.

COOK'S TIP To test if they are cooked, pierce the thickest part of the thigh; the juices should run clear.

Energy 866kcal/3619kJ; Protein 118g; Carbohydrate 0.1g, of which sugars 0.1g; Fat 43.6g, of which saturates 16.1g; Cholesterol 59mg; Calcium 145mg; Fibre 0g; Sodium 1006mg.

Roasted Pheasants

Poland still has a strong tradition of hunting for food, and pheasants are a favourite game bird. Juniper berries, allspice, cloves and bay leaves are the key components of the marinade for this delicious dish. Long marinating ensures the flavours permeate the flesh.

Serves 4

2 medium pheasants, cleaned and
   gutted (ask your butcher to
   do this)
150g/5oz streaky (fatty) bacon, cut
   into thin strips
4–5 dried mushrooms, rinsed
   and soaked in warm water for
   30 minutes
150g/5oz/10 tbsp butter, melted
15ml/1 tbsp plain (all-purpose) flour
300ml/½ pint/1¼ cups sour cream
salt and ground black pepper, to taste
Beetroot Salad (page 195), to serve

For the marinade

175ml/6fl oz/¾ cup dry white wine
200ml/7fl oz/scant 1 cup water
90ml/6 tbsp vinegar
1 large onion, roughly chopped
1 carrot, roughly chopped
½ celeriac, roughly chopped
1 parsnip, roughly chopped
5–8 juniper berries, crushed
4 bay leaves
6 allspice berries
6 whole cloves
5ml/1 tsp sugar
salt and ground black pepper, to taste

1 To make the marinade, put all the ingredients in a large pan and bring to the boil. Once the liquid has boiled, remove from the heat.

2 Place the pheasants in a large dish or stainless steel pan and pour over the hot marinade. Cover and leave to cool, then place in the refrigerator and leave to marinate for 2–3 days, turning the pheasants occasionally.

3 Preheat the oven to 220°C/425°F/ Gas 7. Lift out the pheasants and season all over.

4 Place in a roasting pan with the vegetables from the marinade. Roll up the bacon strips and place inside the cavities of the birds.

5 Drain and chop the mushrooms. Pour the melted butter over the pheasants and sprinkle the mushrooms over the top.

6 Place in the oven and roast for about 1 hour. To test whether they are cooked, pierce the thickest part with a knife; the juices should run clear.

7 Mix the flour with the sour cream, then pour over the pheasants. Cover with foil and cook for a further 10 minutes, or until the sauce is thick.

8 Remove from the oven and leave to rest for 15 minutes. Remove the foil, carve, then serve with the vegetables, sauce and Beetroot Salad.

Energy 1114kcal/4636kJ; Protein 89.9g; Carbohydrate 6.3g, of which sugars 3.4g; Fat 78.3g, of which saturates 40g; Cholesterol 149mg; Calcium 212mg; Fibre 0.1g; Sodium 996mg.

Roast Duck with Fruit Stuffing

Duck is considered a luxury in Poland, and is usually reserved for special occasions. Often, as in this recipe, the duck is roasted, stuffed and served with a range of different fruits.

Serves 4

1 large duck, about 2.75kg/6lb
3 apples, chopped
2 whole oranges, chopped
12 prunes, chopped
12 fresh or dried apricots, chopped
175ml/6fl oz/¾ cup fresh orange juice
30ml/2 tbsp clear honey
Spiced Red Cabbage (page 181),
    to serve

For the marinade
1 lemon
5ml/1 tsp dried marjoram
salt and ground black pepper, to taste

COOK'S TIP Duck is a fatty bird, so it is best roasted with a stuffing that will cut the fat, such as this fresh, fruity one.

1 Squeeze the lemon and mix the juice in a bowl with the majoram and pepper.

2 Wash the duck and pat dry with kitchen paper, then put it into a large dish. Rub the lemon marinade over the duck. Cover and leave to marinate for 2 hours, or overnight in the refrigerator.

3 Preheat the oven to 180°C/350°F/Gas 4. Mix together the apples, oranges, prunes, apricots, orange juice and honey, then stuff into the cavity.

4 Weigh the duck and calculate the cooking time: allow 20 minutes per 500g/1¼lb, plus an extra 20 minutes.

5 Put the duck in a roasting pan and place in the hot oven. To test whether it is cooked, pierce the thickest part with a knife; the juices should run clear.

6 Cover with foil and allow it to rest for about 15 minutes. Remove the fruit from the cavity and carve the meat.

7 Transfer the meat to a serving platter and arrange the fruit around it. Serve with Spiced Red Cabbage.

Energy 468kcal/1983kJ; Protein 43.5g; Carbohydrate 54.1g, of which sugars 54.1g; Fat 13.7g, of which saturates 2.6g;
Cholesterol 220mg; Calcium 99mg; Fibre 7.8g; Sodium 241mg.

Wild Boar with Sweet-and-sour Sauce

Harking back to ancient days when hunters caught wild boar in the forests around Poland, this old Polish recipe involves marinating for several days before roasting and serving it with a flavoursome sauce.

Serves 4–6

1 piece wild boar rump, about
  2kg/4¹/₂lb
115g/4oz/²/₃ cup lard
30ml/2 tbsp plain (all-purpose) flour
15ml/1 tbsp rosehip preserve
5ml/1 tsp ground cinnamon
5ml/1 tsp sugar
5ml/1 tsp salt
redcurrant jelly, to serve

For the marinade
500ml/17fl oz/2¹/₄ cups water
500ml/17fl oz/2¹/₄ cups dry red wine
90ml/6 tbsp vinegar
2 strips of lemon rind
2 onions, sliced
3 large garlic cloves, chopped
1 carrot, chopped
¹/₂ celeriac, chopped
1 parsnip, chopped
15 prunes
10 black peppercorns
10 allspice berries, cracked
4–5 whole cloves
20 juniper berries
4 bay leaves
1 piece fresh root ginger, chopped

1 Place all the marinade ingredients in a stainless steel pan and bring to the boil. Simmer for 5 minutes, then cool.

2 Add the meat to the marinade, cover and chill. Leave to marinate for 3–4 days. This helps to tenderize the meat.

3 Preheat the oven to 180°C/350°F/ Gas 4. Heat the lard in a flameproof casserole. Add the meat and brown all over. Scoop out the vegetables and lemon from the marinade and add to the meat in the casserole.

4 Strain the marinade. Add to the casserole. Cook for 2 hours. Lift out the meat, cover and rest for 15 minutes.

5 Mix together the flour, rosehip preserve, cinnamon, sugar and salt, then add to the casserole. Stir to mix and return to the oven for 10 minutes.

6 Carve the meat into slices, then transfer to plates and spoon over the sauce. Serve with redcurrant jelly.

Energy 655kcal/2734kJ; Protein 73g; Carbohydrate 17.4g, of which sugars 8.8g; Fat 33g, of which saturates 12.5g; Cholesterol 228mg; Calcium 63mg; Fibre 3.3g; Sodium 578mg.

Rabbit in Smetana

Smetana, the Russian version of sour cream, is an ingredient in many of the country's dishes. Cooking rabbit in a sauce of smetana helps to keep the meat tender and also gives it a delicate, mild flavour. In Russia, boiled potatoes are the traditional accompaniment to this dish.

2 Add the shallots and water and half the beef stock to the pan, cover and cook over a low heat for 1–1½ hours, until the meat is tender. If necessary, add a little additional water.

3 Put the rest of the beef stock, the smetana or crème fraîche and the chopped parsley in a jug (pitcher) and mix together.

4 Add the cream and parsley mixture to the meat, bring to the boil, then reduce the heat and simmer for 10–15 minutes.

5 To serve, put the rabbit on a warmed serving dish and spoon over the sauce. Garnish the rabbit with parsley sprigs and accompany it with boiled potatoes, rice or pasta.

COOK'S TIP If you have difficulty in buying rabbit from a supermarket, you can order it from a butcher or often find it at a food market. Chicken can be used instead.

Serves 4–6

40g/1½oz/3 tbsp butter
1 rabbit, total weight about
   1.5kg/3¼lb, boned and cut
   into chunks
12 shallots
45–60ml/3–4 tbsp water
200ml/7fl oz/scant 1 cup beef stock
300ml/1/2 pint/1¼ cups smetana or
   crème fraîche
15g/½oz/¼ cup finely chopped fresh
   parsley, plus 4–5 sprigs, to garnish
salt and ground black pepper
boiled potatoes, rice or pasta,
   to serve

1 Heat the butter in a large frying pan. Add the rabbit pieces and fry over a medium heat, stirring occasionally, for 10 minutes, until browned on all sides. Season with salt and pepper.

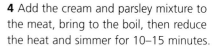

Energy 436kcal/1809kJ; Protein 33.9g; Carbohydrate 6.7g, of which sugars 5g; Fat 30.5g, of which saturates 19.5g; Cholesterol 193mg; Calcium 121mg; Fibre 1.4g; Sodium 129mg.

Venison Ragoût

Bear meat was originally used in this recipe, which dates from the times when bears were hunted for food in Russia, but other game such as elk or venison can be substituted. In some Russian restaurants today bear ragoût made with imported meat is served.

Serves 4

600g/1lb 6oz venison or elk fillet
2 onions
500g/1¼lb turnips
5–6 juniper berries
40g/1¼oz/3 tbsp butter
30ml/2 tbsp rapeseed (canola) oil
1 beef stock (bouillon) cube
60–75ml/4–5 tbsp tomato purée
  (paste)
15ml/1 tbsp plain white (all-purpose)
  flour
2–3 bay leaves
4–5 black peppercorns
500ml/17fl oz/generous 2 cups water
300ml/½ pint/1¼ cups double
  (heavy) cream
salt and ground black pepper
mashed or boiled potatoes to serve

1 Cut the meat into chunky pieces. Chop the onions, dice the turnips and crush the juniper berries. Heat the butter and oil in a flameproof casserole. Add the meat and fry, stirring frequently, for about 10 minutes, until browned on all sides.

2 Add the onions to the pan and fry for 3–5 minutes. Add the turnips and fry, stirring all the time, for a further 5 minutes. Crumble in the stock cube and add the tomato purée.

VARIATION If you do use bear fillet for this recipe, you will need to increase the cooking time by about 1½ hours.

3 Sprinkle the flour over the meat and fry, stirring, for 1 minute. Add the juniper berries, bay leaves, peppercorns and gradually stir in the water. Bring to the boil, then reduce the heat, cover and simmer for about 1½ hours.

4 Stir the cream into the pan and cook for a further 10 minutes. Season to taste and serve hot with boiled or mashed potatoes and Marinated Mushrooms.

Energy 758kcal/3148kJ; Protein 37.6g; Carbohydrate 19.1g, of which sugars 13.7g; Fat 60.7g, of which saturates 32.4g; Cholesterol 199mg; Calcium 139mg; Fibre 4.7g; Sodium 200mg.

Venison with Wine Sauce

Tender venison steaks are the perfect partner to the wild mushrooms that abound in Poland's forests. Here the steaks are cooked simply and served with a rich wine sauce. If venison is out of season or not available you can replace it with beef; sirloin or rump would be the best cuts.

Serves 4

100g/3½oz fresh wild mushrooms, cut in half
4 venison loin steaks, 2cm/¾in thick
25g/1oz/¼ cup plain (all-purpose) flour
25g/1oz/2 tbsp butter
1 large onion, sliced into rings
5ml/1 tsp fresh thyme leaves
5ml/1 tsp juniper berries
5–6 allspice berries
5 bay leaves
4 garlic cloves, crushed
175ml/6fl oz/¾ cup white wine
salt and ground black pepper

1 Brush the mushrooms to remove any grit, and wash the caps briefly if necessary. Dry with kitchen paper. Lightly dust the venison steaks with the flour.

2 Heat the butter in a heavy pan with a lid, then add the onion rings and venison, and fry for 5 minutes, until the onions have softened and the steaks are brown.

3 Add the remaining ingredients to the pan and season to taste. Cover and simmer for 30 minutes.

4 Taste and adjust the seasoning, if necessary. Serve immediately.

Energy 303kcal/1276kJ; Protein 45.1g; Carbohydrate 5.2g, of which sugars 0.4g; Fat 9.6g, of which saturates 4.9g; Cholesterol 113mg; Calcium 24mg; Fibre 0.2g; Sodium 150mg.

Marinated Hare

In this delectable Polish dish, the saddle and thighs of a hare are marinated in buttermilk and vegetables, before being roasted and then baked with a cream sauce. The marinating process helps to tenderize the meat. Wild boar could be used in place of hare in this recipe.

Serves 4

saddle and thighs of 1 hare
120ml/4fl oz/½ cup vinegar
900ml/1½ pints/3¾ cups buttermilk
175g/6oz/¾ cup butter
5 large dried mushrooms, rinsed and
  soaked in warm water for 30
  minutes, thinly sliced
15ml/1 tbsp plain (all-purpose) flour
200ml/7fl oz/scant 1 cup thick
  sour cream
175ml/6fl oz/¾ cup white wine
salt and ground black pepper
cranberry preserve, to serve (optional)

For the marinade:
10–15 juniper berries
2 large onions, cut into slices
½ celeriac, chopped
2 parsnips, chopped
2 carrots, chopped
3 large garlic cloves, crushed
5 bay leaves

1 Place the hare pieces, vinegar and all the marinade ingredients in a large dish and pour in enough buttermilk to cover.

2 Add salt and pepper, cover, and place in the refrigerator. Leave to marinate for 2–3 days. Change the buttermilk after day 1.

3 At the end of the three days, drain off the marinade and buttermilk. Preheat the oven to 180°C/350°F/Gas 4. Transfer the hare pieces to a roasting pan, rub with 15ml/1 tbsp salt, and dot with the butter.

4 Sprinkle the mushrooms over the hare. Cover and roast for 1–1½ hours.

5 Mix the flour with the sour cream and white wine, then add to the roasting pan.

6 Shake the pan so that the hare is covered with the sauce, then cover the pan with foil and replace in the oven. Cook for a further 15–20 minutes, or until the sauce is thick and bubbling.

7 Transfer the pieces of hare to a warm serving dish and spoon over the creamy sauce. Serve immediately, with cranberry preserve, if you like.

COOK'S TIP An important part of Polish cuisine involves marinating game before it is cooked. This process helps to tenderize the meat and also adds flavour to the finished dish.

Energy 581kcal/2423kJ; Protein 62.9g; Carbohydrate 6.9g, of which sugars 3g; Fat 29.5g, of which saturates 8.4g; Cholesterol 40mg; Calcium 118mg; Fibre 0.5g; Sodium 111mg.

MEAT

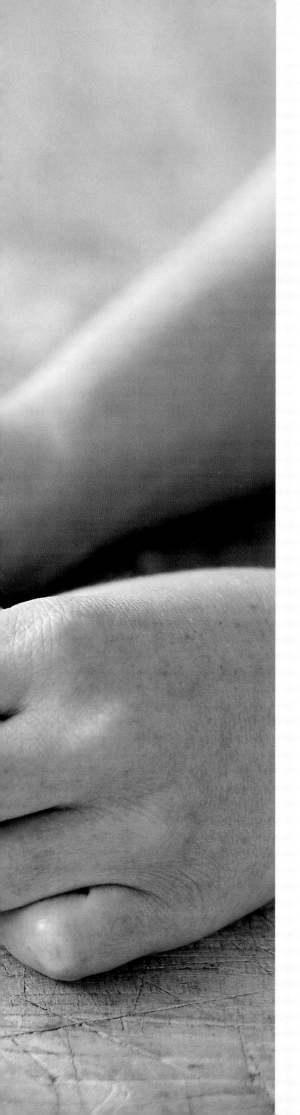

Russians and Poles are both nations of meat lovers, and enjoy it roasted whole or in casseroles. Russian meat recipes often go right back to the days when the large wood-burning stove, which was kept alight the whole year round, was also used for slowly braising delicious stews. Most of these recipes also contain mixtures of vegetables and grains to add bulk and create an entire meal in a pot. Mushrooms, tomatoes, potatoes and cabbage are frequently included for colour and flavour as well as nutritional qualities. Russians are particularly fond of beef and lamb recipes, while Poles have a special love for pork in all its many forms. Both rural communities developed recipes for using all parts of the animal, including offal, which is a highly prized delicacy often eaten as a snack in Poland, and the hearts, which are enjoyed in Russia. The addition of sour cream to many of the following meat dishes helps to give them a particularly Russian and Polish taste.

Little Beef Dumplings

These tiny Siberian dumplings are traditionally accompanied by red wine vinegar, melted butter and ground black pepper. Russians expect to eat about 40 pelmeni at a time, but this is, of course, not obligatory, and here we suggest 20. Leftover pelmeni are delicious fried in butter. It is customary to make pelmeni in advance and freeze them, to be cooked as needed.

Makes 80–100
Serves 4–6

2 eggs
150ml/¼ pint/⅔ cup water
15ml/1 tbsp rapeseed (canola) oil
2.5ml/½ tsp salt
360g/12½oz/3⅛ cups plain white (all-purpose) flour, plus extra for dusting

For the filling
1 onion, total weight 100g/3¾oz
200g/7oz minced (ground) beef
200g/7oz minced (ground) pork
7.5ml/1½ tsp salt
2–2.5ml/⅓–½ tsp ground black pepper
red wine vinegar, melted butter, salt and ground black pepper, and smetana (optional), to serve

COOK'S TIP The best pelmeni are always handmade but, if you want to save time, you can roll the dough through a pasta machine and cut the pieces into rounds using a 5cm/2in round cutter. Fill them with the meat mixture and seal by pressing the edges firmly together.

1 First make the pastry. Put the eggs, water, oil, salt and half of the flour in a food processor and process until well blended. Add the remaining flour, in batches, to form a smooth pastry.

2 Turn the pastry on to a lightly floured surface and knead for 5 minutes. Put in a plastic bag and leave to rest for 30 minutes, or overnight, in a cold place.

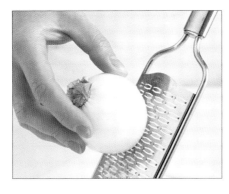

3 To make the filling, finely grate the onion and put it in a bowl. Add the minced beef and pork, salt and pepper and mix together. Set aside.

4 To make the dumplings, cut the pastry into eight pieces. Work with one piece at a time, keeping the remaining pieces in the plastic bag to prevent them from drying out.

5 On a floured surface, roll the piece of pastry into a roll, the thickness of a finger. Cut the roll into 10–12 small pieces.

6 Flatten out each piece to a round, about 3cm/1¼ in in diameter, and then roll out into a thinner round, 5–6cm/2–2½in in diameter.

7 Spread each round with 5m/1 tsp of the meat mixture, leaving a small uncovered edge. Fold and pinch together the rounds to form a half-moon shape.

8 As you make the dumplings, put them on a floured baking sheet. When the sheet is full, put it in the freezer.

9 When the dumplings are completely frozen, transfer them to a plastic bag and keep frozen until required.

10 When you are ready to serve the dumplings, take the amount you need from the freezer and put in a pan of lightly salted boiling water.

11 Simmer until the dumplings float to the surface, then simmer for a further 1 minute. Using a slotted spoon, scoop out of the water and serve immediately, sprinkled with red wine vinegar, melted butter, salt and pepper.

12 A small amount of the cooking water mixed with smetana may be served on the side, if wished.

Energy 381kcal/1605kJ; Protein 20.9g; Carbohydrate 47.9g, of which sugars 1.8g; Fat 13.1g, of which saturates 4.4g; Cholesterol 105mg; Calcium 103mg; Fibre 2.1g; Sodium 74mg.

Roast Beef Roll

This traditional Polish dish is a combination of fine steak and stong-flavoured mushrooms.
Stuffed meat dishes such as this have been a part of Polish cooking since the 17th century, and
they are usually served on festive occasions or as part of a special Polish dinner.

3 Using a mallet, pound the steak to the thickness of your little finger. Spread the stuffing all over the meat, then roll tightly. Tuck the edges in and tie with scalded white cotton thread.

4 Heat the butter in a large pan. Sprinkle the roll with salt, then add to the pan and seal on all sides. Add the stock, cover and simmer for 30 minutes. Preheat the oven to 180°C/350°F/Gas 4.

5 Transfer the beef roll and the juices to a roasting pan and roast for 30 minutes. Add more stock if required.

Serves 4–6

1.3kg/3lb piece boneless rump steak
25g/1oz/2 tbsp butter
120ml/4fl oz/½ cup beef stock
pinch of salt
Buckwheat Kasha (page 192) and a
  green salad or poached beetroots
  (beets), to serve

For the stuffing
50g/2oz/½ cups dried mushrooms,
  soaked in warm water for
  30 minutes
25g/1oz streaky (fatty) smoked bacon
15g/½oz/1 tbsp butter
½ onion, finely chopped
15ml/1 tbsp fresh breadcrumbs
1 egg, beaten
15ml/1 tbsp sour cream
15ml/1 tbsp finely chopped
  fresh parsley
salt and ground black pepper, to taste

1 To make the stuffing, strain the mushrooms and put into a food processor with the bacon. Process to form a paste, then scrape into a bowl.

2 Heat the butter in a pan, then add the onion and fry for 5 minutes. Leave to cool, then add to the bowl with the breadcrumbs, egg, sour cream, parsley and seasoning. Use your hands to knead the mixture to combine.

6 Remove the thread and cut into thin slices. Ladle over the juices and serve with Buckwheat Kasha and a green salad or poached beetroots.

Energy 360kcal/1510kJ; Protein 50.1g; Carbohydrate 2.9g, of which sugars 0.8g; Fat 16.6g, of which saturates 8g; Cholesterol 177mg; Calcium 23mg; Fibre 0.3g; Sodium 267mg.

Kebabs with Plum Sauce

At weekends, Russian families love to go on a picnic. Other family members, friends and colleagues are all invited to go to a sjasliki – cooking food on skewers. The best sjaslik are made over the glowing cinders left from an open fire.

Serves 4

800g–1kg/1¾–2¼lb beef fillet
1 onion, finely sliced
200ml/7fl oz/scant 1 cup red wine
15g/½ oz/1 tbsp butter
salt and ground black pepper
lemon wedges, to garnish

For the plum sauce
300g/11oz fresh green or red plums
400ml/14fl oz/1⅔ cups water
2 garlic cloves
45ml/3 tbsp chopped fresh
  coriander (cilantro)
small pinch of cayenne pepper

1 Cut the meat into chunks. Put in a large bowl with salt and pepper, the onion and wine. Cover with clear film (plastic wrap) and leave in the refrigerator for 3 hours.

2 For the sauce, put the plums in a pan. Add the water, bring to the boil, reduce the heat, then cover and simmer for 20 minutes. Remove the plums from the pan and set aside. Reserve the liquid.

3 When the plums are cool, remove the stones (pits) and put the flesh in a food processor. Add the garlic, coriander and about 75ml/5 tbsp of the plum liquid and blend. Add more liquid to the purée, until it is the consistency of thick cream. Add cayenne pepper and salt to taste.

4 Heat a barbecue, if using, or preheat the grill (broiler). Melt the butter. Thread the marinated meat chunks on to long metal skewers.

5 Brush the meat with the melted butter. Place on the grill and cook the skewers for about 10–15 minutes, turning to cook the meat on all sides.

6 Serve the skewers with the plum sauce and garnish with lemon. Russians would add plain boiled rice and a green salad.

VARIATION You can cook skewers of lamb, such as lamb fillet or boneless loin of lamb, in the same way.

Energy 325kcal/1364kJ; Protein 43.4g; Carbohydrate 8.2g, of which sugars 7.8g; Fat 12.5g, of which saturates 5.6g; Cholesterol 122mg; Calcium 48mg; Fibre 2g; Sodium 95mg.

Burgers with Buckwheat and Fried Onions

Kotletki are Russia's fast food. Russians love them and eat them for both lunch and dinner. Although they can be bought ready-made from the meat counter in the supermarkets, the best kotletki are home-made. Here they are served with buckwheat and fried onions.

Serves 4

1 potato
1 onion
300g/11oz minced (ground) beef
300g/11oz minced (ground) pork
5ml/1 tsp salt
heaped 1.5ml/¼ tsp ground
 black pepper
75g/3oz/1½ cups fresh breadcrumbs
25–40g/1–1½oz/2–3 tbsp butter
30ml/2 tbsp rapeseed (canola) oil
100ml/3½fl oz/scant ½ cup smetana or
 crème fraîche and 4–8 small
 gherkins, to serve

For the buckwheat
350g/12oz/1¾ cups whole
 buckwheat grains
1 litre/1¾ pints/4 cups boiling water
5ml/1 tsp salt
2 large onions
45–60ml/3–4 tbsp sunflower oil

VARIATION The grated potato in the burgers can be replaced with two slices of stale white bread. Remove the crusts and soak in 100ml/3½fl oz/scant ½ cup milk for 5 minutes, until soft.

1 To make the burgers, grate the potato and onion and put in a large bowl. Add the beef, pork, salt and pepper and mix well together until the mixture is smooth.

2 Form the meat mixture into 10–12 equal-sized 2cm/¾in thick burgers and place them on a damp chopping board. (Using a wet surface stops them sticking.)

3 Spread the breadcrumbs on to a plate. Turn the burgers in the breadcrumbs until coated and then place them on a plate or dry chopping board. Set aside.

4 To cook the buckwheat, heat a small frying pan until hot, add the buckwheat and dry-fry for 1–2 minutes. Transfer to a medium pan and add the boiling water and salt. Stir, cover, and cook over a medium heat for 20–30 minutes, until the grains have absorbed all the water.

5 Meanwhile, prepare the onions for the buckwheat. Slice the onions into rings.

6 Heat the oil in a medium frying pan, add the onions and fry, stirring frequently, over a low heat for 5 minutes, or until softened and golden brown.

7 When the buckwheat is cooked, drain and return to the pan. Add the fried onions and stir together.

8 Meanwhile, cook the burgers. Heat the butter and oil in a medium frying pan until hot and the butter has melted. Add three or four burgers at a time and fry, over a medium heat, for 2–3 minutes on each side.

9 Remove from the pan and continue to cook the remaining burgers in the same way. When all the burgers are cooked, return them to the pan, cover with a lid and cook, over a low heat, for 10 minutes.

10 Arrange the burgers in a row on a serving dish and put the buckwheat along each side. Serve hot, with smetana or crème fraîche and gherkins.

Energy 839kcal/3515kJ; Protein 38.9g; Carbohydrate 85.9g, of which sugars 9g; Fat 40.2g, of which saturates 12.9g; Cholesterol 108mg; Calcium 88mg; Fibre 2.9g; Sodium 1284mg.

Beef Stroganoff

This famous dish was created at the time of Catherine the Great by Count Alexander Sergeyevich Stroganov. The Count would invite poor students into his house, and serve them this beef casserole, accompanied by fried potatoes and Salted Cucumbers.

Serves 4

90–105ml/6–7 tbsp rapeseed (canola) oil
6–8 potatoes, peeled and thinly sliced
40–50g/1½–2oz/3–4 tbsp butter
500g/1¼lb beef fillet, very thinly sliced
salt and ground black pepper
Salted Cucumbers (page 79), diced,
  to serve

For the sauce

30–45ml/2–3 tbsp rapeseed (canola) oil
2–3 onions, thinly sliced
1 chicken stock (bouillon) cube
45ml/3 tbsp tomato purée (paste)
15ml/1 tbsp plain white (all-purpose)
  flour
2–3 bay leaves
4–5 black peppercorns
300ml/½ pint/1¼ cups water
200ml/7fl oz/scant 1 cup double
  (heavy) cream
100ml/3½fl oz/scant ½ cup smetana or
  crème fraîche

1 First make the sauce. Heat the oil in a medium pan. Add the sliced onions and fry over a medium heat for 3–5 minutes. Crumble the stock cube into the onions and fry for a further 1–2 minutes.

2 Add the tomato purée to the pan, then the flour and stir well together. Add the bay leaves and peppercorns and then gradually stir in the water and cream.

3 Slowly bring to the boil, stirring, until the sauce thickens. Simmer for a further 10 minutes. Stir in the smetana or crème fraîche.

4 Meanwhile, fry the potatoes. Heat the oil in a large frying pan. Add the sliced potatoes and fry for 10–15 minutes, turning occasionally.

5 Cover the pan and cook for a further 10–15 minutes, until tender. Season the potatoes with salt to taste.

6 To cook the beef, heat the butter in a frying pan. Add the slices of beef, in batches, and cook quickly, over a high heat, for about 1 minute until browned. Transfer to a plate, season, and keep warm. Repeat until all the meat is cooked.

7 When you are ready to serve, reheat the sauce, add the beef and heat through gently for 2–3 minutes. Serve immediately with the fried potatoes, accompanied by diced Salted Cucumbers.

Energy 919kcal/3810kJ; Protein 32.5g; Carbohydrate 36g, of which sugars 11.7g; Fat 72.6g, of which saturates 34.6g; Cholesterol 194mg; Calcium 94mg; Fibre 3.4g; Sodium 177mg.

Beef Goulash

In Poland, beef is relatively expensive and not always easy to obtain, so the Poles make the most of cheaper cuts with recipes such as this rich goulash, in which the meat is cooked slowly, mushrooms are added to bulk the dish out, and it is enriched with cream.

Serves 4–6

45ml/3 tbsp oil
1.3kg/3lb braising steak
2 large onions, chopped
4 garlic cloves, chopped
2.5ml/¹/₂ tsp salt
2.5ml/¹/₂ tsp ground black pepper
3 allspice berries
2.5ml/¹/₂ tsp paprika
4 fresh bay leaves
1 beef stock (bouillon) cube
5 dried wild mushrooms, rinsed
  and soaked in warm water for
  30 minutes
175ml/6fl oz/³/₄ cup dry red wine
60ml/4 tbsp plain (all-purpose) flour
250ml/8fl oz/1 cup sour cream

1 Preheat the oven to 160°C/325°F/Gas 3. Rinse the meat, then pat dry on kitchen paper and cut into 2.5cm/1in cubes.

2 Heat the oil in a flameproof casserole, add the meat and brown on all sides over a high heat. Remove to a plate using a slotted spoon.

3 Add the onions and garlic to the hot oil in the casserole and fry gently for 5 minutes, or until golden brown. Return the meat to the pan and add the salt, pepper, spices, bay leaves and stock cube. Pour in enough water to just cover.

4 Put the casserole in the preheated oven and cook for about 1¹/₂–2 hours, until the meat is tender.

5 Drain and slice the mushrooms and add to the casserole with the wine. Cook for a further 30 minutes.

6 Mix the flour with the sour cream and stir through the goulash. Cook for a further 10 minutes. Serve.

Energy 508kcal/2119kJ; Protein 50g; Carbohydrate 13.4g, of which sugars 4.6g; Fat 26.4g, of which saturates 11.2g; Cholesterol 162mg; Calcium 78mg; Fibre 1g; Sodium 161mg

Little Beef Pies

These golden little pastries are called pirojki in Russian, and they are an important part of the zakuski table. Pirojki are also served as an accompaniment to soups. In this recipe they are filled with beef, but other fillings such as salmon, potato or cabbage can be used.

Makes 24 little pies

Serves 6–8
1 large onion
30–45ml/2–3 tbsp rapeseed
  (canola) oil
400g/14oz minced (ground) beef
100ml/3½fl oz/scant ½ cup beef stock
30ml/2 tbsp smetana or crème fraîche
1 egg
salt and ground black pepper

For the dough
50g/2oz/¼ cup butter
200ml/7fl oz/scant 1 cup milk
45ml/3 tbsp water
1 small (US medium) egg plus
  1 egg yolk
2.5ml/½ tsp salt
7.5ml/1½ tsp caster (superfine) sugar
5g/⅛ oz easy-blend (rapid-rise)
  dried yeast
400g/14oz/3½ cups plain (all-purpose)
  flour

1 To make the filling, finely chop the onion. Heat the oil in a medium frying pan, add the onion and fry for 5 minutes until softened and golden brown.

2 Add the beef and fry, stirring frequently, for about 10 minutes, until browned.

3 Add the stock to the pan, stir through and then add the smetana or crème fraîche. Stir together, then cover and simmer gently, stirring occasionally, for 10–15 minutes. Leave to cool.

4 Meanwhile, put the egg in a pan, cover with cold water and bring to the boil. Reduce the heat to low and simmer for 10 minutes. When the egg is cooked, immediately drain and put under cold running water. Remove the shell from the egg, then finely chop.

5 When the beef has cooled, stir in the chopped egg. Season with salt and pepper to taste. Set aside, while you make the dough.

6 To make the dough, melt the butter in a pan. Add the milk and water to the pan and heat it to 45°C/110°F. Remove from the heat.

7 Whisk the whole egg in a bowl with the salt and sugar. Add the milk mixture to the egg. Mix the yeast with the flour and stir, a little at a time, into the egg mixture.

8 Knead the dough in the bowl for 5 minutes. Cover with a dish towel and leave to rise in a warm place for 30 minutes, until doubled in size.

9 Grease a large baking sheet. Turn the dough on to a lightly floured surface and knead for 2–3 minutes. Cut the dough into 24 equal-sized pieces and form each piece into a ball. Leave to rest for 5–10 minutes.

10 Flatten each ball to a round measuring 10cm/4in in diameter. Spread 25ml/1½ tbsp of the beef filling in the centre of each round of dough. Fold together and seal the edges at the top. Put them, upside-down with the join facing down, on the baking sheet.

11 Preheat the oven to 230°C/450°F/ Gas 8. Whisk the egg yolk with 15ml/1 tbsp water and brush on top of the pies. Leave to rest for 20 minutes.

12 Bake the pies in the oven for 12–13 minutes, until golden. Transfer to a wire rack and leave to cool.

13 Serve the pirojki warm or at room temperature, on their own or with a bowl of hearty Russian soup.

Energy 411kcal/1719kJ; Protein 17.4g; Carbohydrate 41.7g, of which sugars 3.4g; Fat 20.5g, of which saturates 9g; Cholesterol 117mg; Calcium 120mg; Fibre 1.7g; Sodium 108mg.

Russian Beef-stuffed Cabbage Rolls

Cabbage, whether green or red or white, is a staple food in Russian cuisine, especially in the winter time. These stuffed cabbage rolls, called golubtsy, are made in large quantities and will be happily eaten by the family for two to three days in a row.

Serves 4

1 spring or winter cabbage head
100g/3 ³/₄oz/¹/₂ cup long grain rice
1 onion
30ml/2 tbsp rapeseed (canola) oil
300g/11oz minced (ground) beef
150ml/¹/₄ pint/²/₃ cup water
40–50g/1¹/₂–2oz/3–4 tbsp butter
200ml/7fl oz/scant 1 cup beef stock
200ml/7fl oz/scant 1 cup smetana or
  crème fraîche, plus extra to serve
45–60ml/3–4 tbsp finely chopped
  fresh dill
salt and ground black pepper

1 Cut out the woody stem from the centre of the cabbage head, about 5cm/2in deep. (This will make it easier to break off the cabbage leaves during cooking, see step 3.)

2 Put the cabbage head upside-down in the pan and pour over enough boiling water to completely cover the cabbage. Season with salt.

3 Bring the water back to the boil, then reduce the heat and simmer, breaking off the cabbage leaves one by one as they gradually turn soft.

4 Using a slotted spoon, remove the last cooked leaves from the water, then drain on kitchen paper.

5 Place one leaf at a time on a chopping board and, using a sharp knife, remove the thick stem of the leaf to allow it to flatten but remain in one piece. (This will make it easier to roll the leaves.) You need 12–14 prepared leaves in total.

6 Bring a separate large pan of boiling salted water to the boil, add the rice and stir to loosen the grains at the bottom of the pan. Simmer for about 12 minutes, until tender. Drain into a sieve (strainer) and rinse under cold running water.

7 Meanwhile, finely chop the onion. Heat the oil in a small frying pan, add the onion and fry for 5–10 minutes, until softened and golden brown. Turn into a large bowl and leave to cool.

VARIATION Making cabbage rolls is time consuming so Russians often make Lazy Golubsy. Instead of making rolls, finely shred the cabbage and fry it together with the minced (ground) beef and cooked rice. Add salt and pepper and serve with smetana or crème fraîche.

8 When the onion is cool, add the cooked rice, minced beef and water to the onion. Season well with salt and pepper and mix well together.

9 Place 1–1¹/₂ tablespoons of the mixture in the centre of each cabbage leaf. Fold in the sides and roll lengthways, forming a tight roll.

10 Heat the butter in a frying pan until melted. Add the cabbage rolls and fry for 5–10 minutes, until golden brown. Transfer the rolls to a flameproof casserole, arranging them side-by-side. Add the beef stock, cover, and cook over a low heat for 20 minutes, if using a spring cabbage, and 30–40 minutes if using a winter cabbage.

11 Using a slotted spoon, arrange the cabbage rolls on a serving dish. Stir the smetana or crème fraîche into the stock, bring to the boil and boil for 3–4 minutes. Spoon the sauce over the rolls and garnish with finely chopped dill. Serve with smetana or crème fraîche.

Energy 558kcal/2313kJ; Protein 19.2g; Carbohydrate 28.3g, of which sugars 7.7g; Fat 40.9g, of which saturates 24.1g; Cholesterol 129mg; Calcium 130mg; Fibre 3.2g; Sodium 163mg

Veal Stroganoff

'Stroganoff' dishes are thought to have originated in the 19th century in St Petersburg, where the beef dish was created and named after Count Alexander Sergeyevich Stroganov. The recipe was rapidly assimilated into Polish cuisine, and this version has become a much-loved classic.

4 Add the mushrooms and fry for a further 5 minutes. Transfer the vegetables to a plate and keep warm.

5 Pour the remaining oil into the frying pan and heat. When the oil is hot, add the floured meat strips and stir-fry over a high heat for about 2 minutes, until the meat is brown.

6 Return the vegetables to the pan and add the brandy, mustard, veal or beef stock and seasoning.

7 Simmer for 1 minute, then add the sour cream. Simmer for 1 minute more, until thick and glossy. Serve immediately, garnished with parsley, accompanied by buttered egg noodles or rice.

Serves 4–6

900g/2lb veal fillet
15g/¹/₂oz/2 tbsp plain (all-purpose) flour
2.5ml/¹/₂ tsp cayenne pepper
2.5ml/¹/₂ tsp hot paprika
60ml/4 tbsp vegetable oil
2 small onions, finely chopped
4 garlic cloves, finely chopped
8–10 fresh wild mushrooms, wiped clean and halved
150ml/¹/₄ pint/³/₄ cup brandy
5ml/1 tsp Polish or Dijon mustard
400ml/14fl oz/1²/₃ cups veal or beef stock
400ml/14fl oz/1²/₃ cups sour cream
salt and ground black pepper, to taste
30ml/2 tbsp chopped fresh flat leaf parsley, to garnish
cooked egg noodles or rice, to serve

1 Slice the veal into thin strips – this is easier if you freeze it for 30 minutes first.

2 Mix together the flour, cayenne pepper and paprika in a bowl, and toss the strips of meat in it. Set aside.

3 Heat half the oil in a heavy pan, then add the onions and garlic. Fry gently for 5 minutes, or until soft and brown.

Energy 511kcal/2124kJ; Protein 33.7g; Carbohydrate 9.9g, of which sugars 6.3g; Fat 31.6g, of which saturates 13.6g; Cholesterol 133mg; Calcium 97mg; Fibre 1g; Sodium 434mg.

Veal Kidney Gratin

This spicy gratin with Salted Cucumbers is a real winter warmer, best served steaming hot, straight from the oven. It is served with rice or a piece of good bread. Accompany the dish with a full-bodied red wine for a perfect combination of flavours.

Serves 4

600g/1 lb 6oz veal kidneys
1 onion
150g/5oz button mushrooms
25g/1oz/2 tbsp butter
45ml/3 tbsp rapeseed or
  sunflower oil
4 Salted Cucumbers (page79), peeled
  and diced
45ml/3 tbsp tomato purée
7.5mll/1½ tsp plain white
  (all-purpose) flour
100ml/3½fl oz/scant ½ cup white wine
300ml/½ pint/1¼ cups double
  (heavy) cream
125g/4¼ oz Cheddar cheese
pinch of cayenne pepper
salt
45ml/3 tbsp chopped fresh parsley,
  to garnish

1 Preheat the oven to 240°C/475°F/Gas 9. Dice the kidneys. chop the onion and slice the mushrooms.

2 Heat the butter in a large pan until melted, add the kidneys and fry over a high heat, stirring frequently, until browned on all sides. Remove the kidneys from the pan and keep warm.

3 Return the frying pan to the heat, add the oil and the onion and stir-fry for 2–3 minutes, then add the mushrooms and fry for 10 minutes, stirring occasionally.

4 Stir the Salted Cucumbers and the tomato purée into the mushrooms.

5 Sprinkle the flour into the mushroom mixture and stir until mixed, then stir in the wine. Gradually add in the cream, a little at a time, until smooth.

6 Bring the sauce to the boil, stirring. Reduce the heat and simmer for 2–3 minutes. Add cayenne pepper and salt.

7 Divide the fried kidneys between four ovenproof ramekins and pour the sauce over each. Grate the cheese and sprinkle it over the tops.

8 Bake in the oven for 5 minutes, or until the cheese is golden brown. Serve hot, garnished with parsley.

Energy 735kcal/3094kJ; Protein 40g; Carbohydrate 84g, of which sugars 2.5g; Fat 28.9g, of which saturates 15.4g; Cholesterol 184mg; Calcium 42mg; Fibre 1.5g; Sodium 369mg

Veal Stew with Pearl Barley

This rustic dish from Russia, made with a good piece of meat, is easily prepared for Sunday dinner. Serve it with Salted Cucumbers and a sauerkraut salad.

Serves 4

75g/3oz/6 tbsp butter
600g/1lb 6oz lean, tender, boneless
  stewing veal, diced
2 onions, chopped
10 medium potatoes, peeled and cut
  in half lengthways
200–300ml/7–10fl oz/1–1 ¼ cups
  beef stock
3 sprigs flat leaf parsley
2 bay leaves
4–5 black peppercorns
salt and ground black pepper
Salted Cucumbers (page 79) and a
  sauerkraut salad, to serve

For the pearl barley
15ml/1 tbsp rapeseed (canola) oil
300g/11oz/heaped 1½ cups pearl
  barley
1 litre/1¾ pints/4 cups water
25g/1oz/2 tbsp butter

1 To prepare the pearl barley, heat the oil in a pan. Add the barley and stir-fry for 30 seconds. Add the water, bring to the boil then reduce the heat, cover and simmer for 50 minutes, until tender.

2 Heat 40g/1½oz/3 tbsp of the butter in a flameproof casserole. Add the pieces of meat, in batches if necessary, and fry over a medium heat for about 15 minutes, until browned on all sides.

3 Add the remaining butter, onions and potatoes to the pan and cook over low heat for 10 minutes, occasionally stirring. Add the stock, parsley, bay leaves, salt and peppercorns to the pan. Cover and simmer for 30 minutes.

4 Drain the pearl barley and transfer to a serving dish. Stir in the butter until melted and add salt to taste. Serve with the stew, Salted Cucumbers and a sauerkraut salad.

Energy 735kcal/3094kJ; Protein 40g; Carbohydrate 84g, of which sugars 2.5g; Fat 28.9g, of which saturates 15.4g; Cholesterol 184mg; Calcium 42mg; Fibre 1.5g; Sodium 369mg

Fried Calf's Brains

Rich, creamy, and nutritious calf's brains are a real treat. In this classic Polish recipe they are fried with onions, eggs and breadcrumbs, and served on toast.

Serves 4

675g/1½ lb calf's brains
40g/1½ oz/3 tbsp butter
1 large onion, finely chopped
2 eggs, beaten
60ml/4 tbsp fresh breadcrumbs
8 slices hot buttered toast
salt and ground black pepper, to taste
chopped fresh parsley, to garnish

1 Thoroughly rinse the brains under cold running water. Remove the membrane and finely chop.

2 Heat the butter in a large frying pan, add the onion and cook for about 5 minutes, or until golden brown.

3 Add the brains and fry for 5 minutes, stirring, until golden brown.

4 Add the eggs and breadcrumbs and cook for a further 2 minutes, stirring, until the eggs are cooked. Season to taste with salt and pepper.

5 Place the pieces of toast on four serving plates, then top with the hot brain mixture and garnish with chopped parsley.

Energy 521kcal/2172kJ; Protein 27.1g; Carbohydrate 26.5g, of which sugars 2.1g; Fat 34.9g, of which saturates 14.6g; Cholesterol 3850mg; Calcium 90mg; Fibre 1g; Sodium 768mg.

Krakow-style Calf's Liver

Flavoursome and very nutritious, liver is popular all over Poland, especially calf's liver. In this recipe it is served with a white mushroom sauce, giving a lovely contrast of colours and textures. You will need to get your butcher to remove the membrane, or do this yourself, before cooking.

Serves 4–6

900g/2lb calf's liver, rinsed, membrane removed, and sliced into thin pieces
60ml/4 tbsp vegetable oil
chopped fresh parsley, to garnish
black pepper

For the sauce
45ml/3 tbsp butter
1 large onion, sliced
175g/6oz/2½ cups button (white) mushrooms, wiped clean and chopped
15g/½oz/2 tbsp plain (all-purpose) flour
175ml/6fl oz/¾ cup dry white wine
250ml/8fl oz/1 cup sour cream
salt and ground black pepper

1 To make the sauce, heat the butter in a pan, then add the onion and mushrooms. Cook for 5–8 minutes, or until the onion has softened.

2 Stir in the flour and cook for 1 minute. Add the wine and cook for a further 3 minutes. Add the sour cream and season to taste. Keep the sauce warm.

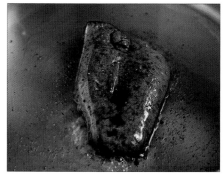

3 Sprinkle the liver with plenty of black pepper. Heat the oil in a frying pan, add the liver and cook for 1–2 minutes on each side, until brown on the outside but still a little pink in the middle.

4 Transfer to serving plates, pour over the sauce and garnish with fresh parsley. Serve immediately.

Energy 410kcal/1705kJ; Protein 29.5g; Carbohydrate 6g, of which sugars 3g; Fat 27.9g, of which saturates 11.7g; Cholesterol 596mg; Calcium 67mg; Fibre 0.3g; Sodium 288mg.

Baked Lamb

In Russian restaurants, this delicious all-in-one dish of lamb with potatoes, aubergines and tomatoes is cooked in individual dishes, which are brought straight from the oven to the table. Here it is cooked in a single ovenproof dish for convenience.

Serves 4

1 mild chilli
600g/1lb 6oz potatoes, peeled
  and diced
1 large onion, chopped
1 aubergine (eggplant), sliced
800g/1¾lb boneless lamb
45ml/3 tbsp chopped fresh parsley
4 bay leaves
6–8 black peppercorns
45ml/3 tbsp chopped fresh coriander
  (cilantro)
3 garlic cloves, chopped
50g/2oz/¼ cup butter
75ml/5 tbsp tomato purée (paste)
1 litre/1¾ pints/4 cups beef stock
3 tomatoes, sliced
salt and ground black pepper

VARIATION The aubergines can be replaced with 2 additional large onions.

1 Preheat the oven to 180°C/350°F/Gas 4. Chop the chilli, discarding the core and seeds. Put the potatoes and onions in a greased roasting pan.

2 Cut the lamb into bitesize chunks. Sprinkle the lamb, aubergine, chilli, parsley, bay leaves, peppercorns, coriander and garlic evenly over the potatoes.

3 Melt the butter in a small pan. Add the tomato purée and fry for 1 minute. Stir in the stock, a little at a time, and bring to the boil. Season to taste.

4 Pour the tomato sauce over the meat and the vegetables. Bake in the oven for about 1 hour. Top the bake with the sliced tomatoes, return to the oven and bake for a further 10 minutes. Serve hot.

Energy 631kcal/2640kJ; Protein 45.3g; Carbohydrate 38.6g, of which sugars 13.9g; Fat 34g, of which saturates 17.2g; Cholesterol 179mg; Calcium 94mg; Fibre 5.8g; Sodium 324mg.

Uzbekistani Pilaff

The cities of Uzbekistan were once important points on the Silk Road from China to Europe, and rice is still a staple part of the diet. Pilaffs, both savoury – consisting of rice, vegetables, meat and spices – and sweet – containing apricots and raisins – are very popular.

Serves 4

- 60–75ml/4–5 tbsp rapeseed (canola) oil
- 600g/1lb 6oz lean boneless lamb steak, cut into bitesize pieces
- 700ml/1 pint 3½fl oz/scant 3 cups water
- 5ml/1 tsp salt
- 2 carrots
- 2 onions
- 350–400g/12–14oz/1¾–2 cups long grain rice
- 1 whole garlic, with the dry outer skin removed, but left intact
- 5 sprigs fresh parsley, to garnish

1 Heat 15ml/1 tbsp of the oil in a flameproof casserole. Add the lamb and fry, stirring frequently, for about 10 minutes, until brown on all sides.

2 Add the water and salt to the pan, bring to the boil, then reduce the heat and simmer for about 40 minutes, until the meat is just tender.

3 Meanwhile, finely dice the carrots and finely chop the onion. Heat the remaining oil in a separate pan. Add the carrots and onions and stir-fry for about 5 minutes, until softened. Add the rice and stir-fry for about 1 minute, until translucent.

4 Transfer the rice mixture to the lamb and add the whole garlic. Bring to the boil, then reduce the heat, cover and simmer for about 20 minutes, until the rice is tender and has absorbed almost all of the liquid.

5 Serve the pilaff immediately, heaped on to a warmed dish, garnished with parsley.

COOK'S TIP The Uzbekistanis rinse their rice several times in water before cooking it. This reduces the amount of starch and prevents the rice from becoming sticky.

Energy 735kcal/3065kJ; Protein 37.2g; Carbohydrate 81.7g, of which sugars 9.8g; Fat 28.6g, of which saturates 9.2g; Cholesterol 114mg; Calcium 66mg; Fibre 2.9g; Sodium 150mg.

Roast Lamb with Garlic, Rosemary and Thyme

Simply roasting lamb with a selection of aromatic ingredients brings out the best in the meat. In this delicious recipe the lamb is rubbed with a mixture of butter, pepper, cloves and allspice, which lend a distinctive spicy Polish note to the meat.

Serves 6

2kg/4½lb leg of lamb
fresh rosemary
fresh thyme
10 garlic cloves, cut into slivers
5ml/1 tsp black peppercorns
6 whole cloves
6 allspice berries
20g/¾oz butter, softened
redcurrant jelly, to serve

1 Preheat the oven to 200°C/400°F/Gas 6. Place the leg of lamb in a roasting pan. Separate the rosemary into sprigs, and cut the thyme stalks into sections.

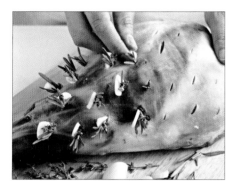

2 Make about 20–30 small, deep slits all over the meat, then push a small sprig of rosemary and thyme and a sliver of garlic into each.

3 Using a pestle and mortar, grind the peppercorns, cloves and allspice to a coarse powder. Combine the powder with the softened butter and smear all over the lamb.

4 Place the roasting pan in the hot oven and cook for 15 minutes. Reduce the heat to 180°C/350°F/Gas 4 and roast the lamb for a further 1½ hours, or until cooked but still slightly pink.

5 Remove the joint from the oven, cover with foil and allow it to rest for at least 15 minutes.

6 Cut the meat into generous slices and serve immediately with redcurrant jelly.

Energy 562kcal/2340kJ; Protein 50.4g; Carbohydrate 0.4g, of which sugars 0.3g; Fat 39.9g, of which saturates 14.1g; Cholesterol 200mg; Calcium 36mg; Fibre 0.6g; Sodium 171mg.

Roast Fillet of Pork with Prunes

Pork is the national meat of Poland, and this recipe of roasted marinated pork fillet stuffed with prunes is a wonderful example of how its delectable flavour can be fully appreciated. Serve with salads for a light lunch, or with Buckwheat Kasha for a more sustaining meal.

2 Preheat the oven to 180°C/350°F/Gas 4. Pour the oil into a roasting pan and put in the oven to heat.

3 Take the pork fillet out of the marinade and lay the chopped prunes along half of the opened-out fillet. Fold the top half over and tie together using string.

4 Place in the hot oil and put into the oven. Roast for about 1½ hours, or until the meat is cooked, basting occasionally with the meat juices.

5 Remove the meat from the oven and allow to rest, covered in foil, for 15 minutes. Remove the string and cut into slices. Spoon over the cooking juices and serve immediately with lettuce and Beetroot Salad.

Serves 4–6

1.8kg/4lb pork fillet (tenderloin)
2.5ml/½ tsp dried marjoram
15ml/1 tbsp caraway seeds
4–5 bay leaves
90ml/6 tbsp white wine
30ml/2 tbsp vegetable oil
225g/8oz ready-to-eat prunes, chopped
salt and ground black pepper, to taste
lettuce and Beetroot Salad (page 195), to serve

VARIATION This delicious stuffed pork joint also makes an impressive Sunday lunch: serve it with roast potatoes and some greens or spiced red cabbage.

1 Partially cut the pork lengthways leaving one long side attached. Rub with salt, pepper and marjoram, then sprinkle with caraway seeds. Put into a dish and add the bay leaves, then pour over the wine. Leave to marinate for about 2 hours.

Energy 537kcal/2247kJ; Protein 63.1g; Carbohydrate 12.8g, of which sugars 12.8g; Fat 15.8g, of which saturates 7.9g; Cholesterol 207mg; Calcium 38mg; Fibre 2.1g; Sodium 233mg.

Breaded Pork Cutlets

Easy to make and quick to cook, this recipe for pork cutlets dipped in breadcrumbs and simply fried is particularly popular in Poland. Coating the cutlets means that the pork stays moist and tender, without drying out. Serve with mashed potato and red cabbage for a real Polish meal.

Serves 4

4 boneless pork cutlets, fat on, each
  weighing about 225g/8oz
2.5ml/½ tsp salt
2.5ml/½ tsp ground black pepper
115g/4oz/1 cup plain (all-purpose)
  flour
2 eggs, beaten
65g/2½oz/1 cup fine fresh
  breadcrumbs
1 tbsp each of chopped fresh
  rosemary, dill and sage
75ml/5 tbsp vegetable oil
fresh parsley sprigs, to garnish
lemon wedges, mashed potato and
  sauerkraut or red cabbage, to serve

1 Cut slits in the rind of the pork cutlets to prevent them from curling during cooking. Using a meat mallet, rolling pin or the base of a frying pan, pound each cutlet lightly on each side to flatten, then sprinkle each side with salt and pepper.

2 Put the flour and beaten eggs in separate bowls. In another bowl, mix the breadcrumbs with the chopped herbs.

3 Dip the pork cutlets first in the flour, then the egg and then into the breadcrumb mixture.

4 Heat the oil in a frying pan until it is smoking hot, then add the breaded pork and fry on a high heat for 4–5 minutes.

5 Turn the cutlets and cook the other side for another 4–5 minutes until golden brown and crispy all over. Reduce the heat and cook for a further 2 minutes to ensure the pork is cooked right the way through.

6 Garnish with parsley and serve immediately with mashed potato and sauerkraut or red cabbage, and with lemon wedges for squeezing over.

COOK'S TIP It is important that you serve the cutlets immediately, as they will become tough if they are left to stand.

Energy 591kcal/2475kJ; Protein 55.9g; Carbohydrate 34.9g, of which sugars 0.9g; Fat 26.2g, of which saturates 5.6g; Cholesterol 237mg; Calcium 92mg; Fibre 1.3g; Sodium 317mg.

Roast Loin of Pork with Apple Stuffing

A spit-roasted sucking pig, basted with butter or cream, roasted in the oven or outside on a spit, and served with an apple in its mouth, was a classic dish for the Russian festive table. This roasted loin with crisp crackling makes a smaller-scale alternative.

Serves 6–8

1.75kg/4lb boned loin of pork
300ml/½ pint/1½ cups dry cider
150ml/¼ pint/⅔ cup sour cream
7.5ml/1½ tsp sea salt

For the stuffing
25g/1oz/2 tbsp butter
1 small onion, chopped
50g/2oz/1 cup fresh white
  breadcrumbs
2 apples, cored, peeled and chopped
50g/2oz/scant ½ cup raisins
finely grated rind of 1 orange
pinch of ground cloves
salt and ground black pepper

1 Preheat the oven to 220°C/425°F/Gas 7. To make the stuffing, melt the butter in a pan and gently fry the onion for 10 minutes, or until soft. Stir into the remaining stuffing ingredients.

2 Put the pork, rind side down, on a board. Make a horizontal cut between the meat and outer layer of fat, cutting to within 2.5cm/1in of the edges to make a pocket.

3 Push the stuffing into the pocket. Roll it up lengthways and tie with string. Use a sharp knife to score the rind.

4 Pour the cider and sour cream into a casserole, in which the joint just fits. Stir to combine, then add the pork, rind side down. Cook, uncovered, in the oven for 30 minutes.

5 Turn the joint over, so that the rind is on top. Baste with the juices, then sprinkle the rind with sea salt. Cook for 1 hour, basting after 30 minutes, but don't baste after this time, to give the skin a chance to crisp.

6 Reduce the oven temperature to 180°C/350°F/Gas 4. Cook for a further 1½ hours. Leave the joint to stand for 20 minutes before carving.

Energy 504kcal/2114kJ; Protein 67.3g; Carbohydrate 12.3g, of which sugars 7.6g; Fat 19.8g, of which saturates 8.3g; Cholesterol 185mg; Calcium 59mg; Fibre 0.5g; Sodium 205mg

Ukrainian Sausages

These sausages from the Ukraine are called kovbasa – they can be grilled, fried or baked and are wonderful as an appetizer or a main course for lunch or dinner. This pork and beef version can be made several days in advance and kept refrigerated; they can also be cooked from frozen.

Serves 4

450g/1lb pork, such as shoulder
225g/8oz chuck steak
115g/4oz pork back fat
2 eggs, beaten
30ml/2 tbsp peperivka (see Cook's Tip)
  or pepper vodka
2.5ml/½ tsp ground allspice
5ml/1 tsp salt
about 1.75 litres/3 pints/7½ cups
  chicken stock
fresh parsley, to garnish
mashed potato, to serve

COOK'S TIP Spicing whisky with peppers to make peperivka is an old tradition in the Ukraine. Add 3 whole cayenne peppers, pricked all over with a fine skewer, to 150ml/¼ pint/⅔ cup whisky or bourbon and leave for at least 48 hours.

1 Mince (grind) the meats and pork back fat together, using the coarse blade of a mincer (grinder), then mince half the mixture again using a fine blade. You can also use a food processor for this.

2 Combine both the meat mixtures with the eggs, peperivka or pepper vodka, allspice and salt. Check the seasoning by frying a small piece of the mixture, then tasting it. Adjust if necessary.

3 Form the meat mixture into four sausages, about 20cm/8in long. Wrap in a double layer of butter muslin and tie securely with string.

4 Bring the stock to a gentle simmer in a large pan. Add the sausages and simmer gently, turning frequently, for 35–40 minutes, or until the juices run clear when the sausages are pierced with a skewer.

5 Leave the sausages in the stock for 20 minutes, then remove and leave to cool. Remove the muslin and sauté the sausages in oil to brown them. Garnish with parsley and serve with mashed potato, topped with butter.

COOK'S TIP Butter muslin is an unbleached linen cloth, which can be bought from most kitchen shops. It is fine enough for the cooking process but robust enough to hold the sausage together.
  Peperivka is vodka infused with whole cayenne peppers. To make your own, place 3 washed, dried and pricked peppers in a jar and fill with vodka. Leave for 48 hours before using.

Energy 436kcal/1816kJ; Protein 44.1g; Carbohydrate 0g, of which sugars 0g; Fat 26.5g, of which saturates 9.6g; Cholesterol 227mg; Calcium 28mg; Fibre 0g; Sodium 170mg

Pork Rib Stew with Cabbage

This delicious stew makes the most of an economical cut of pork and the ubiquitous white cabbage, combining flavoursome ribs with a simple broth. It makes the most of typical Polish flavourings – caraway, paprika and garlic – to enhance a warming all-in-one supper dish.

Serves 4–6

40g/1½ oz/¼ cup bacon dripping or
  40ml/2½ tbsp vegetable oil
1.8kg/4lb pork spare ribs
900ml/1½ pints/3¾ cups beef stock
6 black peppercorns
4 bay leaves
5ml/1 tsp caraway seeds
5ml/1 tsp paprika
2 large onions, roughly chopped
2–3 carrots, roughly chopped
3–4 garlic cloves, roughly chopped
175ml/6fl oz/¾ cup dry white wine
1 white cabbage, quartered and
  core removed
chopped fresh parsley or dill,
  to garnish
boiled new potatoes, to serve

1 Heat the bacon dripping or oil in a heavy pan, add the spare ribs and cook over a high heat for 5 minutes, or until brown all over.

2 Add the stock, peppercorns, bay leaves, caraway seeds, paprika, onions, carrots, garlic and white wine.

3 Cover the pan and simmer over a low heat for about 1½ hours. Add the cabbage and cook for a further 30 minutes, until tender.

4 Ladle on to plates, garnish with parsley or dill and serve immediately with boiled new potatoes.

Energy 539kcal/2241kJ; Protein 45g; Carbohydrate 6.1g, of which sugars 5.9g; Fat 35.1g, of which saturates 11.2g; Cholesterol 159mg; Calcium 62mg; Fibre 2.2g; Sodium 161mg.

Honey-roast Ham

This stunning baked ham is often prepared for a Polish Easter Sunday, when the strict Lenten fast is broken with a lavish feast. It can be served hot or cold with a selection of pickles, such as gherkins or beetroot, and horseradish sauce.

Serves 4–6

2.75–3.6kg/6–8lb ham
20 whole cloves
225g/8oz/1 cup clear honey
sweet gherkins, pickled beetroot
    (beets) and horseradish sauce,
    to serve

For the marinade
1 litre/1¾ pints/4 cups water
250ml/8fl oz/1 cup cider vinegar
1 onion, sliced
4–5 bay leaves
8 whole cloves
2 cinnamon sticks
8 allspice berries
4–5 dried chillies
5ml/1 tsp yellow mustard seeds
15ml/1 tbsp sugar

1 To make the marinade, put all the ingredients in a large pan with a lid. Weigh the ham and calculate the cooking time, allowing 20 minutes per 450g/1lb of meat.

2 Put the ham in the pan, cover with a lid and simmer for 2–2¾ hours, or until the rind on the ham has lifted away from the meat slightly. Remove the meat from the pan.

3 Preheat the oven to 220°C/425°F/Gas 7. Carefully remove the skin from the ham and discard. Score the fat on the ham with a diamond pattern using a large, sharp knife.

4 Warm the honey gently in a small pan to make a glaze. Do not boil.

5 Place the ham in a roasting pan and press a clove into the centre of each diamond. Brush the ham with honey, then place in the oven and roast for 20–25 minutes until the fat is brown and crispy.

6 Serve hot or cold, with sweet gherkins, pickled beetroot and horseradish sauce.

Energy 595kcal/2482kJ; Protein 68g; Carbohydrate 0g, of which sugars 0g; Fat 35.9g, of which saturates 12g; Cholesterol 242mg; Calcium 26mg; Fibre 0g; Sodium 3442mg

Hunter's Stew

Considered by some to be the national dish, Hunter's Stew, or 'bigos', is one of the most treasured of the Polish recipes. Hearty and sustaining, this stew can be found in many different forms throughout the country, and was originally a game recipe, hence its name. Bigos is cooked in large quantities so it can be reheated – the flavours intensify each time – and is a very good dish to cook in advance.

Serves 6–8

1kg/2¼ lb fresh cabbage, finely
  shredded
10 dried mushrooms (boletus)
2 onions, chopped
500g/1¼ lb smoked sausage, sliced
1kg/2¼ lb sauerkraut, drained
2 cooking apples, peeled, cored
  and diced
10 prunes
10 juniper berries, crushed
3–4 bay leaves
10 peppercorns
2.5ml/½ tsp salt
750ml/1¼ pints/3 cups boiling water
500g/1¼ lb roast pork, diced
500g/1¼ lb roast beef, diced
500g/1¼ lb boiled ham, diced
150ml/¼ pint/¾ cup dry red wine
5ml/1 tsp honey
wholemeal (whole-wheat) or rye
  bread and chilled vodka, to serve

1 Place the cabbage in a heatproof colander and wilt the leaves by carefully pouring boiling water over it.

2 Rinse the mushrooms, then place them in a bowl with enough warm water to cover. Leave to soak for 15 minutes, then transfer to a pan and cook in the soaking liquid for 30 minutes. Strain, reserving the cooking liquid, then cut the mushrooms into strips.

3 Put the onions and smoked sausage in a small frying pan and fry gently, until the onions have softened. Remove the sausage from the pan and set aside.

4 Put the wilted cabbage and drained sauerkraut in a large pan, then add the cooked onions, along with the mushrooms, mushroom cooking liquid, apples, prunes, juniper berries, bay leaves, peppercorns and salt. Pour in the boiling water, then cover and simmer for 1 hour.

5 Add the cooked sausage to the pan with the other cooked, diced meats. Pour in the wine and add the honey.

6 Cook, uncovered, for a further 40 minutes, stirring frequently. Taste and adjust the seasoning as required. Remove from the heat.

7 Allow the stew to cool, then cover it and transfer to the refrigerator. Leave it overnight. Return to the boil and simmer for 10 minutes to heat through. Serve with wholemeal or rye bread and a glass of chilled vodka.

VARIATION Any meat, such as duck, lamb or venison, works well in this recipe.

COOK'S TIP When reheating, make sure the stew is brought to the boil and thoroughly simmered before serving.

Energy 546kcal/2279kJ; Protein 50.4g; Carbohydrate 24.6g, of which sugars 19.8g; Fat 26.4g, of which saturates 9.7g; Cholesterol 149mg; Calcium 213mg; Fibre 7.7g; Sodium 2122mg.

Polish Stuffed Cabbage Rolls

Golabki, meaning 'little pigeons', are one of the most popular dishes in Poland. Simple to prepare, cheap and very tasty, they can be made ahead in large quantities and reheated.

Serves 4

1 small cabbage
1 small (US medium) egg, beaten
2.5ml/¹/₂ tsp freshly grated nutmeg
10ml/2 tsp chopped fresh parsley
10ml/2 tsp vegetable oil
400g/14oz can chopped tomatoes
60ml/4 tbsp boiling water
salt and ground black pepper, to taste

For the stuffing

100g/3³/₄oz/¹/₂ cup long grain rice
15g/¹/₂oz/¹/₄ cup dried wild
   mushrooms, rinsed and soaked in
   warm water for 30 minutes
15ml/1 tbsp butter
¹/₂ large onion, finely chopped
225g/8oz/1 cup minced (ground) pork
225g/8oz/1 cup minced (ground) beef
1 garlic clove, finely chopped

1 To make the stuffing, bring a large pan of lightly salted water to the boil and cook the rice, according to instructions on the packet. Once the grains are tender, drain and rinse under cold water to prevent them from cooking further.

2 Drain the mushrooms and chop them finely. Heat half the butter in a large pan, then add the onion and fry gently until golden brown.

3 Add the pork, beef, garlic, mushrooms and seasoning. Cook, stirring, until the meat is browned all over, then remove from the heat and leave to cool slightly.

4 Bring a large pan of lightly salted water to the boil and cook the whole cabbage for 10–15 minutes, or until you can insert a knife into the centre easily, but the leaves are not too soft. Lift the cabbage out of the water and leave to cool slightly.

5 Preheat the oven to 190°C/375°F/Gas 5. Add the egg, nutmeg and parsley to the meat mixture and stir to combine well. When it is cool enough to handle, separate the cabbage into individual leaves. Use the tough outside leaves to line an ovenproof dish. Drizzle with oil.

7 Place a spoonful of the filling in each of the remaining cabbage leaves, fold over the edges and roll to form a tight package. Arrange the rolls in a single layer on the oiled cabbage leaves in the dish.

8 Pour over the tomatoes and boiling water, and dot the remaining butter over the top. Cover the dish with a lid or foil. Cook in the oven for about 1 hour. Serve with spoonfuls of the tomato sauce.

Energy 414kcal/1725kJ; Protein 27.6g; Carbohydrate 28.7g, of which sugars 8.2g; Fat 21g, of which saturates 8.5g; Cholesterol 126mg; Calcium 99mg; Fibre 3.4g; Sodium 133mg.

VEGETABLE AND SIDE DISHES

Despite their hearty appetite for meat, Russians in particular have been very inventive when it comes to vegetable dishes. Many of these recipes work well either as an accompaniment to a meat course, or as a meal in their own right. Often the recipes are based on very simple ingredients, but when the vegetables are fresh, well seasoned, and cooked in delicious puff pastry, or in tiny dumplings, they are completely irresistible.

Both Poland and Russia share a love of cabbage, and for the Russians there is no better way to serve it than as sauerkraut. This sharp mixture of fermented cabbage with vinegar makes a satisfying stew for a cold day or a light salad for warmer weather. Sauerkraut is also very popular in Poland. After sauerkraut, perhaps the next best-loved vegetable is the mushroom, which Russians and Poles enjoy picking wild. Then, of course, there is the potato, cooked in many equally enjoyable ways from dumplings to fried potato cakes and beyond!

Cheese Dumplings

Vareniki (meaning 'boiled things') are dumplings, thought to have been inspired by Chinese influences in the Ukraine, which come in all kinds of varieties. These cottage cheese versions can also be made with Italian ricotta, or another fresh cheese, and are similar to gnocchi.

Serves 4

500g/1¼lb/2½ cups ricotta cheese or cottage cheese
2 eggs
200g/7oz/1¾ cups plain white (all-purpose) flour
2 litres/3½ pints/8 cups water
25g/1oz/2 tbsp butter
salt
smetana or crème fraîche, to serve

COOK'S TIP When the dumplings have been boiled, it is important to rinse them under cold running water immediately for a couple of seconds. This is partly to stop them cooking, and also to rinse off some of the starch and stop them from sticking together.

VARIATION Serve these dumplings with fried bacon for non-vegetarians, or as a dessert with smetana and sugar.

1 Put the cheese, eggs and a pinch of salt in a bowl and mix well together. Add the flour and fold in until it is thoroughly combined. The dough should be soft and form into a ball. Remove the ball from the bowl and put on a floured surface.

2 Cut the dough into eight equal pieces and roll each into a sausage shape. Cut each sausage into 2cm/¾in sections.

3 Bring a large pan of water to the boil and add 5ml/1 tsp salt. Put half of the dumplings in the pan and simmer for 2 minutes, until they float to the surface.

4 Using a slotted spoon, remove the dumplings from the pan, transfer to a colander and put under cold running water for a few seconds. Cook the second batch in the same way.

5 Heat the butter in a large pan. Add the drained dumplings and sauté them until thoroughly warmed through and slightly golden. Serve immediately with a bowl of smetana or crème fraîche.

Energy 803kcal/3328kJ; Protein 11.8g; Carbohydrate 38.9g, of which sugars 0.8g; Fat 68g, of which saturates 41.3g; Cholesterol 227mg; Calcium 208mg; Fibre 1.6g; Sodium 450mg.

Grated Potato Dumplings

These Polish dumplings contain a mixture of mashed and grated potato, which gives them an interesting texture. They make an ideal accompaniment to many casseroled or braised meat dishes and are served with delicious little fried cubes of cured pork fat.

Serves 4

1kg/2¼ lb potatoes, peeled
2 eggs, beaten
pinch of salt
115g/4oz plain (all-purpose) flour,
    plus extra for dusting
15ml/1 tbsp potato flour
150g/5oz pork fat (boczek), cut into
    1cm/½ in cubes

1 Chop half the potatoes into chunks, then add to a pan of lightly salted boiling water. Cook for 10 minutes, or until soft. Drain the potatoes, then mash in a bowl.

2 Grate the remaining raw potatoes and squeeze in a sieve (strainer) or in a dish towel to remove the excess liquid. Add to the mashed potato in the bowl.

3 Add the eggs, a pinch of salt and the flours to the bowl, and knead thoroughly to form a dough.

4 Using floured hands, roll spoonfuls of the dough into balls.

5 Bring a large pan of lightly salted water to the boil, then add the dumplings. Cook for 4–5 minutes, or until the dumplings float to the surface of the water.

6 Meanwhile, fry the cubes of pork fat in a hot pan for about 4 minutes, or until golden brown all over. Transfer the cooked dumplings to a serving plate and spoon over the fried pork fat cubes.

COOK'S TIP If you can't find Polish boczek, use a thick slice of pancetta or cured pork belly instead.

Energy 658kcal/2746kJ; Protein 10.3g; Carbohydrate 65.6g, of which sugars 3.7g; Fat 41.1g, of which saturates 16.2g; Cholesterol 130mg; Calcium 71mg; Fibre 3.5g; Sodium 64mg.

Little Deep-fried Potato Pies

Pirojki are an indispensable part of the Russian zakuski table, but can also be served as accompaniments to soup, when a little hole is made in the top and a spoonful of soup is poured in. Pirojki can be baked, but here they are fried so the pastry is deliciously crisp.

Makes 24
Serves 6–8

For the dough
50g/2oz/¼ cup butter
200ml/7fl oz/scant 1 cup milk
45ml/3 tbsp water
1 small (US medium) egg plus
  1 egg yolk
2.5ml/½ tsp salt
7.5ml/1½ tsp caster (superfine) sugar
5g/⅛oz easy-blend (rapid-rise) dried
  yeast
400g/14oz/3½ cups plain white
  (all-purpose) flour
rapeseed (canola) oil for frying

For the filling
500g/1¼lb floury potatoes
45–60ml/3–4 tbsp rapeseed
  (canola) oil
2 onions, finely chopped
salt and ground black pepper

1 To make the dough, melt the butter in a pan. Add the milk and water and heat it to 45°C/110°F. Remove from the heat. Whisk the whole egg in a large bowl with the salt and sugar.

2 Add the warm milk mixture to the egg. Mix the yeast with the flour and stir it, a little at a time, into the egg and milk mixture to form a soft dough.

3 Knead the dough in the bowl for 5 minutes. Cover with a dish towel and leave to rise in a warm place for 30 minutes, until it has doubled in size.

4 Meanwhile, prepare the filling: peel and cut the potatoes, put in a pan of salted cold water, bring to the boil, then reduce the heat and simmer for 15–20 minutes, until the potatoes are soft.

5 Drain, return to the pan, then leave for 2–3 minutes to allow the steam to evaporate. Mash the potatoes until smooth then transfer to a bowl.

6 Heat the oil in a small frying pan, add the onions and fry, stirring frequently, for about 5 minutes until softened and golden brown.

7 Add the onions to the mashed potatoes and mix. Season with plenty of salt and pepper. Set aside.

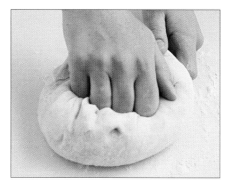

8 Grease a large baking sheet. Turn the dough on to a lightly floured surface and knead for 2–3 minutes. Cut the dough in 24 equal-sized pieces and form each piece into a ball. Leave to rest for 5–10 minutes. Flatten each ball to a round measuring 10cm/4in in diameter.

9 Spread 25ml/1½ tbsp of the potato filling in the centre of each round of dough. Fold together and seal the edges at the top. Put them, upside-down with the join facing down, on a floured wooden chopping board.

10 Half fill a deep pan with oil, and heat to 180°C/350°F, or until a small piece of dough when dropped in, rises to the surface immediately. In batches of around four or five, fry the pies in the oil for 2–3 minutes, turn them over gently, and then cook for a further 2–3 minutes, until golden brown.

11 Remove the pies from the pan with a slotted spoon, and place on kitchen paper to drain. Cook all the pies in this way, and serve immediately.

COOK'S TIP The pirojki dough can be made in an electric mixer, fitted with a dough hook, if wished.

Energy 349kcal/1467kJ; Protein 8.5g; Carbohydrate 55.1g, of which sugars 6.3g; Fat 12g, of which saturates 4.6g; Cholesterol 64mg; Calcium 127mg; Fibre 3.1g; Sodium 69mg.

Potato Cakes with Mushroom Sauce

Potatoes are the perfect accompaniment to many Russian dishes and are served fried, boiled, mashed and in gratins, with fish, meat or vegetables. Russians believe potatoes and mushrooms make the perfect combination, and those who do not pick their own mushrooms dry bought ones at home and thread them on a string.

Serves 4

1kg/2¼lb floury potatoes
50g/2oz/¼ cup butter
100ml/3½fl oz/scant ½ cup warm milk
1 egg, beaten
75g/3oz/1½ cups fresh white
  breadcrumbs
15ml/1 tbsp rapeseed (canola) oil
salt

For the mushroom sauce

1 onion, peeled and finely chopped
15ml/1 tbsp rapeseed (canola) oil
25g/1oz/2 tbsp butter
250g/9oz fresh porcini
15ml/1 tbsp plain white (all purpose)
  flour
300ml/½ pint/1¼ cups smetana or
  crème fraîche
salt and ground black pepper

1 For the mushroom sauce, put the soaked mushrooms and the water in a pan and simmer for 40 minutes. Using a slotted spoon, remove the mushrooms from the pan, reserving the water.

2 Heat the oil in a large frying pan, add the onion and fry, stirring frequently, for 3 minutes, or until golden brown.

3 Add the butter and mushrooms and fry, stirring all the time, for a further 5 minutes. Sprinkle the flour over the mushrooms and stir until mixed.

4 Gradually stir all the reserved water into the mushroom and flour mixture, a little at a time, until smooth. Slowly bring to the boil, stirring all the time, until the sauce boils and thickens. Reduce the heat and simmer for 10 minutes.

5 Add the smetana or crème fraîche and simmer for a further 5 minutes. Season with salt and pepper to taste.

6 Peel and cut the potatoes into even pieces. Put in a pan of salted water, bring to the boil, then reduce the heat and simmer for 20 minutes, until soft. Drain, return to the pan and mash until smooth.

7 Add 15g/½oz/1 tbsp of the butter and the milk to the potatoes and mix together until smooth. Leave to cool.

8 Once the potatoes are cool, add the beaten egg and mix thoroughly. Season the potatoes with salt to taste.

9 Wet your hands under cold water, take a handful of the mashed potato and form into a cake. Repeat with the remaining mashed potato to make eight cakes.

10 Spread the breadcrumbs on a plate and turn the cakes in the breadcrumbs to coat on both sides. Set aside.

11 To cook the potato cakes, heat the remaining 40g/1½oz/3 tbsp butter and the oil in a large frying pan, add the cakes and fry over a medium heat, for about 3–5 minutes on each side, turning once, until they are golden brown.

12 Gently reheat the mushroom sauce, and serve the potato cakes hot, accompanied by the sauce.

Energy 389kcal/1637kJ; Protein 8.9g; Carbohydrate 56g, of which sugars 5g; Fat 16g, of which saturates 7.7g; Cholesterol 76mg; Calcium 79mg; Fibre 2.9g; Sodium 274mg.

Potato and Cheese Dumplings

The Polish version of Russian pirojki are pierogi, and they are just as popular. Made from simple, cheap ingredients, they can be served immediately after they are cooked, or allowed to cool and then fried in a little butter. They can be filled with a number of different ingredients.

Serves 4–6

500g/1¼lb plain (all-purpose) flour, plus extra for dusting
2.5ml/½ tsp salt
2 eggs, beaten
45ml/3 tbsp vegetable oil
250ml/8fl oz/1 cup warm water
chopped fresh parsley, to garnish
thick sour cream, to serve

For the filling

15g/½oz/1 tbsp butter
½ large onion, finely chopped
250g/9oz peeled, cooked potatoes
250g/9oz/1¼ cups curd or cream cheese
1 egg, beaten
salt and ground black pepper, to taste

1 To make the filling, heat the butter in a small pan, add the onion and cook for about 5 minutes, or until softened.

2 Push the cooked potatoes through a ricer, or mash in a large bowl. Add the curd cheese and stir to combine. Add the egg, onion and seasoning to taste to the potato mixture and mix well.

3 To make the dough, sift the flour into a large bowl, then add the salt and the two eggs. Pour in the oil and water, and mix to form a loose dough.

4 Turn on to a floured surface and knead for about 10 minutes, until the dough is soft and doesn't stick to your hands.

5 Divide the dough into four equal pieces, then roll each one out thinly with a floured rolling pin. (Cover the portions you are not working on with a dish towel to prevent them from drying out.) Cut the dough into 5–6cm/2–2½in circles using a pastry (cookie) cutter.

6 Place a heaped teaspoonful of the cheese filling mixture in the centre of each of the circles of dough, then fold over the dough and press firmly to seal the edges. The dumplings should be neat and well filled, but not bursting.

7 Bring a large pan of lightly salted water to the boil, add the dumplings and cook for about 4–5 minutes, or until they rise to the surface.

8 Cook for a further 2 minutes, once they have risen, then remove with a slotted spoon and place in a warmed serving dish. Garnish with chopped parsley and serve with thick sour cream.

Energy 419kcal/1768kJ; Protein 11.7g; Carbohydrate 71.6g, of which sugars 2.3g; Fat 11.5g, of which saturates 2.9g; Cholesterol 100mg; Calcium 136mg; Fibre 3.1g; Sodium 57mg.

Mashed Potato Dumplings

These soft little dumplings from Poland are similar to Italian gnocchi and can be served with different toppings. Here they are served with a crisp breadcrumb topping, adding texture and colour to the dumplings. They make an excellent accompaniment to braised meats.

3 Transfer the potato dough to a lightly floured surface and, with damp hands, shape into walnut-sized balls. Flatten the balls slightly and make a small indentation in the centre.

4 Bring a large pan of lightly salted water to the boil, then drop in the dumplings and cook for 5 minutes, or until they are firm to the touch.

Serves 4–6

5 potatoes, scrubbed
225g/8oz/2 cups plain (all-purpose) flour
1 egg, beaten
2.5ml/½ tsp salt
45ml/3 tbsp butter
45ml/3 tbsp fresh white breadcrumbs

1 Cut the scrubbed potatoes into quarters, leaving the skin on for an authentic texture. Place in a pan of boiling water and cook for 10–15 minutes, or until tender. Remove from the heat, drain and leave to cool.

2 Push the potatoes through a ricer, or mash to a paste with a potato masher. Add the flour, egg and salt, and knead to combine.

5 Meanwhile, melt the butter in a frying pan, add the breadcrumbs and fry for about 3 minutes, stirring constantly, or until the breadcrumbs are brown.

6 Drain the dumplings and arrange on a serving dish. Sprinkle the browned breadcrumbs over the top, and serve immediately.

VARIATION Try topping the dumplings with crispy fried onions instead of the toasted breadcrumbs. Slice an onion into thin rounds and fry in olive oil in a large frying pan until crispy. Add a crushed clove of garlic, if you wish.

Energy 313kcal/1321kJ; Protein 7.5g; Carbohydrate 56g, of which sugars 2.8g; Fat 8.1g, of which saturates 4.4g; Cholesterol 48mg; Calcium 69mg; Fibre 2.8g; Sodium 240mg.

Spiced Red Cabbage

Red cabbage is one of the staples of Polish cooking, and this spiced dish has its equivalent in most of the countries of eastern and northern Europe and Scandinavia. The cabbage is braised with apples and spices and makes the perfect accompaniment to goose or duck.

Serves 4–6

1 tbsp butter
1 large onion, sliced
1 red cabbage
2 cooking apples, peeled, cored and cut into cubes
7.5ml/1½ tsp caraway seeds
4–5 bay leaves
5–6 allspice berries
30ml/2 tbsp clear honey
juice of 1 lemon
1 glass dry red wine
6 whole cloves
salt and ground black pepper, to taste
chopped chives or parsley, to garnish

1 Melt the butter in a frying pan over a medium heat.

2 Add the sliced onion to the frying pan and fry gently for 5 minutes, or until the onion has softened and is golden brown.

3 Finely shred the cabbage and place in a large, heavy pan, together with 1 litre/1¾ pints/4 cups boiling water.

4 Add the fried onion to the cabbage with the remaining ingredients. Stir well and cover. Cook over a medium heat for 15–20 minutes.

5 Check the mixture towards the end of the cooking time. The cabbage should be tender, the apples should have broken down and the liquid should have reduced by about half.

6 If there is too much liquid, cook uncovered for a further 5 minutes.

7 Add salt and ground black pepper to taste, if you wish.

8 Serve garnished with chopped chives or parsley, or keep in the refrigerator until needed. This dish is even better served the next day, and can also be frozen.

Energy 112kcal/469kJ; Protein 2g; Carbohydrate 17.1g, of which sugars 15.5g; Fat 2.4g, of which saturates 1.3g; Cholesterol 5mg; Calcium 55mg; Fibre 3.1g; Sodium 25mg.

Fried Mushrooms with Root Vegetables

Russians check their hand-picked mushrooms carefully and reserve the most beautiful specimens for drying or marinating. The rest are often cut into pieces and fried in butter or used in soup. This is a traditional side dish, which makes a good accompaniment to most meat dishes

Serves 4

350g/12oz fresh mushrooms, such as porcini, cut into small pieces
65g/2½oz/5 tbsp butter
2 onions, peeled and chopped
1 turnip, finely diced
3 carrots, finely diced
3–4 potatoes, finely diced
60–75ml/4–5 tbsp finely chopped fresh parsley
100ml/3½fl oz/scant ½ cup smetana or crème fraîche
salt and ground black pepper

1 Heat a large frying pan, add the mushrooms and cook over a medium heat, stirring frequently, until all the liquid has evaporated. Add half of the butter and the onions and stir-fry for 10 minutes.

2 In a separate frying pan, heat the remaining butter until melted. Add the diced turnip, carrots and potatoes, and fry for 10–15 minutes, until soft and golden brown. Do this in two or three batches if you don't have a big enough frying pan, as the vegetables need to stay in a single layer.

3 Mix the mushrooms and the fried root vegetables together, cover the pan and cook for about 10 minutes, until the vegetables are tender. Season to taste.

4 Sprinkle the chopped parsley into the pan. Stir in the smetana or crème fraîche and reheat gently. Serve hot.

Energy 361kcal/1503kJ; Protein 5.8g; Carbohydrate 31g, of which sugars 11.1g; Fat 24.7g, of which saturates 15.5g; Cholesterol 63mg; Calcium 94mg; Fibre 5.7g; Sodium 150mg.

Sautéed Wild Mushrooms

Poland is the largest producer of wild mushrooms in Europe, and as in Russia, collecting them is a national pastime. This recipe of fried onions and mushrooms in a sour cream sauce allows the earthy flavours to shine through. It can be served with fried or roasted meat.

Serves 4

60ml/4 tbsp butter
2 large onions, halved and sliced
15ml/1 tbsp plain (all-purpose) flour
250ml/8fl oz/1 cup sour cream
450g/1lb/6½ cups fresh wild
   mushrooms
salt and ground black pepper, to taste
15ml/1 tbsp chopped fresh parsley,
   to garnish

1 Melt the butter in a large frying pan, then add the onions. Cook gently for 5 minutes, or until they begin to brown slightly. Stir in the flour and sour cream.

2 Meanwhile, brush the wild mushrooms to remove any grit, and wash the caps only briefly if necessary. Dry the mushrooms with kitchen paper and slice them thinly.

3 Add the sliced mushrooms to the onion sauce and season to taste. Simmer gently over a low heat for 15 minutes. Garnish with chopped parsley and serve immediately.

Energy 303kcal/1253kJ; Protein 5.5g; Carbohydrate 13.7g, of which sugars 8.4g; Fat 25.6g, of which saturates 15.8g; Cholesterol 69mg; Calcium 98mg; Fibre 2.8g; Sodium 125mg.

Dumplings Stuffed with Mushrooms

These tiny stuffed dumplings are traditionally served in Poland as an accompaniment to borscht or clear soup, or as a light snack with a shot of 95 per cent proof Polish spirit or vodka. Uszka means little ears in Polish, and it is generally thought that the smaller the dumplings the greater the skill of the cook who made them.

Serves 4–6

225g/8oz/2 cups plain (all-purpose) flour, plus extra for dusting
2.5ml/½ tsp salt
1 egg, beaten
30–45ml/2–3 tbsp lukewarm water
chopped fresh parsley, to garnish (optional)

For the filling
115g/4oz/2 cups dried mushrooms, rinsed and soaked in warm water for 30 minutes
25g/1oz/2 tbsp butter
1 onion, very finely chopped
15ml/1 tbsp fresh white breadcrumbs
30ml/2 tbsp finely chopped fresh parsley
1 egg, beaten
salt and ground black pepper, to taste

1 Soak the dried mushrooms in warm water for 30 minutes.

2 To make the filling, drain the soaked mushrooms and chop very finely.

3 Gently heat the butter in a large frying pan, add the onion and sauté for 5 minutes, or until softened.

4 Add the chopped mushrooms to the pan and cook for about 10 minutes, or until the liquid has evaporated and the mixture begins to sizzle.

5 Turn the mushroom mixture into a large bowl, then add the fresh white breadcrumbs, chopped parsley and beaten egg.

6 Season to taste and mix together to form a firm paste, then set aside and leave to cool slightly. (This mixture can be kept in the refrigerator at this stage for up to 24 hours.)

7 Sift the flour into a large bowl, mix in the salt, then make a dip in the middle with the back of a wooden spoon. Pour the beaten egg into the dip and mix into the flour adding enough lukewarm water to form a stiff dough.

COOK'S TIP As with Russian pelmeni, these tiny dumplings can be frozen and then cooked as needed. To do this, at the end of step 6 simply place each dumpling on to a greased baking tray, then freeze. When frozen, transfer to freezer bags. To serve, drop into boiling water and cook for 5–8 minutes.

8 Turn the dough out on to a lightly floured surface and knead until it is pliant but fairly stiff. Leave to rest for 30 minutes. Roll out the dough thinly, to a thickness of about 3mm/⅛in, then cut into 5cm/2in squares.

9 Place a small amount of the mushroom filling in the centre of each square of dough. Fold one corner over the filling diagonally and press the edges together. Fold the two bottom corners of the triangle to the middle and press together to form a 'pig's ear' shape.

10 Bring a large pan of lightly salted water to the boil. Drop in the dumplings and cook for about 3–5 minutes, or until they float to the surface.

11 Lift out the dumplings with a slotted spoon and place on a warmed serving dish. Garnish with chopped parsley, if you like, and serve immediately.

Energy 198kcal/835kJ; Protein 6.4g; Carbohydrate 32g, of which sugars 1.3g; Fat 5.9g, of which saturates 2.8g; Cholesterol 72mg; Calcium 70mg; Fibre 1.5g; Sodium 70mg.

Puff Pastry Cabbage Pie

Crisp puff pastry with a very soft cabbage filling is a favourite dish for Russians to eat on a Saturday night when the whole family is gathered around the table. Russian hostesses pride themselves on their pastry-making, but buying a sheet of ready-made puff pastry is acceptable!

Serves 4–6

300–400g/11–14oz cabbage
40–50g/1½–2oz/3–4 tbsp butter
3 eggs
1 sheet ready-made chilled puff
  pastry, measuring about
  40x20cm/16x8in
salt

For the glaze
1 egg yolk
5ml/1 tsp water
15ml/1 tbsp fresh white breadcrumbs

COOK'S TIP This pie is made with one large sheet of ready-made puff pastry, which can be bought chilled in one roll. The size should be about 40x20cm/16x8in. However, if your pastry sheets are smaller, it is possible to put three smaller sheets together and seal them into one large one.

3 Preheat the oven to 220°C/425°F/Gas 7. Put the sheet of pastry on a dampened baking tray. Spread the cabbage and egg mixture lengthways on one half of the pastry sheet. Brush the edges with water and fold the other side over to enclose. Seal together by pressing with a fork along the join. It should look like a tightly packed loaf.

1 Discard the outer leaves and hard stalk of the cabbage, cut in half and chop finely. Heat the butter in a medium frying pan over a low heat, add the cabbage and stir-fry for 25 minutes until soft, but don't allow it to brown. Set aside to cool.

2 Put the eggs in a pan, cover with cold water and bring to the boil. Reduce the heat and simmer for 10 minutes, then drain and put under cold running water. Remove the shells from the eggs, then chop and put in a large bowl. Add the cabbage, season to taste, and mix.

4 To make the glaze, whisk together the egg yolk and water. Brush the pastry with the mixture and make some small holes in the top with a fork. Sprinkle the top of the pastry with the breadcrumbs.

5 Bake the pie in the oven for 12–15 minutes, until the pastry is crisp and golden brown. Leave the baked pie to rest for 5–10 minutes, then cut into portions and serve.

COOK'S TIP Make sure that the brand of puff pastry you buy is a high quality, all-butter one, or at least containing a high proportion Pif butter.

Energy 333kcal/1388kJ; Protein 7.9g; Carbohydrate 25.3g, of which sugars 3.3g; Fat 23.6g, of which saturates 4.5g; Cholesterol 143mg; Calcium 80mg; Fibre 1.2g; Sodium 276mg.

Sauerkraut Stew with Prunes

Dried fruits are often used in Russian cuisine, not only for desserts but also in main courses.
In this dish they add a delicious sweetness to the contrasting sour taste of the sauerkraut.
Serve the dish as a main course with potatoes or to accompany baked ham.

3 Add the sauerkraut to the pan and fork it through to mix with the fried onions and melted butter.

4 Add the peppercorns and bay leaf to the sauerkraut and onion mixture. Add the garlic bulb, without peeling or separating into cloves.

5 Transfer the sauerkraut mixture into an ovenproof dish. Add the water and sugar, and season with salt.

6 Bake the sauerkraut in the oven, stirring occasionally. After 30 minutes, stir in the prunes. Return to the oven and bake for a further 20 minutes, stirring two or three times during cooking.

COOK'S TIP Keeping the garlic whole and unpeeled gives a very sweet, gentle garlic tone to the sauerkraut. If you prefer a stronger taste, stir in an additional crushed clove of garlic at the same stage as you add the prunes.

Serves 4

700g/1lb 10oz sauerkraut
2 large onions, sliced
75–100g/3–3¾oz/6–7½ tbsp butter
5 black peppercorns
1 bay leaf
1 whole garlic bulb, about 10 cloves
200ml/7fl oz/scant 1 cup water
15ml/1 tbsp sugar
8 dried prunes
salt

1 Preheat the oven to 200°C/400°F/ Gas 6. Rinse the sauerkraut under running water if you find it too sour.

2 Heat the butter in a medium pan until melted. Add the sliced onions and fry for 5–8 minutes, stirring occasionally, until soft and golden brown.

COOK'S TIP Sauerkraut is available bottled or canned from large supermarkets.

Energy 239kcal/986kJ; Protein 4.2g; Carbohydrate 21.2g, of which sugars 18.3g; Fat 15.7g, of which saturates 9.8g; Cholesterol 40mg; Calcium 142mg; Fibre 7g; Sodium 1298mg.

Fried Potatoes with Eggs and Onions

A large pan with fried potatoes and onions can make a whole meal for a Russian family, often served with smetana, bread, Salted Cucumbers and maybe a couple of fried eggs. Fried potatoes are also the most common accompaniment to Russian fish and meat dishes.

Serves 4

6–8 potatoes, total weight 1kg/2¼lb, peeled and cut into slices or wedges
60–75ml/4–5 tbsp sunflower oil
50g/2oz/¼ cup butter
1–2 onions, sliced into rings
4 eggs
salt
4 Salted Cucumbers (page 79), sliced, and smetana or crème fraîche, to serve

4 Add the fried onions to the cooked potatoes and season well with salt. Wipe out the small frying pan and return to the heat.

5 Melt the remaining butter in the frying pan and fry the eggs. Place on top of the potatoes and serve with Salted Cucumbers and smetana or crème fraîche.

1 Pat the sliced potatoes dry with kitchen paper. Heat the oil in a very large frying pan, add the potatoes and fry for 3 minutes. Shake the pan or turn the potatoes and fry for a further 5–10 minutes, until golden.

2 Cover the pan with a lid, or with a double thickness of foil, and cook over a low heat for 5–10 minutes, until the potatoes are tender.

3 Meanwhile, heat half of the butter in a small frying pan, add the onions and fry, stirring, for 5–10 minutes until golden.

Energy 477kcal/1990kJ; Protein 11.8g; Carbohydrate 48.2g, of which sugars 8.9g; Fat 27.8g, of which saturates 9.6g; Cholesterol 217mg; Calcium 71mg; Fibre 3.9g; Sodium 176mg.

Courgettes with Smetana

Russians who have their own dacha (country house) grow their own vegetables. Courgette plants usually produce a glut, so during the season they are preserved, salted or marinated, fried and mixed with caviar and also sautéed and served in a creamy, mild smetana sauce.

Serves 4

4 small courgettes (zucchini)
45–75ml/3–5 tbsp plain white
  (all-purpose) flour
30ml/2 tbsp rapeseed (canola) oil
45ml/3 tbsp chopped fresh parsley
200ml/7fl oz/scant 1 cup smetana or
  crème fraîche
salt and ground black pepper
rye bread to serve

VARIATION Try using dill instead of parsley if serving this with fish.

1 Cut the courgettes into 1cm/½in thick slices. Coat the slices in the flour.

2 Heat the oil in a large frying pan, then add the courgettes, working in batches if necessary to keep to a single layer, and fry for about 1 minute on each side or until golden brown. Remove from the pan and keep warm until all the courgettes are fried.

3 Return all the courgettes to the pan. Season the courgettes with plenty of salt and pepper and sprinkle with the chopped parsley.

4 Add the smetana or crème fraîche to the pan, cover and simmer over a low heat for about 5 minutes until the courgettes are soft.

5 Serve the courgettes warm, straight from the pan with rye bread.

COOK'S TIP Courgettes can be frozen. Slice them, blanch in boiling water, dry on kitchen paper, then freeze in a single layer on baking trays. When frozen transfer to freezer bags.

Energy 312kcal/1290kJ; Protein 5.7g; Carbohydrate 13.4g, of which sugars 4.5g; Fat 26.5g, of which saturates 14.4g; Cholesterol 56mg; Calcium 111mg; Fibre 2.5g; Sodium 17mg.

Vegetable Ragoût

Russians prefer to eat their vegetables very soft and very hot. Both are illustrated in this recipe, which may seem simple but, with the addition of vegetable stock and butter, is a very tasty and economical way to serve vegetables. Serve the ragoût with dark rye bread and butter.

Serves 4

3–4 carrots
1 swede (rutabaga)
1 turnip
1 parsnip
10ml/2 tsp sunflower oil
1 large onion, finely chopped
100–200ml/3½–7fl oz/scant ½–1 cup
  vegetable stock or lightly salted
  water
105ml/7 tbsp finely chopped fresh
  parsley
15g/½oz/1 tbsp butter
dark rye bread and butter, to serve

1 Cut the carrots, swede, turnip and parsnip into small chunks. Heat the oil in a flameproof casserole, add the chopped onion and fry over a medium heat, for 3–5 minutes until softened.

2 Add the carrots, swede, turnip and parsnip to the pan and fry, stirring frequently, for a further 10 minutes. Add the stock and bring to the boil. Cover with a lid and simmer for 20 minutes.

3 Add the chopped parsley and the butter to the pan and stir until the butter has melted. Season with salt to taste and serve hot.

VARIATION Add 100g/3¾oz/scant 1 cup fresh or frozen peas to the ragoût 3 minutes before adding the chopped fresh parsley and butter.

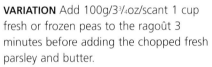

Energy 122kcal/506kJ; Protein 2.6g; Carbohydrate 15.9g, of which sugars 13.3g; Fat 5.7g, of which saturates 2.3g; Cholesterol 8mg; Calcium 137mg; Fibre 6.3g; Sodium 68mg.

Buckwheat Kasha

Kasha has been eaten in Poland and other Eastern European countries for centuries as a staple accompaniment to all kinds of roasts and stews. It is often simply served with standard or soured milk, which may be an acquired taste but is thought to be delicious all over the country.

Serves 4–6

300g/11oz/1½ cups buckwheat
500ml/17fl oz/2¼ cups water
pinch of salt
60ml/4 tbsp vegetable oil or
   45g/1½ oz lard

1 Put the buckwheat in a large, heavy pan and add the water, salt and oil or lard.

2 Bring to the boil and cook over a low heat for about 20 minutes, or until the buckwheat has absorbed all the water and the grains are soft.

3 Serve the kasha immediately.

COOK'S TIP Kasha can be made with other grains, but the buckwheat version has a stronger flavour than most. It forms part of the traditional Christmas Eve supper.

Energy 180kcal/746kJ; Protein 2.9g; Carbohydrate 25.7g, of which sugars 0g; Fat 7.8g, of which saturates 0.9g; Cholesterol 0mg; Calcium 10mg; Fibre 1.35g; Sodium 0mg.

Polish-style Cucumber Salad

According to legend, this simple salad, 'miseria', was a favourite dish of Queen Bona Sforza, an Italian princess who married the Polish king Sigismund I in the 16th century. Homesick for her native Italy, the dish made her cry, hence its Polish name, derived from the Latin for 'misery'.

Serves 4–6

2 medium cucumbers
2.5ml/¹/₂ tsp salt
120ml/4fl oz/¹/₂ cup sour cream
juice from ¹/₂ lemon
2.5ml/¹/₂ tsp sugar (optional)
1.5ml/¹/₄ tsp ground black pepper
15ml/1 tbsp chives, to garnish

1 Peel the cucumbers, slice them thinly and place in a sieve (strainer).

2 Sprinkle over the salt, leave for a few minutes, then rinse to remove the salt and pat dry with kitchen paper.

3 To make the dressing, mix together the sour cream, lemon juice, sugar, if using, and black pepper.

4 Fold in the cucumber, then place in the refrigerator and leave for 1 hour. Serve as an accompaniment, garnished with chopped dill or chives.

Energy 53kcal/216kJ; Protein 1.3g; Carbohydrate 2.6g, of which sugars 2.6g; Fat 4.1g, of which saturates 2.5g; Cholesterol 12mg; Calcium 44mg; Fibre 0.7g; Sodium 13mg.

Apple and Leek Salad

Fresh and tangy, this simple Polish salad of sliced leeks and apples with a lemon and honey dressing can be served with a range of cold meats or smoked fish as part of a summer meal. For the best result, make sure you use slim young leeks and tart, crisp apples.

Serves 4

2 slim leeks, white part only, washed
  thoroughly
2 large apples
15ml/1 tbsp chopped fresh parsley
juice of 1 lemon
15ml/1 tbsp clear honey
salt and ground black pepper, to taste

COOK'S TIP When buying leeks, look for slim ones with firm white stems and bright green leaves. Avoid those that are discoloured in any way. If you can't find young leeks use older ones but blanch them in boiling water, then rinse in cold running water. This gives a milder flavour.

1 Thinly slice the leeks. Peel and core the apples, then slice thinly.

2 Put in a large serving bowl and add the parsley, lemon juice, honey and seasoning to taste.

3 Toss well, then leave to stand in a cool place for about an hour, to allow the flavours to blend together.

Energy 59kcal/252kJ; Protein 1.9g; Carbohydrate 12.5g, of which sugars 11.8g; Fat 0.6g, of which saturates 0.1g; Cholesterol 0mg; Calcium 27mg; Fibre 3.4g; Sodium 4mg.

Beetroot Salad

The fresh, sweet and nutty flavour of beetroot makes the ideal partner for horseradish, and this salad is often served as a side dish with cold meats, such as ham and Polish sausage. Beetroot is believed to have beauty-enhancing and aphrodisiac properties.

Serves 4–6

4–5 medium beetroot (beets), washed but not peeled
15ml/1 tbsp sugar
60–75ml/4–5 tbsp freshly grated horseradish
juice of 1 lemon
1 glass dry red wine
2.5ml/½ tsp salt
cold meats, to serve

1 Put the beetroot, in their skins, in a large pan, and cover with water. Bring to the boil and cook the beetroots for about 1 hour, or until tender. Remove from the heat and leave to cool.

2 When the beetroot are cool, peel off the skin with your fingers or a sharp knife. Grate the flesh into a large bowl.

3 Add the sugar, horseradish, lemon juice, red wine and salt to the shredded beetroot. Mix together, then transfer to a jar. Store in a cool place for up to 4 months. Serve with cold meats.

Energy 60kcal/253kJ; Protein 1.5g; Carbohydrate 9g, of which sugars 8.5g; Fat 0.1g, of which saturates 0g; Cholesterol 0mg; Calcium 20mg; Fibre 1.6g; Sodium 221mg.

Polish-style Lettuce Salad

This light salad makes an excellent accompaniment to pork or poultry dishes. The egg yolks make a lovely rich dressing – choose free-range eggs with a good golden yolk, if you can. You should serve the salad as soon as it is dressed, as if left for too long it will wilt.

Serves 4-6

2 medium lettuces
200ml/7fl oz/scant 1 cup sour cream
juice of 1 lemon, or 2 tbsp vinegar
1 tbsp sugar
5ml/1 tsp salt
2 hard-boiled eggs
chopped chives and dill, to garnish

1 Divide the lettuces into separate leaves. Wash carefully under running water, then pat completely dry with kitchen paper or a clean dish towel.

2 To make the dressing, in a large bowl, mix together the sour cream, lemon juice or vinegar, sugar and salt.

3 Peel the eggs and carefully separate the yolks from the whites. Crumble the yolks and fold them into the dressing.

4 Just before serving, place the lettuce leaves in a large bowl. Pour the dressing over the leaves, and mix gently with two forks. Transfer to a serving dish.

5 Thinly slice the egg whites and arrange over the top, with the chopped chives and dill. Serve immediately.

Energy 112kcal/465kJ; Protein 3.6g; Carbohydrate 5g, of which sugars 5g; Fat 8.8g, of which saturates 4.8g; Cholesterol 83mg; Calcium 61mg; Fibre 0.6g; Sodium 39mg

Celeriac Salad

This salad combines raw celeriac with onion, apples and carrots in a simple dressing. It goes especially well with cold chicken and turkey. Because the vegetables are raw, it is also bursting with goodness, and adds a fresh crunch to accompany winter dishes.

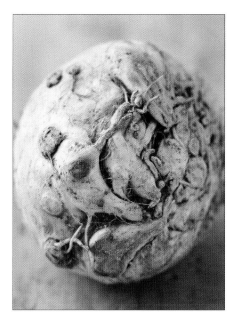

Serves 4

1 medium celeriac
1 small onion
2 large apples, peeled and cored
2 carrots
juice from 1 lemon
15ml/1 tbsp clear honey
15ml/1 tbsp olive oil
30ml/2 tbsp mayonnaise
15ml/1 tbsp chopped fresh parsley
salt and ground black pepper

1 Finely shred the celeriac, onion, apples and carrots. Transfer to a large bowl and toss to combine.

2 In a separate bowl, combine the lemon juice, honey, olive oil, mayonnaise, and salt and pepper to taste. Pour over the vegetables, add the parsley and toss to combine. Taste and adjust the seasoning as necessary.

Energy 149kcal/623kJ; Protein 1.4g; Carbohydrate 17.1g, of which sugars 16.6g; Fat 8.9g, of which saturates 1.2g; Cholesterol 6mg; Calcium 74mg; Fibre 3.8g; Sodium 55mg.

Sauerkraut Salad with Cranberries

Cabbage is a staple ingredient in Russia and the best soured cabbage can be bought in the market halls, where you are invited to taste both the cabbage and the brine. It is not unusual for a customer to taste up to ten different kinds before making a decision.

Serves 4–6

500g/1¼lb sauerkraut
2 red apples, cut into wedges
100–200g/3¾–7oz/scant 1–1¾ cups
   fresh cranberries or lingonberries
30ml/2 tbsp sugar
60–75ml/4–5 tbsp sunflower oil
2–3 sprigs fresh parsley, to garnish

1 Put the sauerkraut in a colander and drain thoroughly. Taste it, and if you find it is too sour, rinse it under cold running water, then drain well. Transfer to a large bowl and add the apple slices.

2 Add the apples and the cranberries or lingonberries to the sauerkraut. Add the sugar and oil and mix well. Transfer to a serving bowl and garnish with parsley.

Energy 105kcal/437kJ; Protein 1.3g; Carbohydrate 8.8g, of which sugars 8.8g; Fat 7.4g, of which saturates 0.9g; Cholesterol 0mg; Calcium 49mg; Fibre 3.1g; Sodium 493mg.

Fresh Spring Salad

This pretty salad can be served as an accompaniment to most meat and fish dishes. It is a typical home-made Russian dish and is hardly ever served in restaurants. Prepare this salad no more than an hour in advance and only add the dressing just before it is served.

Serves 4

2 eggs
1 large cos or romaine lettuce
1 cucumber, peeled and finely sliced
10 radishes, finely sliced
1 bunch spring onions (scallions),
  finely sliced
45ml/3 tbsp chopped fresh dill,
  to garnish

For the dressing
200ml/7fl oz/scant 1 cup smetana or
  crème fraîche
juice of 1 lemon
15ml/1 tbsp sugar
pinch of salt

1 First make the dressing. Put the smetana or crème fraîche and lemon juice in a small bowl and whisk together.

2 Add the sugar and salt to the bowl and whisk again until the sugar is completely dissolved. Set aside.

3 Put the eggs in a pan, cover with cold water and bring to the boil. Reduce the heat to low and simmer for 10 minutes. Drain and put under cold running water. Remove the shells and slice the eggs.

4 Cut the lettuce into pieces and put in a serving dish. Layer the salad by placing the cucumber on top of the shredded lettuce, then the radishes, then the sliced egg and finally the spring onions.

5 Just before serving, spoon the dressing over the salad and garnish with chopped fresh dill.

Energy 268kcal/1107kJ; Protein 6g; Carbohydrate 8.7g, of which sugars 8.5g; Fat 23.5g, of which saturates 14.5g; Cholesterol 152mg; Calcium 96mg; Fibre 1.8g; Sodium 55mg.

DESSERTS AND DRINKS

Despite the hearty nature of many Polish main courses, a
dessert is often also served, generally based on fruit and
so not too filling but sweet enough to round off the meal.
Russians, too, enjoy something sweet to finish dinner, but
their desserts more often consist of little cakes or pies.
More substantial Polish desserts are based on curd cheese
and eggs. Polish Cheesecake is a light baked mixture
made with whisked eggs, while Pancakes with
Vanilla Cheese are folded round a similar mixture of
curd cheese with raisins and vanilla. Russian desserts
also often include fruit, either the widely available
ones such as cherries, blueberries and apples, or
more exotic fruits from one of the warmer former
Soviet republics – grenadines, grapes or watermelon.
These are combined in delicious concoctions such
as cherry compote, or vanilla ice cream with frozen
berries and warm fudge sauce.

Bread and Apple Bake

Bread has always been the basic, staple food of Russian cuisine. It is treated with great respect, bought fresh each day and used to the last crumb. This recipe makes a new dish out of old bread – frugal, simple but very good. Sweet, dessert apples are best for this recipe.

Serves 6–8

a loaf of 2–3 days old white bread
60g/2¼oz/4½ tbsp cold butter
1 egg
150ml/¼ pint/⅔ cup milk
6–8 apples
130g/4½oz/⅔ cup caster (superfine)
  sugar

1 Preheat the oven to 200°C/400°F/ Gas 6. Use 10g/¼oz/1½ tsp of the butter to grease a 20cm/8in flan tin (pan).

2 Slice the loaf fairly thickly; you will need around 10 slices. Cut off the crusts.

3 Break the egg into a bowl and beat lightly. Add the milk to the bowl and whisk together. Cut five of the bread slices in half.

4 Dip the halved slices of bread, one at a time, into the milk mixture and place in the flan tin so that they cover the edges. Dip the remaining uncut bread slices in the milk mixture and place tightly in the bottom of the tin.

5 Cut the remaining 50g/2oz/4 tbsp butter into small cubes. Peel and core the apples and cut the flesh into small pieces.

6 Put half of the apples on top of the bread, sprinkle with half of the sugar and half of the butter cubes. Top with the remaining apples, sugar and butter.

7 Bake in the oven for 15 minutes. Lower the temperature to 180°C/ 350°F/Gas 4 and bake for a further 35 minutes, until golden brown. Serve warm, straight from the tin.

Energy 245kcal/1038kJ; Protein 4.6g; Carbohydrate 41.8g, of which sugars 26.1g; Fat 7.9g, of which saturates 4.3g; Cholesterol 41mg; Calcium 77mg; Fibre 1.6g; Sodium 240mg.

Apple Pie

Russians like to finish the day with vechernij chaj – evening tea. Chocolate confectionery, cookies, berries and spoonfuls of jam may be served. If something more substantial is required, a large home-baked pie is served with the steaming hot tea.

Serves 4–6

40–50g/1½–2oz/3–4 tbsp butter
5–6 cooking apples, peeled and sliced
45ml/3 tbsp raisins
1 sheet ready-made chilled puff
  pastry, measuring about
  40x20cm/16x8in
1 egg yolk
5ml/1 tsp water

1 Melt the butter in a medium frying pan. Add the apples and stir-fry, over a low heat, for 5 minutes, until soft. Remove the pan from the heat, add the raisins and mix together. Set aside and leave to cool.

2 Preheat the oven to 220°C/425°F/Gas 7. Put the sheet of pastry on a greased baking tray. Carefully place the apple filling on just half of the pastry, leaving one side free of filling, and a 5cm/2in border around the other three edges.

3 Brush the edges of the pastry with water or milk and fold over the other half to enclose the filling.

4 Whisk the egg yolk and water together to make a glaze. Brush the pastry with the mixture and make some small holes in the top with a fork.

5 Bake the pie in the oven for 12–15 minutes, until golden brown. Allow the pie to rest for 5–10 minutes then cut into slices and serve with a spoonful of smetana or crème fraîche.

Energy 393kcal/1650kJ; Protein 4.1g; Carbohydrate 56.3g, of which sugars 27.7g; Fat 18.4g, of which saturates 11.4g; Cholesterol 46mg; Calcium 68mg; Fibre 2.5g; Sodium 136mg.

Small Blueberry Pies

Delicious little blueberry pies are perfect as a dessert after a Sunday lunch. Alternatively, serve them in the afternoon; seat your guests in the garden and bring out the samovar. Serve these home-made temptations on a Russian tray decorated with fresh flowers, with lots of hot tea.

Makes 10

For the dough
50g/2oz/¼ cup butter
200ml/7fl oz/scant 1 cup milk
45ml/3 tbsp water
2.5ml/½ tsp salt
7.5ml/1½ tsp caster (superfine) sugar
1 small (US medium) egg
400g/14oz/3½ cups plain white (all-purpose) flour
large pinch of easy-blend (rapid-rise) dried yeast

For the filling
300–350g/11–12oz/2¾–3 cups blueberries, fresh or frozen
25g/1oz/2 tbsp caster (superfine) sugar
15ml/1 tbsp potato flour

For the glaze
150ml/¼ pint/⅔ cup smetana or crème fraîche
45ml/3 tbsp caster (superfine) sugar
icing (confectioners') sugar, for dusting

1 To make the dough, melt the butter in a small pan. Add the milk, water, salt and sugar and heat until warm to the finger. Pour the mixture into a large bowl. Add the egg and mix together.

2 Put the flour and yeast in a large bowl and mix together. Stir in the butter mixture, a little at a time, until combined.

3 Knead the dough in the bowl for at least 5 minutes. Cover the bowl with a dish towel and leave the dough to rise in a warm place for 30 minutes, until it has doubled in size.

4 Turn the dough on to a lightly floured surface. Cut the dough into 24 equal-size pieces and form each piece into a ball. Leave to rest for 5–10 minutes.

5 Meanwhile, prepare the filling. Put the blueberries in a bowl, add the sugar and potato flour and mix together.

6 Preheat the oven to 200°C/400°F/Gas 6. Grease a large baking tray. Flatten each ball to a round measuring about 15cm/6in in diameter.

VARIATION You can vary the fillings for these little pies depending on what fruit is in season: blackberries would work well, as would raspberries or apricots, or try finely chopped apples and a sprinkle of cinnamon. Adjust the amount of sugar to suit the fruit you use.

7 Place the rounds on the baking tray. Place 45ml/3 tbsp of the blueberry mixture in the centre of each round, then fold a small edge up around the mixture.

8 Bake the pies in the oven for 10–15 minutes, until golden brown.

9 Meanwhile, make the glaze. Put the smetana or crème fraîche and the sugar in a bowl and mix together.

10 When the pies are baked, gently spoon a little of the glaze over each pie. Dust the tops with sifted icing sugar. Serve hot or cold.

Energy 371kcal/1559kJ; Protein 4.4g; Carbohydrate 55.8g, of which sugars 25.7g; Fat 16g, of which saturates 4.9g; Cholesterol 8mg; Calcium 93mg; Fibre 3.2g; Sodium 228mg.

Crêpes with a Cheese Filling

Russians love pancakes of all kinds, and these crêpes are deliciously light and crisp. If you omit the sugar and add salt and pepper, this can be adapted to a savoury dish for a main course.

Serves 4

50g/2oz/¼ cup butter
3 eggs
2.5ml/½ tsp salt
2ml/⅓ tsp caster (superfine) sugar
200ml/7fl oz/scant 1 cup warm water
185g/6½oz/1⅔ cups plain white
  (all-purpose) flour
350ml/12fl oz/1½ cups milk
rapeseed (canola) oil, for brushing,
  and frying
smetana or crème fraîche, and caster
  (superfine) sugar, to serve

For the filling
500g/1¼lb/2½ cups fresh cheese, such
  as ricotta or cottage cheese
2 egg yolks
30–45ml/2–3 tbsp caster (superfine)
  sugar

1 Melt the butter. Whisk the eggs, salt and sugar together in a bowl. Add the water, then gradually whisk in the flour.

2 Stir the milk into the egg and flour mixture, a little at a time, and then add the melted butter.

3 Heat a non-stick frying pan over a medium heat. Brush it with a little oil and pour in a thin layer of batter. As soon as the surface has set, turn the crêpe over and cook the other side.

4 Fry the remaining crêpes in the same way, brushing the pan with oil each time and stacking when cooked.

5 To make the filling, put the cottage cheese or ricotta cheese and egg yolks in a bowl and mix together. Add sugar to taste. Place 45ml/3 tbsp of the filling in the centre of each crêpe and fold over to create an envelope.

6 Heat the oil in a frying pan. Add the envelopes, joint-side down, and fry, over a medium heat, for 1–2 minutes. Turn and fry the other sides for 1–2 minutes, until golden brown. Serve the pancakes with smetana or crème fraîche and sugar.

Energy 1054kcal/4371kJ; Protein 17.5g; Carbohydrate 48g, of which sugars 12.7g; Fat 89.6g, of which saturates 47.9g; Cholesterol 394mg; Calcium 332mg; Fibre 1.4g; Sodium 547mg.

Pancakes with Vanilla Cheese

Pancakes are always popular, and these delicious Polish ones are no exception. Filled with a rich rum and raisin cheese mixture, the pancakes are dusted with icing sugar.

Serves 4–6

115g/4oz/1 cup plain (all-purpose) flour
45ml/3 tbsp sugar
pinch of salt
3 eggs, plus 2 yolks
350ml/12fl oz/1½ cups milk
225g/8oz/1 cup curd (farmer's) cheese
40g/1½oz/¼ cup raisins
45ml/3 tbsp rum
10ml/2 tsp vanilla sugar or 5ml/1 tsp vanilla extract
45ml/3 tbsp vegetable oil
45ml/3 tbsp icing (confectioners') sugar, for dusting

1 Sift the flour into a large bowl. Stir in the sugar and salt, and make a well in the centre. In a jug (pitcher) whisk together the 3 eggs and the milk.

2 Gradually add the milk mixture to the flour, beating constantly, until smooth.

3 Put the egg yolks, curd cheese, raisins, rum and vanilla sugar or extract in a bowl and beat well.

4 Heat enough oil to just coat the base of a small frying pan over a high heat and add a ladleful of the pancake batter.

5 Cook for about 1 minute, until golden underneath, then flip over and cook on the other side. Slide on to a plate and keep warm. Continue until you have used all the batter.

6 Place a spoonful of the curd cheese mixture in the centre of each pancake and fold the edges over. Dust the pancakes with icing sugar and serve immediately.

Energy 330kcal/1383kJ; Protein 11.5g; Carbohydrate 31.3g, of which sugars 16.7g; Fat 16.8g, of which saturates 6g; Cholesterol 182mg; Calcium 126mg; Fibre 0.7g; Sodium 68mg.

Baked Cheesecake

Russians love their tea and tea drinking is an ancient Russian tradition. It is popular to have parties where nothing but tea and sweet accompaniments are served. These include cherry jam, gooseberry jam and whole strawberry jam (put in the tea or eaten from special plates), chocolates, fudge and soft spicy ginger cookies. The highlight of the tea is a cheesecake, flavoured with raisins, preserved peel and lemon.

Serves 6–8

15g/½oz/1 tbsp butter
45ml/3 tbsp fresh white breadcrumbs
4 eggs
100g/3¾oz mixed (candied) peel
500g/1¼lb/2 cups cottage or ricotta cheese
90g/3½oz/½ cup caster (superfine) sugar
50g/2oz/scant ½ cup raisins
grated rind of 1 lemon
45ml/3 tbsp semolina
icing (confectioners') sugar, for dusting
smetana, crème fraîche or whipped cream, and fresh berries, such as strawberries, raspberries, blueberries or redcurrants, to serve

3 Add the cottage or ricotta cheese, sugar, raisins, lemon rind and semolina and mix well together.

4 Whisk the egg whites until they are stiff and hold their shape, then carefully fold into the cheese mixture. Spoon the mixture into the prepared tin.

1 Preheat the oven to 180°C/350°F/Gas 4. Use the butter to grease the bottom and sides of a 20cm/8in loose-bottomed cake tin (pan), then pour in the breadcrumbs and tip and shake until the insides of the tin are well coated with the breadcrumbs.

2 Separate the egg yolks from the egg whites into two separate large bowls. Finely chop the candied peel and add to the egg yolks.

5 Bake the cake in the oven for 30–40 minutes, until a skewer, inserted in the centre, comes out dry. Leave the cake to cool in the tin.

6 Slide a knife around the edge of the cake and carefully remove it from the tin. Place on a serving plate and dust with sifted icing sugar.

7 Serve the cheesecake with smetana, or crème fraîche or whipped cream, and fresh berries.

Energy 297kcal/1239kJ; Protein 7.6g; Carbohydrate 27.2g, of which sugars 19g; Fat 18g, of which saturates 9g; Cholesterol 83mg; Calcium 56mg; Fibre 1.1g; Sodium 139mg.

Polish Cheesecake

There are many versions of cheesecake in Poland, including this light, baked version. The raisins and semolina sink to the bottom of the cheesecake and form a kind of base during cooking.

Serves 6–8

500g/1¼ lb/2¼ cups curd (farmer's) cheese
100g/3¾oz/scant ½ cup butter, softened
2.5ml/½ tsp vanilla extract
6 eggs, separated
150g/5oz/¾ cup caster (superfine) sugar
10ml/2 tsp grated lemon rind
15ml/1 tbsp cornflour (cornstarch)
15ml/1 tbsp semolina
50g/5oz/⅓ cup raisins or sultanas (golden raisins) (optional)
icing (confectioners') sugar, to dust

1 Preheat the oven to 200°C/400°F/Gas 6. Grease and line a 20cm/8in round cake tin (pan).

2 Cream together the curd cheese, butter and vanilla in a large bowl until combined.

3 In a separate large bowl, whisk the egg whites with 15ml/1 tbsp sugar, until stiff peaks form.

4 In a third bowl, whisk the egg yolks with the remaining sugar until the mixture is thick and creamy.

5 Add the egg yolk and sugar mixture to the curd cheese and butter mixture with the lemon rind and stir to combine.

6 Gently fold in the egg whites, then the cornflour, semolina and raisins or sultanas, if using, taking care not to knock the air out of the mixture.

7 Transfer the mixture to the prepared tin and bake for 1 hour, or until set and golden brown.

8 Leave to cool in the tin, then dust with icing sugar and serve in slices.

COOK'S TIP It is important to use good quality curd cheese in this recipe; it should not taste sour at all.

Energy 347kcal/1448kJ; Protein 10.8g; Carbohydrate 24.8g, of which sugars 21.6g; Fat 23.6g, of which saturates 13.4g; Cholesterol 196mg; Calcium 34mg; Fibre 0g; Sodium 131mg.

Baked Coffee Custards

Unlike their eastern European neighbours, the Polish have a passion for both drinking and cooking with coffee. Here, it is used to lift a simple baked custard to new heights.

Serves 4

300ml/½ pint/1¼ cups full-fat
  (whole) milk
25g/1oz ground coffee (not instant)
150ml/¼ pint/⅔ cup single
  (light) cream
3 eggs
30ml/2 tbsp caster (superfine) sugar
whipped cream and unsweetened
  cocoa powder, to decorate

1 Preheat the oven to 190°C/375°F/ Gas 5. Put the milk in a heavy pan and bring to the boil. Add the coffee, remove from the heat and leave to infuse for 10 minutes.

2 Strain the flavoured milk into a clean pan, add the cream and gently heat until just simmering.

3 Beat the eggs and sugar in a bowl until pale and fluffy. Pour over the hot milk mixture, whisking constantly.

4 Pour the custard mixture into individual heatproof bowls or coffee cups and cover tightly with foil. Place them in a roasting pan and pour in enough boiling water to come halfway up the bowls or cups.

5 Carefully place the roasting pan in the oven and cook for about 30 minutes, or until the custards are set. Remove from the roasting pan and leave to cool completely. Transfer to the refrigerator and chill for at least 2 hours.

6 Just before serving, decorate with whipped cream and cocoa powder.

Energy 207kcal/860kJ; Protein 8.5g; Carbohydrate 12g, of which sugars 12g; Fat 14.3g, of which saturates 7.6g; Cholesterol 174mg; Calcium 147mg; Fibre 0g; Sodium 96mg.

Chocolate and Coffee Mousse

A light but intensely chocolatey mousse is always a popular way to end a meal. This Polish version is made with a good strong chocolate and flavoured with coffee and rum, Polish spirit or vodka. You can omit these, depending on your preference.

Serves 4–6

250g/9oz dark (bittersweet) chocolate (minimum 70 per cent cocoa solids)
60ml/4 tbsp cooled strong black coffee
8 eggs, separated
200g/7oz/1 cup caster (superfine) sugar
60ml/4 tbsp rum, or 95 per cent proof Polish spirit or vodka

VARIATION For a slightly less intense mousse, whip 300ml/½ pint/1¼ cups double (heavy) cream until soft peaks form, then fold into the mixture at the end of step 3.

1 Break the chocolate into small pieces and melt in a heatproof bowl over a pan of gently simmering water. Ensure the water does not touch the base of the bowl, or the chocolate may seize.

2 Once the chocolate has melted, stir in the cold coffee. Leave to cool slightly.

3 Beat the egg yolks with half the sugar until it is pale, thick and creamy. Add the rum, spirit or vodka and the chocolate.

4 Whisk the egg whites in a separate bowl until stiff peaks form. Stir in the remaining sugar, then fold into the chocolate mixture. Spoon into glasses. Chill for at least an hour before serving.

Energy 464kcal/1951kJ; Protein 10.6g; Carbohydrate 61.3g, of which sugars 60.9g; Fat 19.1g, of which saturates 9.1g; Cholesterol 256mg; Calcium 70mg; Fibre 1.1g; Sodium 98mg.

Baked Apples with Cinnamon and Nuts

Cream cake may be one of the most popular desserts in Russia, but health conscious young Russians of today appreciate lighter desserts and are as happy to serve baked apples – another old traditional Russian classic dessert.

2 Preheat the oven to 220°C/425°F/ Gas 7. Using a vegetable peeler, peel the apples. Remove the cores, leaving the base of the apple intact. Put the apples in an ovenproof dish.

3 Divide the filling into four, and stuff the apples. Melt the butter in a small pan and pour over the apples to coat.

4 Bake the apples in the oven for about 20 minutes, until soft, but before they collapse. Serve hot, with vanilla ice cream.

Serves 4

4 large, firm apples
15g/½oz/1 tbsp butter
vanilla ice cream, to serve

For the filling
25g/1oz/2 tbsp butter
90ml/6 tbsp blanched almonds
 or hazelnuts
30ml/2 tbsp sugar
5ml/1 tsp ground cinnamon

VARIATION Instead of flavouring with cinnamon, use the same quantity of ground cardamom or vanilla extract.

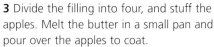

1 To make the filling, melt the butter. Grind or finely chop the almonds or hazelnuts and put in a bowl. Add the sugar, cinnamon and melted butter and mix together.

Energy 294kcal/1229kJ; Protein 5.3g; Carbohydrate 22.8g, of which sugars 22.2g; Fat 20.9g, of which saturates 6.2g; Cholesterol 21mg; Calcium 66mg; Fibre 4.1g; Sodium 67mg.

Poached Pears with Chocolate

Many types of pear are grown in Poland, and they are either simply eaten raw or gently poached and served with a rich chocolate sauce, as in this recipe. Once cooked, these pears can be frozen in their syrup. To use from frozen simply defrost and then make the chocolate sauce.

Serves 4

4 firm pears, peeled
250g/9oz/1¼ cups caster (superfine) sugar
600ml/1 pint/2½ cups water
500ml/17fl oz/2¼ cups vanilla ice cream

For the chocolate sauce
250g/9oz good-quality dark (bittersweet) chocolate (minimum 70 per cent cocoa solids)
40g/1½ oz unsalted butter
5ml/1 tsp vanilla extract
75ml/5 tbsp double (heavy) cream

1 Cut the pears in half lengthways and remove the core. Place the sugar and water in a large pan and gently heat until the sugar has dissolved completely.

2 Add the pear halves to the pan, then simmer for about 20 minutes, or until the pears are tender but not falling apart.

3 Lift out of the sugar syrup with a slotted spoon and leave to cool.

4 To make the chocolate sauce, break the chocolate into small pieces and put into a pan.

5 Add the butter and 30ml/2 tbsp water. Heat gently over a low heat, without stirring, until the chocolate has melted.

6 Add the vanilla extract and cream, and mix gently to combine.

7 Place a scoop of ice cream into each of four glasses.

8 Add two cooled pear halves to each and pour over the hot chocolate sauce. Serve immediately.

COOK'S TIP Like apples, there are two types of pear: softer dessert varieties and those that can be cooked. Use firm ones, as they will hold their shape when poached, rather than disintegrating.

Energy 1014kcal/4255kJ; Protein 8.8g; Carbohydrate 145.1g, of which sugars 143.2g; Fat 46.7g, of which saturates 29.6g; Cholesterol 81mg; Calcium 206mg; Fibre 4.9g; Sodium 152mg.

Plum Dumplings

These traditional sweet dumplings are served everywhere in Poland during the autumn, when plums are at their best. They are sometimes eaten as a meal on their own!

Serves 4

675g/1½lb potatoes, peeled
250ml/8fl oz/1 cup sour cream
75g/3oz/6 tbsp butter
2 eggs, beaten
250g/9oz/2¼ cups plain (all-purpose) flour, plus extra for dusting
8 plums
90g/3½oz/¾ cup icing (confectioners') sugar, mixed with 30ml/2 tbsp ground cinnamon
45ml/3 tbsp breadcrumbs
icing (confectioners') sugar and cinnamon, for dusting

1 Cut the potatoes into even pieces and cook in a pan of lightly salted boiling water for 10–15 minutes, or until soft. Drain, cool, then mash in a large bowl.

2 Add the sour cream, 25g/1oz/2 tbsp butter, eggs and flour to the mashed potato and stir to combine thoroughly.

3 Turn the dough out on to a lightly floured surface and knead lightly.

4 Cut a slit down one side of each plum and remove the stone (pit), keeping the plum intact. Push a teaspoonful of the sugar and cinnamon mixture inside each.

5 On a well-floured surface, roll out the potato dough until it is about 5mm/¼ in thick. Divide into eight 10cm/4in squares.

6 Place a plum in the centre of each square, then bring up the dough and pinch the edges together to completely seal the plum in the dough.

7 Bring a pan of water to the boil, and add the dumplings in batches. Cook for 8 minutes, until they rise to the surface. Remove with a slotted spoon, transfer to a bowl and keep warm while you cook the remaining dumplings.

8 Heat the remaining butter in a large frying pan, add the breadcrumbs and fry until golden brown. Add the dumplings, turn to coat in the crumbs, then transfer to a serving plate and dust with icing sugar and cinnamon. Serve immediately.

Energy 510kcal/2147kJ; Protein 11.1g; Carbohydrate 72.6g, of which sugars 18.6g; Fat 21.6g, of which saturates 12.4g; Cholesterol 115mg; Calcium 147mg; Fibre 5.3g; Sodium 190mg.

Strawberry Mousse

A popular dessert in homes all over Poland, where strawberries are often grown in the garden, this light fruit mousse is an excellent way to enjoy the strawberry season when they are at their least expensive. You can also mix in some raspberries to this recipe for a little added tartness.

Serves 4

250g/9oz strawberries, hulled
90g/3³/₄ oz/¹/₂ cup caster (superfine) sugar
75ml/2¹/₂fl oz/¹/₃ cup white wine
75ml/2¹/₂fl oz/¹/₃ cup cold water
15ml/1 tbsp powdered gelatine or 8 sheets leaf gelatine
60ml/4 tbsp boiling water
300ml/¹/₂ pint/1¹/₄ cups double (heavy) cream
fresh mint leaves, to decorate

1 Chop most of the strawberries, reserving a few whole ones for decoration.

2 Transfer the chopped strawberries to a food processor or blender, add the sugar and wine, and blend to a smooth purée.

3 Put the cold water in a large bowl and sprinkle over the gelatine (or immerse leaf gelatine). Leave for 5 minutes, then add the boiling water and leave for 2–3 minutes, or until the gelatine has completely dissolved.

4 Add the strawberry mixture to the gelatine and mix to combine. Chill for about 30 minutes, or until the mixture has thickened.

5 Lightly whip the cream until soft peaks form, then gently fold into the thickened strawberry mixture.

6 Spoon the mousse into serving glasses and chill overnight in the refrigerator. Just before serving, decorate with a halved strawberry and some mint leaves.

Energy 478kcal/1987kJ; Protein 7.2g; Carbohydrate 29.4g, of which sugars 29.4g; Fat 40.4g, of which saturates 22.5g; Cholesterol 98mg; Calcium 62mg; Fibre 0.7g; Sodium 34mg

Wild Strawberries with Whipped Cream

Smaller and with a more intense flavour than their domestic cousins, wild strawberries require little in the way of preparation. In this delectable dish they are simply served with a dollop of slightly sweetened cream and garnished with mint.

Serves 4

475ml/16fl oz/2 cups double
  (heavy) cream
50g/2oz/¼ cup vanilla sugar
275g/10oz/2½ cups wild strawberries
fresh mint leaves, to decorate

1 Whip the double cream with the sugar until soft peaks form.

2 Wash and hull the berries, then divide among four serving dishes.

3 Spoon over the sweetened whipped cream and decorate with fresh mint. Serve immediately.

COOK'S TIP Tiny wild strawberries grow on grassy banks, heaths and open woodland and have a beautifully sweet flavour. The plant, which has hairy stems and runners, is low-growing and the leaves are toothed, shiny and grow in groups of three. Look for the ripe berries in mid- to late summer.

Energy 657kcal/2712kJ; Protein 2.5g; Carbohydrate 19.2g, of which sugars 19.2g; Fat 63.8g, of which saturates 39.7g; Cholesterol 163mg; Calcium 76mg; Fibre 0.8g; Sodium 31mg.

Pashka

This classic Russian recipe is a special Easter treat. The fresh cheese and dried fruit dessert is made by mixing the ingredients together, putting them in a lined mould and letting all the liquid drain away, creating a firm, dome-shaped pudding. The traditional shape is a pyramid, made in a wooden mould, but a coffee filter-holder or a clean plastic flower pot work equally well. Paskha needs to be made a few days in advance.

Serves 6–8

500g/1¼lb/2½ cups ricotta cheese or cottage cheese
75g/3oz/6 tbsp unsalted butter, softened
275g/10oz/1½ cups caster (superfine) sugar
30ml/2 tbsp vanilla sugar
150ml/¼ pint/⅔ cup whipping cream
30ml/2 tbsp smetana or crème fraîche
2 egg yolks
40g/1½oz/generous ¼ cup raisins
grated rind 1 lemon
glacé (candied) orange or lemon and blanched almonds, to decorate

1 If using cottage cheese, push the cheese through a sieve (strainer). Put the ricotta or cottage cheese in a sieve and stand the sieve over a bowl. Leave to drain overnight in a cold place.

2 Line a clean 750ml/1¼ pints/3 cups coffee filter, or a flower pot with a drainage hole, with damp muslin (cheesecloth) allowing the edges of the muslin to overhang the edges.

3 Transfer the drained cheese into a bowl, add the butter, sugar and vanilla sugar and beat together until smooth.

4 Pour the whipping cream into a separate bowl and whisk until it forms soft peaks.

5 Stir the whipped cream into the cheese mixture, then add the smetana or crème fraîche and egg yolks. Whisk until fluffy and smooth. Add the raisins and grated lemon rind and stir together.

6 Spoon the mixture into the lined holder and fold the edges of the muslin into the centre. Cover with a small saucer that fits inside the holder and put a 500g/1¼lb weight on top. Stand in a bowl or soup plate and leave in a cold place, to drain, for one to three days.

7 Remove the weight and saucer. Unfold the muslin and very carefully turn the paskha out on to a serving plate. Remove the muslin. Serve the Paskha decorated with glacé fruits and nuts.

Energy 369kcal/1544kJ; Protein 9.3g; Carbohydrate 41.9g, of which sugars 41.9g; Fat 19.1g, of which saturates 11.5g; Cholesterol 100mg; Calcium 118mg; Fibre 0.1g; Sodium 256mg.

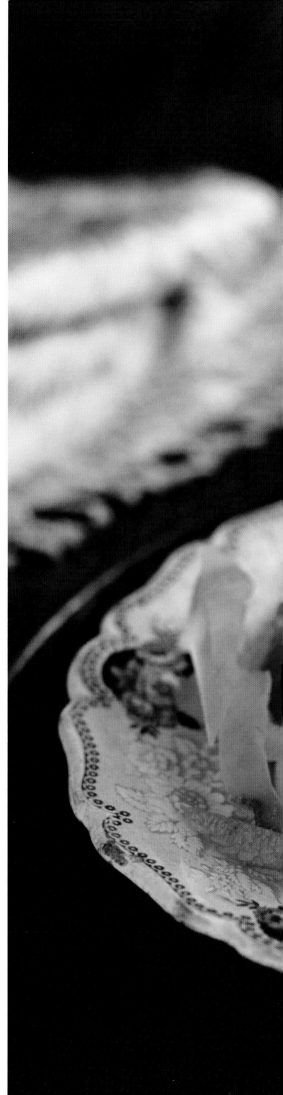

Pear and Raspberry Compote

This simple dessert combines seasonal fruit with typical Polish flavourings, cinnamon and cloves, to make a nutritious dish that can be eaten on its own or served with vanilla ice cream or whipped cream. Omit the raspberry liqueur if you are making this for children.

3 Add the pears to the pan and simmer gently over a low heat for 15–20 minutes, or until the pears are tender.

4 Lift the pears out of the pan with a slotted spoon and arrange on a serving dish. Leave to cool.

5 Meanwhile, remove the cinnamon and cloves from the syrup in the pan.

6 Blend half the raspberries in a food processor, then push through a sieve (strainer) set over a bowl and add the juices to the syrup in the pan.

Serves 4–6

900ml/1½ pint/3¾ cups water
350g/12oz/1¾ cups sugar
1 large cinnamon stick
4–5 whole cloves
900g/2lb pears, peeled, cored and
    cut into quarters
275g/10oz/1⅔ cups fresh
    raspberries, rinsed
60ml/4 tbsp raspberry liqueur

1 Place the water and sugar in a heavy pan and heat gently until the sugar has completely dissolved.

2 Add the cinnamon stick and cloves to the mixture, increase the heat and boil for 4 minutes, stirring, until the mixture becomes syrupy.

VARIATION If you don't have any raspberry liqueur use the same amount of brandy.

7 Stir in the remaining raspberries and the raspberry liqueur.

8 Pour the sauce over the pears and leave to cool completely before chilling in the refrigerator. Alternatively, serve the compote warm.

Energy 331kcal/1408kJ; Protein 1.6g; Carbohydrate 81.9g, of which sugars 81.9g; Fat 0.3g, of which saturates 0.1g; Cholesterol 0mg; Calcium 63mg; Fibre 4.8g; Sodium 11mg.

Dried Fruit Compote

Russian suppers almost always consist of three dishes – a soup, the main dish and a dessert. To round off an evening meal, a compote is the most popular final course. You can mix the fruit ingredients to suit your own taste or according to what is available.

Serves 4

250g/9oz/1¼ cups mixed dried fruits
  including plums, pears, apples
  and apricots
1.5 litres/2½ pints/6¼ cups water
2 cinnamon sticks or bay leaves
60ml/4 tbsp raisins
5ml/1 tsp finely grated lemon or
  orange rind
30–45ml/2–3 tbsp sugar

VARIATION To make the Armenian version of this compote, flavour it with a little brandy in step 5, and add some roughly chopped walnuts just before serving.

1 Keeping the fruit types separate, cut any large pieces of fruit into smaller chunks. Pour the water into a medium pan and bring to the boil.

2 When the water is boiling, add the plums, pears, cinnamon sticks or bay leaves and return to the boil. Reduce the heat and simmer for 10 minutes.

3 Add the apples and apricots to the pan and simmer for a further 10 minutes. Add the raisins and grated rind and simmer for 5 minutes more.

4 Remove the fruit from the pan and transfer to a heatproof serving bowl.

5 Add the sugar to the juices in the pan, bring to the boil, then boil for 5 minutes, stirring from time to time until the syrup thickens slightly.

6 Pour the syrup over the fruit and serve the compote warm or cold.

Energy 169kcal/721kJ; Protein 2.9g; Carbohydrate 41.1g, of which sugars 41.1g; Fat 0.4g, of which saturates 0g; Cholesterol 0mg; Calcium 57mg; Fibre 4.2g; Sodium 18mg.

Apricot Compote with Almonds

As in Russia, traditional winter desserts in Poland are made with dried fruits, such as plums, apples or apricots, because it was once difficult to buy the fresh variety out of season. This rich apricot compote is warming and nutritious, making it especially popular around Christmas.

Serves 6

350g/12oz/¹⁄₂ cup dried apricots, finely chopped
60ml/4 tbsp water
50g/2oz/¹⁄₄ cup caster (superfine) sugar
90ml/6 tbsp 95 per cent proof Polish spirit
75g/3oz/¹⁄₂ cup blanched almonds, chopped
75g/3oz/¹⁄₂ cup chopped candied peel
whipped cream and ground cinnamon, to serve

1 Place the chopped apricots and the water in a heavy pan, bring to the boil and simmer for 25 minutes.

2 Add the sugar and simmer for a further 10 minutes, or until you have a thick jam-like mixture.

3 Remove from the heat and stir in the Polish spirit, almonds and candied peel.

4 Spoon into serving dishes or glasses and leave to cool, then chill in the refrigerator for at least 2 hours. Just before serving, decorate with whipped cream and dust with cinnamon.

Energy 230kcal/973kJ; Protein 5.1g; Carbohydrate 38.3g, of which sugars 37.9g; Fat 7.4g, of which saturates 0.6g; Cholesterol 0mg; Calcium 93mg; Fibre 5.2g; Sodium 46mg.

Frozen Cranberries with Fudge Sauce

Cranberries are a special treat in Russia and this dessert makes the most of their vibrant, tart flavour by serving them with a deliciously sweet fudge sauce. It is worth making double quantities of the sauce and keeping the rest in a jar for pouring over ice cream.

Serves 4

150ml/¼ pint/⅔ cup whipping cream
100ml/3½fl oz/scant ½ cup milk
30-45ml/2–3 tbsp caster (superfine)
  sugar
45ml/3 tbsp treacle (molasses)
15g/½ oz/1 tbsp butter
425–500g/15oz–1¼lb/4–5 cups frozen
  cranberries or lingonberries

VARIATION If frozen cranberries are not available, try serving this fudge sauce with other frozen berries that have a tart rather than sweet flavour, such as a mixture of blackcurrants and raspberries.

1 Pour the cream and milk into a medium pan, add the sugar, treacle and butter, and stir together. Bring to the boil, reduce the heat and simmer for 10-15 minutes, until the mixture is light brown and thick.

2 Put the cranberries or lingonberries in a bowl and leave at room temperature for 10 minutes to thaw slightly. Divide the fruit among four small plates, pour over the fudge sauce and serve.

Energy 264kcal/1100kJ; Protein 2.7g; Carbohydrate 23.2g, of which sugars 23.2g; Fat 18.5g, of which saturates 11.5g; Cholesterol 49mg; Calcium 158mg; Fibre 3.3g; Sodium 70mg

Cranberry Juice

A decanter filled with home-made, sweet and sour cranberry juice is a necessity on the Russian party table, almost as much as the ice-cold vodka and the Russian champagne. These days it can be bought in supermarkets but the home-made variety has a much better taste.

3 Cover the bowl with clear film (plastic wrap) and put in the refrigerator.

4 Put the reserved strained berries in a pan, add the water and bring to the boil. Reduce the heat and simmer for 5 minutes. Strain the berries and discard them, but reserve the juice.

5 Pour the cranberry juices back into the pan. Add the sugar and simmer, stirring all the time, until the sugar has dissolved. Remove the pan from the heat and leave to cool.

6 When cool, mix the juice in the pan with the cold juice from the refrigerator.

7 Return to the refrigerator for 2–3 hours before pouring into a decanter or jug (pitcher) and keep cool until serving time. Serve in tall glasses with ice.

VARIATION Substitute lingonberries for the cranberries, if you wish.

Makes 1.5 litres/2½ pints/6¼ cups to serve 4

500g/1¼lb/5 cups cranberries
1 litre/2½ pints/6¼ cups water
100g/3¾oz/scant½ cup sugar
ice, to serve

1 Put the cranberries in a food processor and blend until smooth.

2 Strain the juice into a bowl, reserving the cranberries.

Energy 143kcal/615kJ; Protein 0.4g; Carbohydrate 37.1g, of which sugars 37.1g; Fat 0.4g, of which saturates 0g; Cholesterol 0mg; Calcium 26mg; Fibre 0g; Sodium 8mg

Honey and Cardamom Drink

It is a well-known fact that Russian gentlemen drink vodka with their food while the women prefer champagne but, for a variation, try this old Russian, alcohol-free honey and cardamom drink as an accompaniment to your Russian meal.

Makes 2 litres/3½ pints/8 cups

150g/5oz/generous ½ cup honey
2 litres/3½ pints/8 cups water
large pinch of dried hops
1 cardamom pod
5ml/1 tsp preserving sugar
10g/¼oz fresh yeast

1 Mix the honey and 350ml/12fl oz/ 1½ cups of the water in a pan. Bring to the boil, then lower the heat and simmer for 2–3 minutes, skimming if necessary.

5 Skim the surface, then pour through a sieve (strainer). Transfer into clean bottles. Store in the refrigerator and drink within a week. Serve chilled.

2 Mix the hops and 150ml/5fl oz/⅔ cup of the water in a separate pan. Bring to the boil, then lower the heat and simmer for 2–3 minutes. Add the honey water.

3 Bring the mixture to the boil and add the remaining water. Remove from the heat and leave the liquid to cool at room temperature until it is about 40°C/104°F.

4 Add the cardamom, sugar and yeast to the pan. Cover and set aside at 8–10°C/ 46–50°F, until the surface is foamy.

Energy 469kcal/1999kJ; Protein 4.2g; Carbohydrate 120.2g, of which sugars 119.8g; Fat 0.1g, of which saturates 0g; Cholesterol 0mg; Calcium 18mg; Fibre 0g; Sodium 22mg.

BAKING

Poles and Russians have a sweet tooth, which is amply satisfied by their many recipes for cakes, cookies and sweet treats. Although people make cakes at home, in Poland especially, bakeries take pride in elaborately decorated confections and pastries to eat as dessert or with coffee as a snack. Afternoon tea is a Russian speciality, with plenty of hot tea – still sometimes served from a samovar – little pots of jam eaten with a spoon, and perhaps a creamy layer cake.

The best cakes and pastries are traditionally made at Christmas and Easter, and both Russia and Poland have special recipes for these festive celebrations, including the traditional Russian Easter cake, kulitj, and Poland's dark, rich Poppy Seed Cake, makowiec. Many of these cakes are made with a yeast dough rather than baking powder, which gives a firm texture and a distinctive flavour that is ideal for combining with dried fruits and spices.

Angels' Wings

This old Polish recipe for deep-fried pastry strips dusted with sugar is traditionally made in large quantities on Fat Thursday, the last Thursday before Lent begins, but also for carnivals, where they are sold in huge quantities.

Serves 4–6

50g/2oz/¼ cup butter, softened
50g/2oz/¼ cup caster (superfine) sugar
3 egg yolks, plus 1 whole egg
250g/9oz/2¼ cups plain (all-purpose) flour, plus extra for dusting
2.5ml/½ tsp bicarbonate of soda (baking soda)
120ml/4fl oz/½ cup sour cream
pinch of salt
30ml/2 tbsp clear honey
45ml/3 tbsp 95 per cent proof Polish spirit or vodka, or rum
15ml/1 tbsp vinegar
vegetable oil, for deep-frying
icing (confectioners') sugar, for dusting

2 Roll out the dough on a floured surface to a rectangle,10cm/4in across, 3mm/⅛in thick. Cut into four 2.5cm/1in strips

3 Cut the dough lengthways, then cut each of these horizontally, on a slight slant, into pieces about 10cm/4in long.

1 Beat the butter and sugar in a large bowl. Add the eggs, flour, bicarbonate of soda, sour cream, salt, honey, Polish spirit, vodka or rum, and the vinegar. Beat to combine and form a smooth dough.

COOK'S TIPS
Add a cube of bread to the hot oil to prevent it from spitting while the cookies are cooking.
   These cookies are delicious eaten warm or cold, but for the best result they should be eaten on the same day.

4 Make a 4cm/1½in lengthways slit in the middle of each strip.Lift the lower end of the pastry and pass it through the slit. Gently pull it through the other side and downwards to create a twist.

5 Heat enough oil for deep-frying to 180°C/350°F/Gas 4, then add the pastry strips in batches of two and fry for 5–8 seconds, until they rise to the surface and are golden brown.

6 Remove from the oil immediately, using a slotted spoon, and drain on kitchen paper. Repeat the process with the remaining pastry. Transfer to a serving dish and dust generously with icing sugar.

Energy 364kcal/1527kJ; Protein 7.7g; Carbohydrate 45.7g, of which sugars 14g; Fat 16.2g, of which saturates 8.3g; Cholesterol 203mg; Calcium 104mg; Fibre 1.3g; Sodium 79mg.

Honey and Almond Cookies

These delectable spiced honey cookies are traditionally made at Christmas, although they are also eaten at other times of the year. They keep well if stored in an airtight container.

Makes 20

225g/8oz/1 cup clear honey
4 eggs, plus 2 egg whites
350g/12oz/3 cups plain (all-purpose) flour
5ml/1 tsp bicarbonate of soda (baking soda)
2.5ml/¹⁄₂ tsp freshly grated nutmeg
2.5ml/¹⁄₂ tsp ground ginger
2.5ml/¹⁄₂ tsp ground cinnamon
2.5ml/¹⁄₂ tsp ground cloves
20 blanched almond halves

1 Beat together the honey and whole eggs until light and fluffy. Sift over the flour, bicarbonate of soda and spices, and beat to combine.

2 Gather the cookie dough into a ball, wrap in clear film (plastic wrap) and chill in the refrigerator for 1 hour, or overnight if making in advance.

3 Preheat the oven to 200°C/400°F/ Gas 6. Roll out the dough on a lightly floured surface to a thickness of 5mm/¹⁄₄in.

COOK'S TIP Ancient Slavic tribes used to make cakes with honey, but it wasn't until the arrival of spices in the 17th century that Polish people starting making these sweet and delicious little morsels.

4 Using a 4cm/¹⁄₂in cookie cutter, stamp out 20 rounds. Transfer the rounds to two lightly greased baking trays.

5 Beat the egg whites until soft peaks form. Brush the tops of the rounds with the egg white, then press an almond half into the centre of each one.

6 Place in the oven and bake for 15–20 minutes, or until they are a pale golden brown. Remove from the oven and allow to cool slightly before transferring to a wire cooling rack.

Energy 112kcal/473kJ; Protein 3.4g; Carbohydrate 22.6g, of which sugars 8.9g; Fat 1.5g, of which saturates 0.4g; Cholesterol 38mg; Calcium 33mg; Fibre 0.5g; Sodium 22mg.

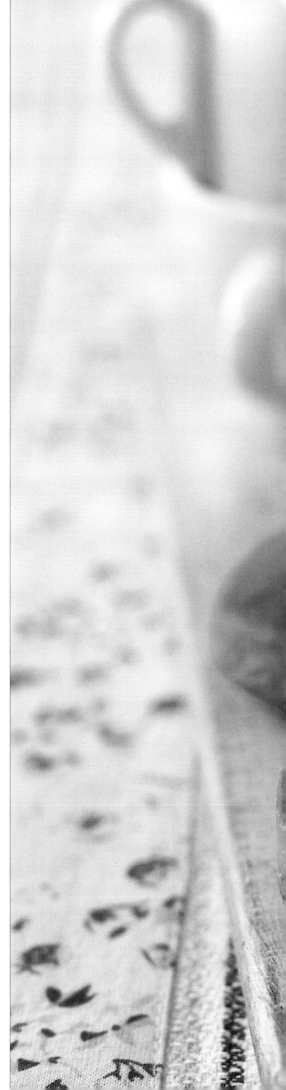

Easter Pastry

Consumed in vast quantities at Easter in Poland, there are many different toppings for these sweet, decorative pastries, including nut paste, almonds, cheese, jams, raisins and coloured icing.

Serves 6

300g/11oz/2²/₃ cups plain (all-purpose) flour
115g/4oz/1 cup icing (confectioners') sugar
250g/9oz/generous 1 cup butter, softened
4 egg yolks

For the filling
500ml/17fl oz/2¹/₄ cups double (heavy) cream
400g/14oz/2 cups caster (superfine) sugar
1 vanilla pod (bean)
400g/14oz/1³/₄ cups unsalted butter, cut into cubes
about 150g/5oz each of almonds and dried fruits, to decorate

1 Sift the flour and icing sugar into a large bowl. Add the softened butter and egg yolks, and mix thoroughly to make a smooth dough.

2 Form the dough into a ball, cover with clear film (plastic wrap) and chill in the refrigerator for 45 minutes.

3 Preheat the oven to 220°C/425°F/Gas 7. Grease a rectangular baking tray. Roll out the pastry and cut a piece that is the same size as the tray. Place on the tray.

4 Cut the remaining pastry into strips and join together. Brush a little water around the edge of the pastry base. Twist the strip of pastry and place around the edge.

5 Bake the pastry base in the oven for about 20 minutes, or until golden brown. Leave to cool slightly, then carefully lift it out on to a large serving dish and cool completely.

6 To make the filling, pour the cream into a heavy pan, then add the sugar and vanilla pod. Gently bring to the boil, then boil for about 5 minutes, stirring constantly, until the mixture is thick.

7 To test whether it is ready, spoon a small amount on to a cold plate. It should set quickly. Remove from the heat and leave to cool slightly.

8 Remove the vanilla pod, then beat in the butter while the cream mixture is still warm. Spread the mixture inside the pastry case, smoothing the top.

9 While the filling is still warm, decorate the top with almonds and dried fruits. You can either simply sprinkle the nuts and fruit over, or you may like to create a pattern.

COOK'S TIP The pastry will keep for up to 3 days in an airtight container in the refrigerator.

VARIATION You can decorate the top with anything you like. Good choices might include crystallized (candied) fruits, drizzles of chocolate, sweets (candies) or coloured icing (frosting). Children, in particular, will enjoy decorating the top.

Energy 1989kcal/8270kJ; Protein 14.9g; Carbohydrate 149.4g, of which sugars 110.6g; Fat 152.2g, of which saturates 86.5g; Cholesterol 480mg; Calcium 270mg; Fibre 4g; Sodium 703mg.

Polish-style Doughnuts

These hot, sweet doughnuts, generously filled with rosehip preserve, are traditionally eaten on Shrove Tuesday, before the restrictions of Lent begin. They are a great favourite throughout Poland. Although they require a little effort to make, the end result is well worth it.

Serves 6

60g/2¼oz fresh yeast
115g/4oz caster (superfine) sugar
500g/1¼lb strong white bread flour, plus extra for dusting
250ml/8fl oz/1 cup full-fat (whole) milk, slightly warmed
8 eggs, separated
75ml/5 tbsp 95 per cent proof Polish spirit or vodka, or rum
15ml/1 tbsp grated lemon rind
pinch of salt
115g/4oz/½ cup butter, melted

For the filling

200g/7oz/⅔ cup rosehip preserve
1kg/2¼lb/6 cups lard or oil
vanilla-flavoured icing (confectioners') sugar (see Cook's Tip)

1 Cream the yeast with 15ml/1 tbsp sugar, then add 115g/4oz/1 cup flour and beat well. Gradually add the warmed milk and mix to a smooth batter.

2 Cover with a clean, damp dish towel and leave in a warm place for 30 minutes, or until foamy and risen.

3 Beat the egg yolks with the remaining sugar until thick and creamy.

4 Sift the remaining flour into a separate bowl, then add the egg yolks and sugar, the yeast mixture, the Polish spirit, vodka or rum, lemon rind and salt.

5 Stir to combine, then knead in the bowl until bubbles begin to form. Pour in the melted butter and knead for a few more minutes, or until firm and elastic. Cover with a damp dish towel, then put in a warm place and leave the dough to rise for 30 minutes.

6 On a lightly floured surface, roll out the dough to a thickness of 1cm/½in. Using a 4cm/1½in cutter, cut out rounds. Gather together any pieces of dough that are not used, then reroll and cut out more rounds. Continue in this way until all the dough has been used.

7 To create the filling, place 2.5ml/½ tsp rosehip preserve in the centre of each round, then bring up and seal the edges to make a ball. Cover with a clean dish towel and leave to rise for 1 hour.

8 Melt the lard in a large, heavy, pan and heat until very hot. The temperature is correct when a small amount of the dough rises immediately when dropped into the fat.

9 Carefully lower the balls into the hot fat, two or three at a time. Fry them on one side for about 2 minutes, or until golden brown, then turn over and fry on the other side for about 2 minutes.

10 Test to see if they are done by inserting a skewer a little way in (taking care not to pierce to the centre); if it comes out clean, the dough is cooked.

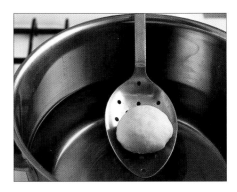

11 Remove the doughnuts from the fryer with a slotted spoon and drain on kitchen paper. Fry the remaining balls in batches.

12 As they are cooked, allow the balls to cool slightly, then dredge them in icing sugar. Serve immediately.

COOK'S TIP You can flavour icing (confectioners') sugar with vanilla by putting some of the sugar in a sealable jar and adding a vanilla pod (bean). Leave for 2 weeks for the flavour to develop.

Energy 883kcal/3703kJ; Protein 18g; Carbohydrate 109.9g, of which sugars 46.4g; Fat 41.5g, of which saturates 19.4g; Cholesterol 312mg; Calcium 223mg; Fibre 2.6g; Sodium 241mg

Plum Cake

This bread-like plum cake is a traditional harvest treat in Poland, and is still enjoyed today. It freezes well, so if you have a glut of plums make a couple of these cakes for enjoying during the winter months!

Serves 6

225g/8oz/2 cups strong white
  bread flour
7g/¼oz dried yeast
50g/2oz/¼ cup caster (superfine)
  sugar, plus 30ml/2 tbsp
150ml/¼ pint/⅔ cup lukewarm water
50g/2oz/⅓ cup cream cheese
50g/2oz/¼ cup unsalted butter
grated rind of 1 lemon
2 eggs, lightly beaten
450g/1lb plums
cream or ice cream, to serve
  (optional)

For the topping
25g/1oz/2 tbsp butter, melted
15ml/1 tbsp demerara (raw) sugar

VARIATION Any kind of plums can be used for this cake, including the golden yellow type. You can also use fresh apricots or even tinned pineapple when fresh plums are out of season.

1 Put 30ml/2 tbsp flour, the yeast and half the sugar in a bowl. Gradually stir in half the water, then cover with a clean, damp dish towel and put in a warm place and leave for about 30 minutes, or until the mixture starts to rise.

2 Cream together the cream cheese and butter, then stir in the lemon rind and beaten egg. Put the remaining flour and sugar in a second bowl. Add the creamed mixture to the flour and sugar.

3 Add the remaining water to the flour and cream mixture and beat until smooth, for about 15 minutes.

4 Grease a 20cm/8in springform cake tin (pan) and put half the mixture in it.

5 Halve the plums and remove the stones (pits). Dust the plums with a little caster sugar and place half on top of the dough. Add the remaining dough, then place the remaining plums on top, cut sides down.

6 Cover with a damp dish towel and leave to rise in warm place for about 40 minutes, or until doubled in size. Preheat the oven to 200°C/400°F/Gas 6.

7 Bake the cake for 30 minutes. Remove from the oven and brush with melted butter for the topping. Sprinkle with demerara sugar, then return to the oven and bake for a further 15 minutes.

8 Remove from the oven and allow to cool slightly before turning out. Serve warm or cold with cream or ice cream.

Energy 311kcal/1308kJ; Protein 6.4g; Carbohydrate 44.5g, of which sugars 15.9g; Fat 13.2g, of which saturates 7.4g; Cholesterol 89mg; Calcium 86mg; Fibre 2.4g; Sodium 102mg

Cottage Cheese Pancakes

Crispy and delicious, these little pancakes – known as blinis – are very popular in Russia as a dessert. They are traditionally served warm, with fresh berries and smetana. Blinis are used for savoury as well as sweet toppings, and can be eaten with almost anything.

2 Heat the oil in a non-stick frying pan, over a medium heat. Pour a tablespoon of the batter into the pan, adding another one or two spoonfuls, depending on the space in the pan.

3 Fry the pancakes for 1 minute then, using a metal spatula, flip them and cook the other side for a further 1 minute.

4 Transfer the pancakes to a warmed plate and keep warm until you have cooked all the batter.

5 Serve warm with cream, smetana or crème fraîche and fresh berries.

COOK'S TIP You can prepare the pancakes in advance and heat them in the oven at 110°C/ 225°F/Gas ¼ for about 5 minutes, until warm, before serving.

Serves 4

225g/8oz/1 cup cottage cheese or ricotta cheese
45ml/3 tbsp plain white (all-purpose) flour
1 egg, plus 1 egg yolk
30ml/2 tbsp vanilla sugar
15ml/1 tbsp icing (confectioners') sugar
30ml/2 tbsp rapeseed (canola) oil
whipped double (heavy) cream, smetana or crème fraîche and fresh berries, such as raspberries, blueberries or redcurrants, to serve

1 Put the cottage or ricotta cheese in a food processor. Add the flour, egg yolk, vanilla sugar and icing sugar and process until smooth.

Energy 171kcal/716kJ; Protein 4.2g; Carbohydrate 20.7g, of which sugars 12.1g; Fat 8.5g, of which saturates 1.5g; Cholesterol 98mg; Calcium 39mg; Fibre 0.4g; Sodium 45mg.

Polish Honey Cake

Many Eastern European cakes, like this Polish one, which is known as 'Tort Orzechowy', are sweetened with honey and made with ground nuts and breadcrumbs instead of flour. This gives them their characteristic rich, moist texture.

Serves 12

15g/¹/₂oz/1 tbsp unsalted butter, melted and cooled
115g/4oz/2 cups slightly dry fine white breadcrumbs
175g/6oz/³/₄ cup set honey, plus extra to serve
50g/2oz/¹/₄ cup soft light brown sugar
4 eggs, separated
115g/4oz/1 cup hazelnuts, chopped and toasted, plus extra to decorate

COOK'S TIP The cake will rise during cooking but then sink slightly as it cools – this is quite normal.

3 Mix the remaining breadcrumbs with the hazelnuts and fold into the egg yolk and honey mixture. Whisk the egg whites in a separate bowl, until stiff, then fold in to the other ingredients, half at a time.

4 Spoon the mixture into the tin. Bake for 40–45 minutes, until golden brown. Leave to cool in the tin for 5 minutes, then turn out on to a wire rack to cool. Scatter over nuts and drizzle with extra honey to serve.

1 Preheat the oven to 180°C/350°F/Gas 4. Brush a 1.75 litre/3 pint/7¹/₂ cup fluted brioche tin (pan), with the melted butter. Top with 15g/¹/₂oz/¹/₄ cup breadcrumbs.

2 Put the honey in a large bowl, set over a pan of barely simmering water. When the honey liquifies, add the sugar and egg yolks. Whisk until light and frothy. Remove from the heat.

Energy 188kcal/791kJ; Protein 4.6g; Carbohydrate 23.5g, of which sugars 16.1g; Fat 9.1g, of which saturates 1.6g; Cholesterol 66mg; Calcium 39mg; Fibre 0.8g; Sodium 108mg

Russian Easter Cake

A traditional Russian Easter dinner almost always starts with zakuski and will finish with kulitj, a cake flavoured with cardamom and vanilla, which is often blessed by the priest.

Serves 8–10

200ml/7fl oz/scant 1 cup milk
350–425g/12–15oz/3–3²/₃ cups plain
  white (all-purpose) flour
185g/6¹/₂oz/scant 1 cup caster
  (superfine) sugar
large pinch easy-blend (rapid-rise)
  dried yeast
115g/4oz/¹/₂ cup butter, plus extra
  for greasing
15ml/1 tbsp vanilla sugar
2.5ml/¹/₂ tsp salt
5ml/1 tsp ground cardamom
3 egg yolks
150g/5oz/1 cup raisins

COOK'S TIPS If preferred, the mixture can be made in a large bowl, rather than in a food processor. Cover the cake with baking parchment, halfway through the cooking time, if it shows signs of becoming too brown.

1 Pour the milk into a small pan and heat until warm to the finger. Remove from the heat. Put 325g/11¹/₂oz/scant 3 cups of the flour, half of the sugar and the yeast in a food processor and mix together.

2 Add the warm milk to the processor and mix until combined. Cover and leave to rise in a warm place for about 30 minutes, until doubled in size.

3 Melt the butter, then mix with the remaining sugar, the vanilla sugar, salt and cardamom.

4 Reserve 15ml/1 tbsp butter mixture, then add the rest to the risen dough and mix together until smooth. Add the egg yolks, one at a time, until combined.

5 Generously grease a 17cm/6¹/₂in round, 10cm/4in deep cake tin (pan) or 1.5 litre/2¹/₂ pint/6¹/₄ cup soufflé dish with butter.

6 Transfer the dough to a lightly floured surface and knead in the remaining flour and the raisins. Put the dough into the prepared tin or dish, cover and leave to rise for 30 minutes.

7 Preheat the oven to 180°C/350°F/Gas 4. Brush the dough with half of the reserved melted butter. Bake in the oven for 30 minutes. Brush with the remaining melted butter and bake for a further 20–30 minutes, until risen and golden brown.

8 Remove from the tin or dish and transfer to a wire rack to cool.

Energy 346kcal/1459kJ; Protein 5.3g; Carbohydrate 57.9g, of which sugars 31.3g; Fat 12g, of which saturates 6.7g; Cholesterol 86mg; Calcium 99mg; Fibre 1.4g; Sodium 92mg.

Polish Easter Cake

Served everywhere on Easter Sunday, this bread-like cake is baked in a bundt tin that is said to resemble an old woman's skirts. This gives it the name babka, Polish for grandmother. Finished with a rum or lemon and sugar glaze, it is as pretty as it is delicious.

Serves 4–6

15ml/1 tbsp dried yeast
120ml/4fl oz/½ cup sour cream,
  slightly warmed
225g/8oz/2 cups strong white bread
  flour, plus extra for dusting
75g/3oz/⅓ cup sugar
3 eggs, lightly beaten
15ml/1 tbsp vanilla extract
2.5ml/½ tsp almond extract
15ml/1 tbsp grated lemon rind
15ml/1 tbsp grated orange rind
40g/1½oz/¼ cup raisins

For the icing
50g/2oz/½ cup icing (confectioners')
  sugar
about 15ml/1 tbsp rum or lemon juice

1 In a bowl, combine the yeast with the sour cream. Sift half the flour into a large bowl, then stir in the sugar.

2 Add the yeast mixture, mix, then cover the bowl with a clean, damp dish towel and leave in a warm place for 1 hour, or until doubled in size.

3 Add the remaining flour with the remaining ingredients. Mix to combine, then transfer to a lightly floured surface and knead for 10 minutes, or until smooth and elastic.

4 Grease and flour a 23cm/9in bundt tin (pan). Place the dough in the mould, cover with a damp dish towel and leave in a warm place for 1 hour, or until doubled in size.

5 Meanwhile, heat the oven to 200°C/400°F/Gas 6. Put the cake in the oven and bake for 1 hour, or until the top is golden brown.

6 Leave the cake to cool slightly in the tin, then turn out on to a wire rack until completely cool.

7 Sift the icing sugar into a large bowl and add the rum or lemon juice. Stir to make a smooth icing with a pouring consistency, add a little more liquid if necessary.

8 Place a plate underneath the cake on the wire rack and drizzle the icing over the cake. Leave the icing to set, then slice the cake and serve.

Energy 299kcal/1262kJ; Protein 7.5g; Carbohydrate 54.4g, of which sugars 25.8g; Fat 7.3g, of which saturates 3.4g; Cholesterol 107mg; Calcium 99mg; Fibre 1.3g; Sodium 50mg.

Poppy Seed Cake

This dark, dense cake, made from a sweet dough rolled with an aromatic poppy-seed filling, is made throughout the year in Poland, but especially at Christmas and Easter. Known as makowiec, it has a distinctive taste, as well as appearance, and is absolutely delicious. The cake's filling needs to be soaked for three hours, so give yourself enough time for this.

Serves 6

45ml/3 tbsp sour cream
50g/2oz fresh yeast or 2 packets active
  dried yeast
400g/14oz/3½ cups strong white
  bread flour
115g/4oz/1 cup icing (confectioners')
  sugar, plus extra for dredging
15ml/1 tbsp grated lemon rind
pinch of salt
150g/5oz/10 tbsp butter, melted
  and cooled
3 eggs, beaten

For the filling

500g/1¼lb/5 cups poppy seeds
200g/7oz/scant 1 cup butter
200g/7oz/1 cup sugar
115g/4oz/1 cup chopped almonds
30ml/2 tbsp currants
60ml/4 tbsp honey
45ml/3 tbsp finely chopped
  candied peel
1 vanilla pod (bean)
3 egg whites, lightly beaten
15ml/1 tbsp rum or cognac

1 To make the filling, place the poppy seeds in a fine mesh sieve (strainer) and rinse under cold running water. Boil a kettle and pour boiling water over the seeds. Drain, then transfer to a bowl. Pour over enough boiling water to cover, then leave to soak for at least 3 hours.

2 Drain the poppy seeds, then grind as finely as possible in a blender or with a pestle and mortar.

3 Melt the butter in a pan, then add the sugar, almonds, currants, honey and candied peel. Scrape the seeds from the vanilla pod into the mixture with the poppy seeds, stir to combine, then fry gently for 20 minutes.

4 Remove from the heat, leave to cool, then stir in the beaten egg whites and rum or cognac.

5 To make the dough, mix the sour cream with the yeast in a small bowl. Sift the flour into a large bowl, then stir in the icing sugar, lemon rind and salt.

6 Make a well in the middle of the dry ingredients, then pour in the cooled melted butter, beaten eggs and the yeast mixture.

7 Mix to combine, then turn out on to a lightly floured surface and knead for about 10 minutes, or until smooth and elastic.

8 Roll out the dough to a thickness of about 5mm/¼ in, then spread evenly with the poppy-seed mixture.

9 Roll up the dough to form a loaf shape and place on a greased baking tray. Cover with a clean, damp dish towel and put in a warm place to rise for 45 minutes.

10 About 10 minutes before the end of the rising time, preheat the oven to 190°C/375°F/Gas 5.

11 Pierce the top of the loaf with a large sharp knife, then put in the hot oven and bake for 45–50 minutes, or until golden brown. Transfer to a wire tray and cool.

12 When the cake is completely cool, use a sieve (strainer) to dredge the cake heavily with icing sugar until completely coated. The cake is now ready to be sliced and served.

COOK'S TIP When the cake is dredged very heavily in sifted icing (confectioners') sugar, it has a festive, frosted effect that makes it perfect as an alternative Christmas cake.

Energy 1302kcal/5437kJ; Protein 21.9g; Carbohydrate 124.4g, of which sugars 72.9g; Fat 83.2g, of which saturates 35.9g; Cholesterol 224mg; Calcium 438mg; Fibre 6.6g; Sodium 459mg.

Walnut Gâteau

This fabulously oppulent walnut cake from Poland is deliciously moist, sandwiched together with a delectable cream, which is flavoured with coffee, vanilla and a dash of Polish spirit, vodka or cognac.

Serves 6–8

8 eggs, separated
125g/5oz/²/₃ cup caster (superfine) sugar
165g/5½oz/scant 1½ cups walnuts, finely chopped
15g/1 tbsp self-raising (self-rising) flour, sifted

For the filling
75g/3oz/²/₃ cup icing (confectioners') sugar, plus extra for dusting (optional)
165g/5½oz/scant 1½ cups walnuts, finely chopped
300ml/½ pint/1¼ cups double (heavy) cream
175ml/6fl oz/¾ cup 95 per cent proof Polish spirit or vodka, or cognac
½ vanilla pod (bean)
30ml/2 tbsp cold strong coffee

1 Preheat the oven to 190°C/375°F/Gas 5. Grease and line a 20cm/8in cake tin (pan). Beat the egg yolks with the sugar until thick and creamy. Stir in the nuts, then fold in the flour.

2 In a separate bowl, beat the egg whites until soft peaks form. Fold a tablespoonful of the egg white into the egg yolk mixture to loosen it, then fold in the remaining egg whites. Pour into the tin and bake for 40–45 minutes, or until risen and brown. Allow to cool, then turn out on to a wire rack.

3 To make the filling, combine the icing sugar and chopped walnuts. Whip the cream until soft peaks form, then fold in the Polish spirit, vodka or cognac with the walnuts and sugar.

4 Split the vanilla pod lengthways, then scrape the seeds into the cream. Add the coffee and stir to combine.

5 Split the cake into two layers. Spread one half with two-thirds of the filling, then position the other layer on top. Spread the remaining cream on top and dust with icing sugar, if using.

Energy 697kcal/2889kJ; Protein 13.2g; Carbohydrate 29.5g, of which sugars 27.9g; Fat 54g, of which saturates 16.4g; Cholesterol 242mg; Calcium 106mg; Fibre 1.5g; Sodium 89mg.

Chocolate and Almond Cake

This rich, dense chocolate cake is filled with a sweet almond paste and coated in glossy dark chocolate icing. It is often served in Poland as a snack with coffee, or as an indulgent dessert for a special occasion. Store in an airtight container in the refrigerator.

Serves 6

6 eggs, separated
115g/4oz/1 cup caster (superfine) sugar
150g/5oz/1¼ cups unsweetened cocoa powder
150g/5oz/1¼ cups ground almonds

For the almond paste
150g/5oz/1¼ cups caster (superfine) sugar
120ml/4fl oz/½ cup water
150g/5oz/1¼ cups ground almonds
15–30ml/1–2 tbsp lemon juice, to taste
½ vanilla pod (bean)

For the icing
115g/4oz good-quality dark (bittersweet) chocolate (minimum 70 per cent cocoa solids), chopped
25g/1oz/2 tbsp unsalted butter, cubed
120ml/4fl oz/½ cup double (heavy) cream
50g/2oz/½ cup icing (confectioners') sugar, sifted

1 Separate each of the 6 eggs, placing the yolks in one large bowl and the whites in another.

2 Add the sugar to the bowl containing the egg yolks. Beat together until the mixture is thick and creamy, then add the cocoa powder and ground almonds, and gently fold together.

3 Grease and line a 20cm/8in springform cake tin (pan). Preheat the oven to 200°C/400°F/Gas 6.

4 Whisk the egg whites until stiff peaks form. Using a metal spoon, gently fold a tablespoonful of the egg white into the egg yolk mixture to loosen it slightly, then fold in the remaining egg whites.

5 Spoon the cake mixture into the tin and smooth the top. Bake for 1 hour, or until a skewer inserted into the centre comes out clean. Leave the cake to cool completely in the tin.

6 To make the almond paste, put the sugar and water in a heavy pan, then heat gently, stirring occasionally, until the sugar has completely dissolved.

7 Bring the sugar and water to the boil and boil for 4–6 minutes, or until a thick syrup forms. Stir in the ground almonds and bring back to the boil.

8 Transfer the paste to a bowl, then add the lemon juice. Split the vanilla pod in half and scrape the seeds into the bowl. Mix well to combine.

9 When the cake has cooled, remove it from the tin and carefully slice into two even layers. Spread the bottom half with the almond paste, then sandwich the second half on top.

10 To make the icing, melt the chocolate and butter in a heatproof bowl over a pan of gently simmering water, ensuring the water does not touch the bowl.

11 Remove the bowl from the heat and gently stir in the cream, then add the sifted icing sugar and stir to combine.

12 Cover the top of the cake with the chocolate icing. Leave to set, then serve cut into slices.

VARIATION If you are making this for a dinner party, you might want to add a splash of rum or brandy to the chocolate icing for an added touch of indulgence.

Energy 892kcal/3726kJ; Protein 23g; Carbohydrate 73.7g, of which sugars 69.3g; Fat 58.4g, of which saturates 19g; Cholesterol 228mg; Calcium 226mg; Fibre 7.2g; Sodium 349mg.

Useful Addresses

AUSTRALIA
Russian Tidbits
113 Koornang Road
Carnegie VIC 3163, Greater Melbourne
Tel: (03) 9572 3911

V & V (Restaurant)
136 Koornang Road, Carnegie VIC 3163
Tel: 613 9568 1621

Polka Deli
22 Post Office Place, Glenroy, Melbourne
Tel: (03) 9304 4700

CANADA
Zia's Deli & Café
2773 Barnet Hwy, Coquitlam
B.C. V3B 1C2, Greater Vancouver
Tel: 604-944-2747
www.coquitlamdeli.com

Wendy's Gourmet Perogies
4532 99th St NW,
Edmonton, AB T66 5H5
Tel: 780-432-3893

NEW ZEALAND
St Petersburg Restaurant
1/333 Parnell Road, Parnell, Auckland
Tel: 09 373 3179
www.russianrestaurant.co.nz

UK
The Apple Tree Polish Deli
18 Lytton Road, New Barnet EN5 5BY
www.theappletreedeli.com

Babushka (Derbyshire)
71 West Bars, Chesterfield S40 1BA
Tel: 01246 555336
www.babushkauk.com

P & K Deli
145 Bond Street, Blackpool
Lancashire FY4 1HG
Tel: 01253 341001
www.pkdeli.co.uk

St Petersburg Restaurant (Manchester)
68 Sackville Street
Central Manchester M1 3NJ
Tel: 01612 366333
www.russiancuisine.co.uk

USA
Ostrowski's Famous Polish Sausage
524 S. Washington St
Fells Point, MD
Tel: 410-327-8935

Polana Inc. (online Polish food)
3512 N. Kostner Ave
Chicago, Illinois 60641
Tel: 773 545 4900
www.polana.com

Green Store Polish Deli
517 McCabe Ave,
Bradley Beach, NJ
Tel: 732-988-4291

Elizabeth's Polish Deli
4108 US Highway 19,
New Port Richey, FL
Tel: 727-842-8535

Pulaski Meat Market
1201 Lenox Ave,
Utica, NY
Tel: 315-732-8007

Moscow on the Hudson
801 West 81st Street,
New York, NY 10033
Tel: 212-740-7397
www.moscowonhudson.com

Babushka
62 Washington Street, Brighton,
MA 02135
Tel: 617-731-9739

Siberia Food Market
259 Main Street, Nashua, NH 03060
Tel: 603-883-4110

Russian Café and Deli
1712 Winchester Blvd,

Campbell, CA 95008
Tel: 408-379-6680

Russianfoods.com
DGV International Inc.
30–60 Review Avenue,
New York, NY 11101
Tel: 917-975-0471
www.russianfoods.com

Markys Gourmet Food Store
687 NE 79th Street, Miami, FL 33138
Tel: 305-758-9288
www.markys.com

Slavic Shop
1080 Saratoga Avenue,
San Jose, CA 95129
Tel: 408-615-8533

Moscow Deli
3015 Harbour Blvd,
Costa Mesa, CA 92626
Tel: 714-546-3354
www.moscowdeli.com

Russian General Store
9629 Hillcroft Street,
Houston, TX 77096
Tel: 713-721-7595

Berezka International Food Store
1215 Commonwealth Avenue
Allston, MA 02134
Tel: 617-787-2837

Bz Bee Market
2322 S El Camino Real
San Mateo, CA 94403
Tel: 650-627-9303

Index

PICTURE ACKNOWLEDGEMENTS
All photography by Jon Whitaker, apart
from the following:
Alamy: 15bl, 17tl, 20t, 21b, 22b, 24t &
bl. Corbis: 14t all, 15t, 15br, 16, 17b, 10
br, 21tr. Istock: pp6, 7tl, 8, 9, 10t, 11, 12,
23t13, 18tr, 19t & b, 20bl, 28t, 30t, 32t,
34t, 38t & bl.
Rex Features: pp18tl & b, 24m, 25b.